SHADOWS OF THE INDIAN

SHADOWS OF THE INDIAN

Stereotypes in American Culture

By

Raymond William Stedman

Foreword by Rennard Strickland

University of Oklahoma Press:Norman

By Raymond William Stedman

The Serials: Suspense and Drama by Installment (Norman, 1971, 1977)
A Guide to Public Speaking (Englewood Cliffs, 1971, 1981)
Shadows of the Indian: Stereotypes in American Culture (Norman, 1982)

Illustration of Pocahontas on page 36 excerpted from the book *Pocahontas in London* by Jan Wahl, Illustrated by John Alcorn. Illustration copyright © 1967 by John Alcorn. Reprinted by permission of Delacorte Press/Seymour Lawrence.

Library of Congress Cataloging in Publication Data

Stedman, Raymond William.
  Shadows of the Indian.

  Bibliography: p.
  Includes indexes.
  1. Indians of North America—Public opinion.
2. Ethnic attitudes—United States. 3. Public opinion—
United States. 4. Stereotype (Psychology) I. Title.
E98.P99S73 1982   306'.08997073   82-40330
        AACR2

CONTENTS

ILLUSTRATIONS

"It's a poor sort of memory that only works backwards,"
the Queen remarked.

Lewis Carroll, *Through the Looking-Glass,* Chapter 4

WHITE MEMORY, RED IMAGES, AND CONTEMPORARY INDIAN POLICY: A FOREWORD

By Rennard Strickland

THE SHADOWS of historical memory are cast backward and forward. Raymond William Stedman's *Shadows of the Indian* is a mirror reflecting back upon white images of the red American. It is an interesting and important book, interesting because of the vividness of the images he has found, important because those images still dominate national Indian policy. In his myth of the cave Plato showed us how shadow images distort reality while creating new and seductive realities of their own. There is a contemporary vitality to the historic shadows Stedman describes. The reader is thus drawn from the present into the future of Indian life, culture, and policy. *Shadows of the Indian* unites the past with the future by illustrating that history and policy are opposite sides of the same coin. One cannot understand the realities of modern Indian life and the prospect for the next generations without understanding the popular images of the past and the present.

Too often books like *Shadows of the Indian* are dismissed as interesting but unimportant. That should not be so in an area like Indian affairs where ongoing policy judgments are being made by elected and appointed officials. "Policy is formed by preconceptions, by long implanted biases," Barbara Tuchman argues. "When information is relayed to policy-makers, they respond in terms of what is already inside their heads and consequently make policy less to fit the facts than to fit the notions and intentions formed out of the mental baggage that has accumulated in their minds since childhood."[1] This is particularly true with regard to the American Indian. For here the "facts" of Indian life are dramatically at odds with the "notions" of the dime-novel and the Saturday-matinee Indian.

Understanding the popular image is important, however, not only for the view it provides of the Indian but also for the view of the society that created the image. *Shadows of the Indian* tells us much about white ideas and ideals, and about European and American literature, art, science, philosophy, theater, and cinema, for each new white generation has reinvented the Indian in the image of its own era. Historically, the Indian himself became a mirror. The Indian image was the reflection of the particular white neurosis of that age. We have seen the Indian taken, in the view of white society, from savage to savior; from the devil incarnate of Puritan sermon to the nonpolluting, horseback riding television Indian of the public-service announcement and to the mystical, drug-world Indian of Carlos Castaneda's people of power; from the last of the Mohicans to the end of the trail; from the good Indian who brought corn to the starving pilgrims to the stoic marine raising the flag on Iwo Jima. As Stedman demonstrates, all these images have at least one thing in common. They are primarily the invention of non-Indians and, as such, represent a historical attempt to define the Indian and Indian policy from a non-Indian perspective.

Let us run quickly through some of these eras and their resulting policies. The early Jeffersonian era had the policy of civilizing Indians, using trading posts, federal factors, and plows and spinning wheels distributed by men who were officially called "the agents of civilization." In another era operation of Indian policy was turned over to the churches, to denominational Christianity—when monies were paid directly to church groups. Who can forget the age of military conquest? Or the time when the "solution" was thought of as "education" or "urban resettlement" or any of a dozen other programs. The important fact is that when white society defined the "Indian problem" as one of saving his soul it turned to men of God; when it viewed the problem as one of securing military victory, it turned to soldiers; when the problem seemed to be one of training and educating, white society

1.Barbara W. Tuchman, *Practicing History: Selected Essays* (New York: Alfred A. Knopf, 1981, p. 289.

turned to teachers. Increasingly, in recent years Indians have turned to lawyers.

In writing about these white definitions and perceptions of Indian reality, Stedman joins a group of distinguished scholars who have doggedly pursued the Indian created by the white imagination. Leslie Fiedler's innovative *The Return of the Vanishing Native* (New York: Stein & Day, 1968) has been particularly well received in the Indian community. Robert F. Berkhofer, Jr.'s *The White Man's Indian* (New York: Alfred A. Knopf, 1978) is a thorough and insightful portrait of the relationship of white ideas and Indian policy. Both Henry Nash Smith's *Virgin Land: The American West as Symbol and Myth* (Cambridge, Mass.: Harvard University Press, Twentieth Anniversary Printing, 1970) and Roy Harvey Pearce's *Savagism and Civilization: A Study of the Indian and the American Mind* (Baltimore: John Hopkins Press, rev. ed., 1965) are classics of intellectual history. Stedman builds upon this rich and rewarding tradition of scholarship by creating a work that is soundly rooted in the history of ideas, but his own language and attitudes are clearly of our age.

Stedman has created a rich tapestry of varied images of the Native American Indian and in so doing he has isolated important themes behind the images. He shows these visions in analytical chapters such as "Men Friday," "Vanishing Americans," "La Belle Sauvage," and "The Enemy." His irreverant and ironic treatment is shown in chapters such as "And You Know What They Do to White Women" and "Lust Between the Bookends." *Shadows of the Indian* clearly demonstrates the often contradictory nature of white images. Stedman's range of examples is particularly unique. The shadows we see are cast by William Shakespeare and Daniel Defore, Jennifer Jones and Boris Karloff, the *Ladies Home Journal* and *Playboy* magazine. The white man's historic images of the Indian have little or nothing to do with the reality of Indian life. Most of these dominant images are fictional creations of the white imagination and ignore what the Indian is truly like. Stedman shows how the conception of the American Indian has been modified by white creators. To see this, we can look at the great ecclesiastical debates on the topic "Are Indians people?" We can look at the literature of the "savage demons," the mass body of books on the so-called Indian captivities, the atrocity literature, the "Our Brothers in Red" pamphlets, the "Lo! The Poor Indian" Romantic paintings, the brown-toned photos of Edward Curtis, and the Boy Scout and Bluebird handbooks.

One has only to look at Hollywood for each version of the newly invented Indian—from the demonic devil torturing the "good guy" on the anthill to the equally inventive use of the Indians as a symbol for American resistance to the Vietnam War. And behind all these models stands the basic image of the Indian as the vanishing American, the last of the Mohicans, the end of the trail, the camera fade into the mainstream, the tragic remnant of *A Century of Dishonor*, and the basket-maker holding on to her people's dying craft. The important word is *dying*—the extinction of a strange, exotic, endangered species.

In Stedman's book there is an important lesson for students of contemporary Indian life and policy. It is the startling realization that the Indian has neither faded nor died. Here is the contemporary clash of white image and Indian reality. The white inventor of Indian stereotypes is coming to the realization that if the modern Indian is going to die it is white society that must kill him; Indians have no intention of committing cultural or economic suicide. The inventor may have thought a self-destruct mechanism existed, but what could not be done with smallpox-infested blankets, frozen trails of tears, attacks on peaceful villages, allotment of Indian lands, imposition of white governmental forms, and legislative termination of tribal existence will not be done by a new round of white-created images. As Mark Twain said, "The report of my death has been greatly exaggerated." The American Indian is alive and well.

Stedman's *Shadows of the Indian* suggests the most disquieting aspect of the current controversies over Indian policy. The problem today is that modern Indians are not behaving in the forms that white society has historically defined as appropriately Indian. White society can define, even absorb and tolerate, a second Wounded Knee, AIM, and Indian violence. Such conduct is definitionally Indian. What cannot be understood is what the modern Indian is seeking to do. Indians are behaving in a way that the white inventor of the Indian image did not imagine; therefore, such conduct is intolerable. The Indian legal, governmental, educational, cultural, and industrial revolution of the last decade has revealed the illusory nature of the central, shared historical belief that the Indian problem was temporary, that the Indian would disappear, and that with him would go the Indian problem. It is hard for whites to imagine Indians who identify themselves with native cultural and tribal values as energy entrepreneurs, as doctors, as lawyers, as business executives, as computer programmers, and as government officials on previously all-white school boards and city councils. It is also difficult for non-Indians to believe that a large percentage of America's natural resources escaped the white grasp and are still in Indian hands. Books like Stedman's *Shadows of the Indian* may help all of us face the real Indian, not in condemning tones or with patronizing attitudes but with what Stedman describes as "the humanness factor." Then, and only then, can national Indian policy escape the baggage of the backward trap of distorted memories.

PREFACE

I BEGAN this book in 1972—well, I began to work on it in a formal way then. The idea had been stirring around inside me for years. The Indians I saw on the screen as a child or read about in books or looked at in halftime shows or circuses or heard about in songs were not anything like the young Indians I played schoolyard games with or their parents and grandparents. To be sure, the Indians of popular culture were picturesque characters; they brought abundant thrills to a matinee moviegoer. Yet they were, I came to realize, not of this world. They had, in fact, never existed anywhere, except in imagination. Nonetheless, the illusory Indians were so authentic to most Americans that no alternate images were acceptable. Even in decades that saw an increased awareness of the sensitivities of minority groups, nothing appeared to change regarding the Indian, who as the twentieth century advanced seemed ever more a figure of the past—and a distorted figure to boot. I suppose that is why in adulthood I started on this book.

While gathering materials here and there—Albert Keiser's *The Indian in American Literature* (1933) was one of the few formal sources available at the outset of my work—I recognized that primary source materials for study were both omnipresent and inexhaustible. Thus I could draw upon multiple areas of literature and popular culture to isolate the pervasive themes and counterfeit images attached to the American Indian long ago, or I could concentrate almost entirely upon one conspicuous area—"The Indian of the Movies," for example. To keep the pervasiveness of stereotyping to the fore, I chose the broader approach (and, conveniently, some other writers came along with a focus on the movie Indian, an important but not exclusive facet of this book).

One thing I had to accept, however: just as an intensive study of one medium did not fit my purpose, a comprehensive historical survey of the Indian in American culture from 1493 to the present did not either. That amalgam of art objects, printed works, plays, mass-media artifacts, and popular-culture phenomena, could not be confronted in one volume without sacrificing direction, or substance; and it is doubtful that a general reader would take to a multivolume exploration of the subject, even if it would allow an author to range from "The Indian as a Hero Model in Eighteenth-Century Literature" to "The Indian as a Detective in Twentieth-Century Fiction."

Focusing, then, upon prevailing themes or images, I have examined each one in single or paired chapters, sometimes with a chronological pattern to the unit, sometimes not. Since an overall frame of reference might be helpful to the reader now and again, I have included a brief chronological listing in which events of history are matched with items of entertainment or literature. It saved an extensive amount of repetition and kept me from some tempting tangents. For those that I did not sidestep, a sincere, but no doubt unrepentant, apology.

RAYMOND WILLIAM STEDMAN

Newtown, Pennsylvania

AUTHORS NOTE

I HAVE USED the word "Indian" throughout this book, primarily because my study treats of images not truly reflected in terminology such as "cowboys and Native Americans." The term "Native American" can be used, of course, in reference to contemporary individuals, but its usage does present problems not always considered (even by those who would just as soon forget about "natives" being "restless tonight" or who remember that the anti-immigrant "Know Nothing" faction grew out of a Native American party that had nothing to do with Indians, literally or figuratively). Today, in an ethnic context, the term Native American is applied to the Indians of the United States—a somewhat parochial orientation that reflects the white man's geography, displaces the southern groups, separates Blackfeet and Apaches from their cousins living across a national border, and presents an unworkable specter for this kind of book: Native Mexicans, Native Canadians, Native Guatemalans, and so on. Moreover, to paraphrase George Abrams, a Seneca anthropologist content with the use of the word "Indian": in the state of Hawaii, with its Polynesian heritage, who is the Native American? The term does not travel well.

Semantic arguments aside, however, "Indian" prevails because it is the word still chosen by Indians themselves for collective purposes (individually, the nations often call themselves "the people"). As yet no truly self-generated move exists to embrace any other term. Being possessed of knowledge of their pre-Columbian heritage, Indians are less concerned about their collective designation than they are about their tribal or national identities. They can be *called* Indians or Native Americans or First Americans, but they *are* Oneidas and Kiowas and Cherokees. As the man from Wales thinks more of being Welsh than of being European, the Indian cherishes his or her specific stock (or stocks). Leaning upon a collective term for the Indian when greater precision is appropriate is not much different from using "European" when it is more appropriate to say "German." It may also be the surest path to burying completely the heritage and identity of the individual Indian groups. Then nothing would stand in the way of the stereo-typers.

ACKNOWLEDGMENTS

DURING the ten years in which this book moved from outline to finished work many people offered advice and assistance. Although an Indian position regarding many of the book's subjects did not exactly crystallize, the variety of opinion and information offered by Kiowa or Seneca or Cherokee was a needed reminder to avoid assuming a universal reaction, overall or within tribal units. I will not attempt to name individuals whose informal responses to literary or media patterns provided insight, but an expression of gratitude can go collectively to those within the American Indian Society of Pennsylvania and corresponding organizations elsewhere in the United States. Contemporary Indians, incidentally, are not necessarily steeped in tribal cultures other than their own. Sharing a campus and classes with members of a dozen or more tribal groups during the spring of 1979, learning as they too learned of arts, mores, and customs, was a warm and memorable experience made possible by Louise Smith and the United American Indians of the Delaware Valley.

From the non-Indian community, anything but miscellaneous were the contributions of Christopher Bursk, Richard Bullock, and Curtis Yeske (colleagues all); Bernard Berg of Ocmulgee National Monument; and the staff of the New Jersey State Museum, who in the closing months of this book brought Blackfoot author Jamake Highwater, Seneca anthropologist George Abrams, and some rarely shown Indian movies almost to the author's back yard. Walter Palmer, of Bucks County, added his creative touch to the photography necessary for the illustrations. Finally, my thanks to Erin, Craig, and Eric Stedman, specimen gatherers *extraordinaire,* and Frederic Manning Smith, who made sure that his sometimes worn-down stepson was able to attend more than one enriching function that otherwise would have been missed.

SHADOWS OF THE INDIAN

*The Indian is doubtless a gentleman, but he is a
gentleman who wears a very dirty shirt, and lives a very
miserable life, having nothing to keep him alive except
the pleasures of the chase and the scalp-hunt—which we
dignify with the name of war.*

Robert Montgomery Bird, preface to the
revised edition (1853) of *Nick of the Woods*

PROLOGUE

BROWNIES they were, at least a dozen of them, clustered beneath
a warm Georgia sun that spring day to poke into Indian life and
lore. With their Scout leader and a few harried mothers the
exuberant nine-year-olds had come to the outskirts of bustling Macon
to tramp the ceremonial mounds and peek into the carefully reconstructed buildings of a thousand-year-old village designated Ocmulgee National Monument. Their thirsts thoroughly slaked by
innumerable dashes to a well-tested water fountain, the young ladies
stood ready to meet the patient park assistant who would be their
guide.

Enriched by a thousand such moments, the "ranger" knew exactly
how to begin: "Tell me, what do you know about Indians?"

Nine hands went into the air. The assistant selected the girl who
seemed to have the largest twinkle in her eye. "I know a lot about
Indians," she asserted. "They wear feathers and put paint on their
faces and yell in real high voices when they attack white people and
kill them with tomahawks!" Her friends nodded in agreement, one of
them grunting, "Ugh, ugh."

"How did you learn those things?" the guide asked.

"Oh, from movies on television. I watch them all the time. And
sometimes we talk about Indians in school."

3

"Have you ever seen a real Indian?"

"No, . . . I don't think so."

The guide pointed to a young member of the park staff coming out of the information area. "That fellow's an Indian," he said. "Sometimes we fish or hunt together. And he's as good a person as you'd ever want to meet. Does he look dangerous?"

Silence. Then a few quick "no's."

"Of course not. Now let me tell you about Indians. . . . "

Before the hour had passed, one more set of budding citizens had for the first time passed beyond the stereotypes and clichés of the Indian image and learned something concrete about the American continent's first inhabitants. But what if they had not come to Ocmulgee? What about those children (or adults) who have no Indian parks to visit, no Indians to see? What about tens of millions of residents of the United States who leave the whole matter to the popular media?

Their viewpoint might not differ much from that of the Brownie at Ocmulgee, or those of the students of Mrs. Lillian Rosen at New York City's Public School 183. Killing, once again, seemed to be an Indian's main function, to judge by her pupils' replies to her questions one day. "If an Indian moved to the city," said one boy, "he'd kill people. He's not smart and he would think people were cowboys and would kill dogs because he would think they were water buffalo or fish." Other comments from Mrs. Rosen's class followed the same line: slaughter and stupidity in imaginary situations. Said the dismayed teacher, "The kids don't have the faintest idea that Indians are real people."[1]

Yet is it surprising that children, and children now grown, have at best a mixed conception of those mysterious peoples they meet through history books or mass media? The Indian portrait of the moment may be bellicose or ludicrous or romantic, but almost never is the portrait we see that of a real person. At one instant a phantom Indian passes before us as a statuelike denizen of forest or prairie, sharing food with the Pilgrims, bowing his head before Manitou, shielding the body of John Smith from death clubs, speaking in periodic sentences of the Happy Hunting Ground or the Great White Father or the encroachment of the Long Knives. Yet in a twinkling that Noble Savage is likely to be cinematically, electronically, or typographically metamorphosed into one, any one, of the "renegades"

[1]Richard Flaste, "American Indians: Still a Stereotype to Many Children," *New York Times*, September 27, 1944, pp. 25, 88, 178.

crowding latter-day Wild West thrillers that judiciously skirt the universal defamation of earlier years.

At any time the switch of a dial, like the change of a theatrical signbill or the turn of a comics page, might bring forth some new model. Perhaps it is one of the feather-and-buckskin comedians who for generations have spiced popular entertainment or a jester in warpaint prancing at the local stadium. What good fun these Old Siwashes have provided! Far more dignified, however, is the faithful Tonto, doing the Lone Ranger's legwork into eternity. Although plagued by problems with English grammar, Tonto (like his cousins) is strong and loyal. Yet for all his steadfastness he lacks the snap of good old Geronimo, sneering heavy in a hundred Western dramas. No character, year after year, stirs up as much fictional dust as does this elusive Apache raider, who wound up writing his memoirs between visits to the reservation's Dutch Reformed Church. Geronimo stands for a whole school of devils incarnate. But we must not forget that equally treacherous creature known as a "half-breed"—Injun Joe of *Tom Sawyer*, for instance—or his reverse image, the seraphic soul of mixed blood we meet in tales of two worlds such as *Ramona*.

They are everywhere before us, the shadow Indians. They wear many fictional hats, but few are flattering. They sing and dance, but rarely as they really did . . . or do. They fight desperately on screen in defense of their asserted rights, but die trying to kill the white hero. They pledge their love to handsome army scouts, but soon their white doeskin dresses are stained with their own blood. They inspire thousands of athletic spectators, but usually disguised as court fools. They strike it rich in middle western oil fields and roar around, overdressed, in long roadsters. They drink too much white man's whiskey and stagger about shouting, "Hallelujah!" Yes, they are fascinating figures, the American Indians. But have we ever seen them?

*Some of them paint themselves black . . . and some paint
themselves white, and others red, and others with what
they have. Some paint their faces, others the whole body,
others the eyes only, others only the nose.*

Christopher Columbus,
in his journal, 1492

1

THE CURIOSITY

IN THE BEGINNING they were curiosities, people unlike any other
human beings the first white visitors to the Americas had ever seen.
European reactions varied, of course. The Norse who tramped
about Newfoundland in 1004 summarily extinguished the lives of the
first American natives whom they came across—and called them
"Skraelings" (an untranslatable explicative). Christopher Columbus,
more alert to potential raw material, immediately gathered a few
specimens for export and called them "Indios" (see chronology in
Appendix). The Columbus misnomer stuck. So did most of the other
misrepresentations attached to the first Americans through the years.

At first, however, there was delight at the collected specimens. All
the way from Seville to Barcelona crowds buzzed about the fascinating
creatures (still thought to be from Asia) whom Columbus was deliver-
ing to Ferdinand and Isabella. Youngsters peeked at them in their
night's lodgings and multitudes lined their way for parade after parade
on the path to the city where the monarchs were holding court. In the
ultimate procession to the throne a squad of Tainos who had survived
the sea voyage, and the land display, put on their finest paint and

6

raiment to serve as the color guard. It was a time of true delight—for the Europeans at least. The Indian wars had not begun. The pageant had.

For those not living on the Spanish peninsula, the introduction to Columbus's handsome *Indios* was, of necessity, second hand. Artifacts were abundant, however: the admiral's romanticized letters about the Indies, word-of-mouth reports from those who had lined the route of Columbus's passing caravan, tales framed in mythological imagery by subsequent travelers to the new lands, quaintly decorated maps, and a hodgepodge of what might be called picturesque souvenirs. Guarded or not, the secrets of America rapidly spread throughout Europe, the clergy lending a hand. Even before the first fanciful drawings of the "American-Native-at-Home" went into circulation, many a European had drawn his own portrait of Los Indios—a people soon revealed as belonging not to the Orient but to a new world. That any such portrait, rooted as it was in the romantic mythology of Europe, might not resemble a single American resident would have been inconceivable to its designer. That it might also differ markedly from the picture formed in the mind of the scholar or the Indies investor next door would have been of little consequence, for what fun it was verbally to dissect and explain those savage innocents! Europe had discovered a new amusement, the Indian.[1]

War, and "insurrection," soon troubled the waters, of course, but all that was far away across the ocean and only sketchily reported. More and more live specimens were brought over for study and display, doing a ceremonial dance here, promenading in the park there. Portugal was the first to see North American Indians. Corte Real's men brought back half-a-hundred Boethuks of Newfoundland in 1501. The next year other northern Indians were presented to England's Henry VII. They were still around in 1504, but their "beast-skin" garments had given way to proper English attire. Although a delighted Italian observer noted that the Boethuk women had "small

[1]While our concern in this book lies primarily with the images of the Indian expressed in the popular culture of the United States, for an excellent and richly illustrated analysis of early impressions of the Indian formed in Europe, a reader could find no better work than Hugh Honour, *The New Golden Land.* To consider how the romantic European mythological concept of the Indian was reconciled with harsher portraits as an American mythology developed, a reader could turn to Richard Slotkin, *Regeneration Through Violence: The Mythology of the American Frontier, 1600–1860.* Some of the more interesting early accounts are outlined in the chronology at the end of this book.

7

breasts," "beautiful bodies," and "pleasant faces," apparently the harsher climate of their homeland made the first North American visitors to Europe less endearing in temperament than Columbus's West Indians. Some Canadian Indians who reached France in 1508 also turned out to be more curious than captivating to their observers.

For the rest of the sixteenth century, with Spain leading the way in treasure hunting and colonization, the European would have as his premier models of the new creatures the attractive residents of Central and South America. Even Englanders saw some of them. In 1532, Henry VIII interrupted his dining long enough to stare at a Brazilian chief who had bones planted in his cheeks and a precious stone set beneath his lower lip. Across the channel Henry II and his French countrymen got to see a whole Brazilian village that had been set up right on the riverbank at Rouen. Half-a-hundred imported natives staged mock fights, shinnied up tree trunks, stalked birds with bows and arrows, paddled about the Seine in canoes, danced a little, and performed routine domestic chores. In an illustration for the commemorative program a pair of native monarchs pro tem could be observed enjoying it all from a hammock stretched between two palm-like trees (it was not long after this effective sales demonstration, not incidentally, that France had a colony in Brazil). By the 1560s, South American Indians were somewhat regular participants in state ceremonials. Montaigne, during a show for Charles IX, met a few of the performers, presumably not the disguised Frenchmen who (it was hinted) became spear carriers to flesh out the cast—a practice continued ever afterward, often with the real Indians shoved into the background.

A generation before those French pageants, Spaniards had enjoyed watching a company of performing athletes from Mexico, assembled in 1528 by Hernan Cortés and shown off in Spain by him. Before delighted audiences, the gymnasts juggled meter-length cylinders with their feet and demonstrated their skill at a complicated kind of handball. During a presentation in Toledo in 1529 a visiting German artist named Christoph Weiditz captured their images with his pen. His series of cartoons (including one portraying the lone woman in the troupe and a two-panel cartoon showing a game of chance employing small chips of wood) may be the oldest firsthand drawings of Indians made in Europe. Later, in 1529, a subsection of the Cortés company performed in Rome for a pleased Pope Clement VII. This splinter group may also have toured the Low Countries. Wherever they went, they carried echoes of the Aztec empire so lately uncovered and conquered. After the splash made by Columbus's Tainos (thought, of course, to be rural Asians), the abortive attempts to export Indian slaves to Spain had threatened to remove the cachet of the American Indian in that country. Proofs that America was actually a new world, and tales of fabled empires, brought back the earlier enthusiasm for Indian-watching.

England's eventual Indians of choice were neither Mexicans nor Brazilians but "Virginians." Their time of prominence, however, reflecting Britain's colonial ventures, did not come till around 1600. Initially the term "Virginian" was applied to any Indian along the coast from Maine to North Carolina, so we do not know exactly the homeland of the Virginians who gave a demonstration of how to handle a dugout canoe on the Thames in 1603. There was no question, though, of the geographical origin of a later Virginian visitor. In 1616 a young woman first called Matoaka, then Pocahontas, then Lady Rebecca, became the darling of the English court, being already proficient in English manners and worship. She dined in royal circles without balancing peas on her knife and generally managed to conceal her displeasure at the stench of London's avenues and the noisiness of its citizenry. The extraordinary young woman delicately embodied England's fascination with the Indian, and in vestigial form still does.

In lands where there was no Pocahontas, some other Indian, real or imagined, would strike fire. In eighteenth-century France, for example, there were Chateaubriand's Atala and Chactas. In nineteenth-century Germany there was Karl May's Winnetou (a "great chief of the Apaches," who kept a copy of *The Song of Hiawatha* in his game bag). And for philosophers everywhere in Europe there was from the beginning the mythical "Noble Savage"—though he was not called that right away. Some minds penetrated the mist, it is true. Shakespeare, in *The Tempest,* used the business in which the comic Trinculo stumbles over the stupefied aborigine, Caliban, to chide Englanders who "when they will not give a doit to relieve a lame beggar . . . will lay out ten to see a dead Indian." Nonetheless, from the Shannon to the Danube, the European imagination had awarded a choice carrel to the American Indian, one not reassigned to this day. An English town still bears the name Indian Queen's. An amusement park in France is called Redskin Valley; a nightclub, the Crazy Horse Saloon; and a highway-manners character, "Sly Bison." Members of Indian clubs assemble regularly in various parts of the Continent. And one of the world's finer collections of Indian memorabilia is in Dresden, Germany.

Oddly enough, the United States, a nation built by immigrants who carried with them impressions of the Indian forged in Europe, found itself at the outskirts of the early celebration. No doubt that was because, for a time at least, it had its Indians close at hand. Initially they were objects to be civilized, or utilized. Then they were obstacles to be pushed beyond the frontier. Finally they were, in the words of Roy Harvey Pearce, "forced out of American life and into American history."[2] Only as they moved beyond the horizon did Indians have to be preserved on canvas or photographic plate or reconstructed in word or pageant for stateside examination. Even then each bit of preservation or reconstruction was likely also to take seed and bear fruit in Europe: James Fenimore Cooper's popular Leatherstocking tales of the 1820s; George Catlin's overseas exhibitions of paintings (and live plains Indians) in the 1840s; Buffalo Bill's Grand Tour with his Wild West Show in the Victorian era; and the limitless array of dime novels, Hollywood epics, and, finally, television Westerns.[3]

Despite all the attention, however, the Indian almost everywhere has remained a curiosity—for not many have seen one up close—but a curiosity with a full complement of stereotype faces.

[2]Roy Harvey Pearce, *Savagism and Civilization*, p. 58.
[3]For an entertaining account of European embellishments of the storybook Indian see Ray A. Billington, "The Wild West Through European Eyes," *American History Illustrated*, August, 1979, pp. 16–23.

Europeans showed an immediate interest in the physical appearance of the people encountered by Columbus and his successors. Artists and writers were quick to supply images, accurate or not. In almost five centuries the situation has changed little. People remain curious about Indians, and purveyors of popular culture continue to exploit that curiosity.

The first published portraits (above left) *of "Los Indios—drawn from imagination or borrowed from woodcuts depicting other "natives"—appeared in 1493, but Columbus's rosy images of America's naked innocents soon had to compete with garish displays of frenetic cannibalism.*

Above: *Brazilians cavort in a fete at Rouen, France, 1551.*

Below: *Some of the Cortés troop as drawn by Christoph Weiditz in 1528, when the touring Aztecs were the delight of Europe.*

FLORIDA'S OFFICIAL STATE PLAY

Cross and Sword

BUFFALO BILL TO THE RESCUE

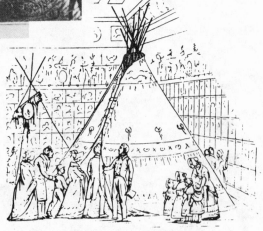

WESTERN INDIANS!

A phantom Sitting Bull seems to be contemplating the show business milieu of which he was briefly a part. The fellow in top hat is Geronimo, on display at an exposition.

15

Jim Thorpe plays in—and is played in—a movie.
Above: Battling with Buffalo Bill *(with Tom Tyler), 1931.*
Below: Jim Thorpe—All American *(with Burt Lancaster), 1951.*

16

Her complexion was a deep Copper, so that her fine
Shape & regular Features made her appear like a Statue
in Bronze done by a masterly Hand.

William Byrd, on seeing a "Dark Angel," *Histories of the*
Dividing Line, 1728

White man, thou shalt not die; or I will die with thee!

James Nelson Barker, *The Indian Princess,* 1808

Pocahontas' body, lovely as a poplar, Sweet as a red
haw in November, or a paw-paw in May.

Carl Sandburg, "Cool Tombs," 1918

2

LA BELLE SAUVAGE

THE SETTING was the Los Angeles Music Center. The occasion, the Academy Awards ceremony in the spring of 1973. No one in attendance doubted that Marlon Brando would win the Best Actor laurel for his performance in *The Godfather*, but there was discomfort in the acute awareness that Brando was not in the hall to receive the award. Worse yet, the actor did not leave matters at boycott, as Oscar winner George C. Scott had two years earlier. Instead, those who witnessed the event in person, or by television, saw a lovely young woman in a light-colored Indian dress walk with dignity to the lectern and advise apprehensive "presenters" Roger Moore and Liv Ullmann that Marlon Brando would not accept his trophy because of the insensitive manner in which Hollywood had portrayed the American Indian through the years. Catcalls interrupted (and obviously disquieted) the young woman, yet her gentle bearing in the face of rudeness soon won her the silence she needed to finish her brief remarks. Then Brando's pretty stand-in, who had identified herself as Sacheen Littlefeather, slipped into the wings. After one or two peevishly restorative barbs by academy hosts, the proceedings once again moved stolidly toward their conclusion.

Across the nation reactions were confusing. Brando's grandstand play—and his sending of a young woman to receive the boos intended for him—drew scorn, of course. After all, the Mafia movie which had brought him the Oscar was scarcely uplifting to the Italian image. Yet even for Brando haters and political reactionaries, there was something about the pristine presence of the Indian woman that partly muted the criticism. *Time* put tongue in cheek concerning the disturbance, in keeping with its conclusion that everything about the evening was a disaster. Acerbic Hubbell Robinson, writing in the conservative *Films in Review,* described the attire of the "Apache girl" as "full Indian regalia," then took to task the missing actor. In contrast to Robinson, columnist Harriet Van Horne was obviously captivated by the "gentle-voiced Apache maiden . . . who appeared on the stage in tribal dress." Once the furor was over, suggested Van Horne, "people will still remember that lovely Littlefeather, in her shining braids, explaining as best she could why the most honored actor of the year was letting the chalice pass." The columnist's "heart went out to that Apache lass in her long braids." And that, she asserted, was "precisely what Marlon Brando had in mind."

Was that what Brando had in mind? If so, he had selected his propaganda device shrewdly, for it was, simply, that of the lovely and selfless Indian princess, possibly the most enduring image this land has known. Brando's braided messenger was Pocahontas and U-le-lah and Minnehaha and Redwing and Sacagawea and Sonseeahray and Summer-Fall-Winter-Spring and, some would say, the allegorical America. She was the female manifestation of the Noble Savage myth, changed little from the image created centuries earlier, and far more endearing and viable in the twentieth century than her male counterpart, the forest nobleman.

In fact, the princess legend crystallized so nearly perfectly during Littlefeather's moment on the stage that it was undamaged when the media began poking at the woman's background. No, Brando did not find his Apache maiden at central casting, though she was a neophyte actress whose real name was Marie Louise Cruz. No, the young woman, who grew up in Salinas, California, was not a phony Indian, but she had never visited a reservation until she was seventeen, when she decided to learn about her background. All these things Sacheen Littlefeather openly admitted to columnist Earl Wilson late in 1974, while at the same time confessing that she had been a drug addict when she was twenty, a three-time attempter of suicide, and a former patient in a mental institution. Between her Oscar appearance and the time of the Wilson column the actress had turned up periodically in national news photos—taking ballet lessons to aid her acting career or being hired by the Los Angeles School Board to make a tape on intercultural relations. Littlefeather's biggest publicity spread, however, occurred in *Playboy* magazine, where she was displayed stark naked on several pages.

While full body exposure in *Playboy* may or may not have represented one more bit of exploitation of the American Indian—depending on who asked whom—it was entirely in keeping with the Indian princess tradition. The singer Buffy St. Marie inexplicably observed it in the 1970s by stripping to the waist for an album cover. In the centuries before *National Geographic* the various woodland maidens of history and legend had provided illustrators with ready excuses for limning bare bosoms. Even grammar-school reference books had their depictions of the seminude Pocahontas draped across John Smith, charms akimbo (and much too fully developed for the child Matoaka in the year of Smith's story). No one, it seems, has ever minded looking at a naked Indian's likeness, be it male or female, the statue at the museum, or the near-bare pseudobrave of the disco-era singing group the Village People. As Hugh Honour has pointed out, however, serious artists sometimes protected themselves in the early colonial period by casting their unclad children of the forest in classical modes. Until explorers stumbled upon the American Indian, the legendary Greek or Roman was Western civilization's only approved nude.

Documentary authority for the bareness (and for the connection of the American Indian to the child-of-nature philosophy, which had been rumbling around Europe even before the first contacts with the New World) was found in the observations of Christopher Columbus. It was "naked people" whom the admiral saw before he went ashore at San Salvador. On landing, he observed that they were also "gentle and peaceful" and of "great simplicity." Columbus magnanimously gave them some baubles to hang around their necks. Recalling that first day, the great navigator described the handsome features and tall bodies of those Tainos, who went "quite naked as their mothers bore them." They carried no weapons except darts, cut themselves by grasping the Spaniards' swords at the wrong end, and were subject to slave raids from the mainland—a pattern for enrichment not over-looked by Columbus. Beyond question those happy islanders would readily embrace Christianity. The second day the explorer saw more Tainos, trim young men who had arrived in swift dugout canoes of all sizes. To Ferdinand and Isabella, Columbus later wrote that these Indians of his were ingenuous, and generous, beyond belief. He could not further permit them to be plied with bits of broken glass, or so he said.

Had Christopher Columbus and company figuratively moved through time to a people embodying man's Arcadian past? Europe's writers and philosophers were ready to think so. So were its artists. Columbus had concurrently discovered the Golden Age, the period Samuel Eliot Morison called "that bright morning of humanity which existed only in the minds of poets."[1] With his tub-thumping descriptions the admiral, setting a pattern for many a successor, was stocking that golden land, and the myth, with noble innocents.

Intellectuals marking the faraway footsteps and landfalls of the New World's explorers seized the glorious opportunity to postulate upon the untouched savage, living as he did in a state of nature. Scores of writers—Peter Martyr, Montaigne, Rousseau, Chateaubriand—to one purpose or another focused upon the innocent creatures depicted by the truth-embroidering Amerigo Vespucci and other early explorers, who, when their only encounters were with Indians of the warmer climes, usually voted a straight ticket (possibly for selfish reasons). Over and over again the inhabitants of the Americas were characterized in firsthand accounts as (1) naked, (2) childlike, (3) willing to share anything they possessed, (4) unaware of religion, and (5) unconcerned with laws or personal property. A sixth element, cannibalism, crept into some accounts—and into hundreds of illustrations—but since the practice did not fit a good-savage motif, it was smoothed over or simply disregarded by many theorists. Appropriating the term which playwright John Dryden had applied to early Europeans in *The Conquest of Granada* (1670), writers two centuries and more after Columbus's voyages extolled the "Noble Savage" and

---

[1]Samuel Eliot Morison, *Admiral of the Ocean Sea*, p. 226.

argued that primitive man, when left alone, was superior to any other creature of civilization. Others, Samuel Johnson, for instance, countered that the whole idea was nonsense. In one form or another the debate continues today. And who was caught in the middle, used by both sides as exhibit A? The actual American Indian.

Pocahontas, of course—and Sacheen Littlefeather—walked in the moccasins of the Noble Savage, the one because she innocently embodied the image, the other because she consciously invoked it. No one can tell, of course, exactly when the portrait of an unspoiled benefactress in feathers was first conceived, or, perhaps, transferred to the Indian. That the ages-old theme of bounty from a virgin goddess (or earthly representative) had simply found a rich growing medium in the untouched New World could well be argued. Yet, whether or not stretching back to prehistory, the ministering-maiden motif had flesh-and-blood representatives early in the colonial era. Columbus apparently missed out on the succor. He kept an aloof distance from the women of the New World, whom he tended to equate with livestock for all his talk of native nobility. But Cortés, in 1519, was not at all opposed to a mental or physical favor or two from a bright and talented Indian woman. It was the slave girl "Doña Marina," given him by the Tabascans on the Mexican coast, who unexpectedly provided the key to his conquest of the mainland. Reputedly the daughter of a native nobleman, Marina (whose Aztec name was Malinche or Malintzin) was Cortés's Rosetta Stone to the language of the Aztecs and his counselor in reading their thoughts. She was his ear to the wall in Montezuma's palace and his agent for winning the hearts of the native allies. She was his companion on the march and his comfort during the night. And later, when she was married to one of his supporters, Marina, beloved by both Indian and white, started off a prominent New World family (two if one counts the son she bore Cortés).

About all that Cortés's benefactress did not do was gain entrance to the history books with a dramatic rescue effort. Not that such heroics are absolutely necessary for inclusion with the Indian princesses, but some sacrificial gesture (like taking the place of Marlon Brando) or romantic tragedy or mournful death does provide a pathway to the memory cells of the general public. Perhaps the pattern was sketched when a European named John found himself captive in a native village in what is now the southern United States. Bound and helpless, he was moments away from death by execution when the cherished daughter of the chief won his life through her tears and pleading. The white man later was reunited with his own kind, not too much the worse for the wear.

The story of John Smith and Pocahontas? Yes and no. In this instance it was the story of Juan (John) Ortiz and a chief's daughter, whom writers later called Princess U-le-lah. The rescue followed Ortiz's capture, incident to Narváez's disastrous Florida expedition of 1528. After years spent with a friendlier Indian group, Juan was delivered to De Soto's party upon their arrival at Tampa Bay in 1539. He went right to work as an interpreter and served the new expedition well until his death in 1642.[2] U-le-lah vanished from history, and, though she beat John Smith's princess to the rescue act by a good seventy-five years, it is mainly as the "Florida Pocahontas" that she is remembered in historical pageants and such. Had the subject of her rescue been a John Smith, and had he lived to write his memoirs, things might have been a little different. But Pocahontas still would have won history's prize. No matter how her personality compared with U-le-lah's, events worked in Pocahontas's favor as far as legend making went. Four years after she saved Smith, Powhatan's daughter was kidnapped by Virginia colonists to keep the "emperor" in line. During her relaxed internment, however, the girl learned English ways from the governor's daughters, accepted Protestant Christianity, and met and married John Rolfe, a widower. Without that period of adjustment and education Pocahontas would not have been able to carry things off in such astonishing fashion when Rolfe took her to England with her tiny son three years later.

Not all the European achievements of Pocahontas stemmed from fortuitous preparation for a swing through royal society. At the base was an obviously impressive presence given to few people. She was called, after all, the Nonpareil of Virginia. Even the dramatic rescue of Smith, which later would add so much to her legend, may have meant nothing to those whom she charmed in England. It was not, in fact, included in Smith's 1608 narrative of his Virginia adventures . . . though she herself was mentioned as Powhatan's daughter, who "not

[2]Before being reunited with his countrymen, Juan Ortiz actually had to be rescued more than once, by a total of four women. For early accounts of the Ortiz ordeal the reader might enjoy Garcilaso de la Vega, *The Florida of the Inca*, and Richard Haykluyt, *Virginia Richly Valued.* The latter volume incorporates the firsthand "gentleman of Elvas" recollection of the De Soto expedition (first published in Portugal in 1557). Haykluyt's book appeared one year after John Smith's first account of the Jamestown venture but fifteen years before Smith's famous Pocahontas story.

only for feature, countenance and proportion much *exceedeth* the rest of the people: but for wit and spirit the only nonpareil of his country." Not until 1624 was the rescue story published, in Smith's *The General Historie of Virginia, New England, and the Summer Isles.* The story is short but vivid. Late in 1607, Smith is captured and brought before Powhatan (Wa-hun-sen-a-cawh), who sits before a fire clad in an enormous raccoon-skin robe. On either side of the "emperor" sit young wenches, while many courtiers line the sides of the arena. As the agitation grows, the "Queen of Appomatoc" brings Smith water to wash his hands, which are dried with feathers. Then, after a feast, it is decided that Smith's brains will be beaten out on two great stones brought in for the occasion. At that point

> Pocahontas the King's dearest daughter, when no entreaty could prevail, got his head in her arms, and laid her own upon his to save him from death: whereat the Emperor was contented he should live to make him hatchets and her bells, beads, and copper.

Shortly afterward Smith is released and escorted back to Jamestown, where every four or five days the young Pocahontas and her attendants bring the colonists provisions "that saved many of their lives." Through "the love of Pocahontas" their spirits are revived and their fear abandoned. Pocahontas turns up here and there in the rest of the account, always in favorable light.

Skeptics would one day say that, as a forgotten hero, John Smith included the dramatic reprieve from Powhatan's executioners in the 1624 narrative to reattach himself permanently to the memory of the fabled woman who had charmed England until her death there of smallpox in 1617. Assuredly Smith was eager to establish contact with Pocahontas when she came to London and he was living in poverty. Yet despite a run of skepticism which budding historian Henry Adams set off in the late nineteenth century (primarily by pointing to the rescue's omission from the 1608 account), current scholarly opinion holds that, just as there is no proof outside Smith's writings that the rescue occurred, there is no proof that it did not. The shrewd colony builder had good reason to keep quiet about Indian trouble in 1608, when the Virginia venture needed no bad publicity. The rescue incident, moreover, was not without precedent (as we have seen from the U-le-lah story). Nor did any Jamestown veteran rise to refute Smith's recollection in 1624. Recently even the earlier derring-do which Smith recounted regarding his part in the Hungarian struggle against the

Turks has proved plausible historically where once it was assumed to be fanciful. Thus John Smith may well have been telling the truth about his near-execution in Powhatan's lodge. But, in the business of legends, it matters not a bit. The association of Pocahontas with the rescue is unbreakable. No one thinks of her without thinking of it. The Indian princess would have laid down her life to save the white man.

Did the Pocahontas of history matter at all? Of course she did. By her extraordinary personality and achievements—for she did help the colonists, and she did manage an incredible social transition—Pocahontas showed Britishers of two lands how remarkable an Indian woman could be. Further, in a country which doted on princesses, she exemplified just what the savants were looking for—an American one. King James, it is said, was angry that Pocahontas was allowed to marry John Rolfe, not because Rolfe was a white man and she an Indian, but because he was a commoner and she a royal daughter. Such concern would have proved awkward, of course, had not Pocahontas, as Lady Rebecca, comported herself the way a princess should. But the fact is, she did. Whatever was being said about the savage state of Virginians, as her people were then called, Pocahontas (nonpareil or not) was living evidence to refute it—at least as far as Indian royalty went.

But was it correct to call her a princess? Except, perhaps, for the Natchez group in the Southeast, Indians in what is now the United States had no perpetual aristocracy in the European sense. Yet in power and domain grand caciques or territorial masters such as Powhatan (who did receive a crown from Britain) were every bit as much kings as were hundreds of ancient monarchs of Europe. And authority often did remain within principal families. To smile at the antique custom of addressing as "Kings" great chiefs who lived in permanent communities may well be to demonstrate prejudice of a subtle nature. Neither hereditary title nor lifetime rule is a necessary prerequisite for kingship: check a dictionary—or ask the Bonapartes. Although democratic government eventually was seen to be the prevailing pattern among the various Indian groups, America's "kings" really disappeared when it became inconvenient politically and economically to have Indian "nations." Nations must be more or less left in place—and their sovereigns left in charge. Moreover, since thoughts of unseating kings made European monarchs nervous, a conceptual turnabout had to precede the absorption of the national territories. It was both advantageous and politic to portray Indians as ill-equipped anarchists with too much land on their hands before

24

taking those lands away. While it was simplistic for Europeans living in the sixteenth and seventeenth centuries to squeeze the government organizations of Indian nations into European monarchial molds, it may be equally simplistic today to perceive nothing even remotely royal in some of the Indian leaders of history, or their daughters.[3]

Semantics aside, many of the famous Indian princesses of fact and fiction were indeed the daughters of chieftains. Often, however, the designation was one of convention, like that of a Kentucky colonel. Thus, Minnehaha, the arrowmaker's daughter in *Hiawatha,* became Princess Minnehaha in various corners of popular culture long before a comic-strip artist played on her name to create Chief Wahoo's friend Princess Minnie Ha-Cha. And since in rougher western societies the princess appellation was extended also to allegedly compliant Indian females, it becomes something of a chore for the average person to separate Indian women who were daughters of chiefs from those who were princesses by virtue of courtesy, or derision. Further confusing the picture has been the tendency of writers to divide Indian women into only two groups: princesses and squaws. "Squaw" (the rough approximation of a word for wife in only one Indian language) is now, apparently, the pejorative of choice for all faceless Indian females— the ones who shuffle along behind "bucks" and say "Ugh." Observe how David Garnett contrasts the painted likeness of Pocahontas to those of other Indian women: "From her portrait, obviously a close likeness, one guesses at a shrewd, observant intelligence and a high vitality. There is nothing of the animal sleepiness seen in the pictures of many squaws."[4]

Through the nation's growing years Pocahontas the Nonpareil— intelligent, guileless, lovely, courageous—turned into Pocahontas the Imitated. Not a season went by that some author, or artist, or playwright, or trademark maker did not call upon her image. Of the many plays built around the daughter of Powhatan during the early decades of the nineteenth century, the first significant one was J. N. Barker's

[3]In a scholarly article of 1974, P. Richard Metcalf reviewed the politics and power structures of some well-known Indian groups through the centuries. Observing the considerable government authority wielded by some Indian leaders, Metcalf proposed that "the belief that aboriginal Indian societies were ruled by concensus is largely a concept of anthropologists, whose native informants often tend to be self-conscious keepers of a tribal heritage which they remember in idealistic terms." Richard P. Metcalf, "Who Should Rule at Home? Native American Politics and Indian-White Relations," *Journal of American History* December, 1974, pp. 664–65.

[4]David Garnett, "John's Royal Wife," *New York Times Magazine,* April 5, 1964.

The Indian Princess; or La Belle Sauvage (1808). Barker, by placing the famous rescue sequence toward the middle of the play, eschewed a convenient melodramatic climax which tempted later writers, emphasizing instead the Pocahontas–John Rolfe romance—for which the playwright shifted to a wondrously overdone blank verse. Several songs dot *The Indian Princess,* along with some offstage naughtiness involving naked damsels. Through an expository sequence, derived directly from John Smith's account in 1624, Pocahontas's maids of honor entertain several Englishmen with a "Virginian mascarado," performed one midnight in "gloomy wood." Except for "a small difference of hue," the costume of the evening is that which "madam Eve" had on before she ate the apple. Aside from this slavered-over bacchanal, in which the bodies of her ladies-in-waiting "glisten'd most gorgeously under the moon," Barker's princess is so much the genteel Western damsel (even before getting to know the colonists) that, full of remorse for putting an arrow into a lovely flamingo, she announces that she will no longer hunt the creatures of the forest. When awakened to love later on, Pocahontas becomes a soaring romantic.

By comparison with this maiden, the heroine of the second major Pocahontas play is conservative and colorless. Whereas Barker's *The Indian Princess* stood alone in its era, however, George Washington Parke Custis's *Pocahontas; or The Settlers of Virginia* (1830) triggered a craze for Indian plays. Custis moved the rescue to the end of the drama, and the colonists into prominence, but he also created a tragically noble Indian war leader, Metacoran, who worshiped the princess as ardently (and hopelessly) as he resisted the tide of colonialism. Pocahontas herself, in Custis's play, is as much southern belle as Indian princess, which is not surprising, since the Virginia-planter playwright was the grandson of Martha Washington and the father-in-law of Robert E. Lee.

In the 1800s far too many Pocahontases—not to mention pseudo-Pocahontases—tripped across the stage for us to look at them all. Not surprisingly, the superabundant porcelain princesses (like their stuffed-shirt Indian-chief counterparts) soon became a glut on the proscenium market. John Brougham's popular burlesque *Po-Ca-Hon-Tas; or The Gentle Savage* (1855 and later) completed the Indian-play coup de grace begun with his parody *Metamora; or The Last of the Polywogs* (1847). A popular afterpiece for many years, *Po-Ca-Hon-Tas,* with its puns, iconoclastic humor, and general irreverancy, was not unlike one of the long, music-sprinkled schoolroom or cabinet-meet-

26

ing sequences in the early Marx Brothers movies. Even the characters' names would have suited the Marx pattern: Barnabas Binnacle, the Right Honorable Quash-Al-Jaw, Ip-Pah-Kak, and Dro-May-Jah (a high official). The burlesque began with a prologue that devastated *The Song of Hiawatha:*

> Ask you—How about these verses?
> Whence this song of Pocahontas,
> With its flavor of Tobacco,
> And the Stincweed—the Mundungus.

Brougham's spoof promised a look at what really happened "in Virginia, on Wednesday, Oct. 12, A.D. 1607, at twenty-six minutes past 4 in the afternoon." With songs, grand scenas, complicatos, intrusive choruses, gymnastics, duettos impetuosos, and more ethnic humor than a modern audience could be comfortable with, *Po-Ca-Hon-Tas* revealed John Rolfe as a stage Dutchman—"Mein cootness gracious, was is das I see"—and Powhatan as a pompous matchmaker who drove his daughter to wail:

> The king who would enslave his daughter so,
> Deserves a hint from Mrs. Beecher Stowe!

When, after a string of puns, Jonsmith puts his head on the execution stone, Pocahontas rushes in "heroineically distressed and dishevelled —followed by sailors":

POCAHONTAS: Husband! for thee I *scream!*

SMITH: *Lemon* or *Vanilla?*

And that's how the rescue really happened, we are told, just before the final duet: "Prima Donna Waltz."

Philip Moeller wrote a twentieth-century spoof, *Pokey; or The Beautiful Legend of the Amorous Indian* (1918), and vaudeville (and television vaudeville) kept the funny-rescue idea from dying, but Brougham's play removed the story from consideration in legitimate theater. In drama Pocahontas was through as a serious character well before the twentieth century. She was viable in New York only when disguised as some other fair maiden ready to effect a rescue or to die for her lover. But that still left many other arenas in which the real Pocahontas (or, more often, suitable facsimiles) could perform. Historical pag-

27

eants never forgot the Indian-princess motif and use it today. More important to the survival of the legend, however, were the popular media that were developing just as the conventional theater was discarding the Indian play. The story papers and their offshoots, the dime novels, liked Pocahontas. To use her fully, they merely had to move her west along with the nineteenth-century frontier and give her an assortment of new names. Traveling Wild West shows seldom were without an Indian maiden but seemed to operate on the principle that where one was good a dozen would be better.

Then came the movies. Just before World War I, celluloid princesses (or maidens) ran around like mice: *Pocahontas* (1908), *An Indian Maiden's Choice* (1910), *The Indian Maiden's Sacrifice* (1910), *Broncho Billy and the Indian Maid* (1912), *The Indian Maid's Warning* (1913), and so on. Thrown in were various white princesses (Pearl White included) and far too many "squaws"—more than a dozen in 1911 movie titles alone (in that era the word "squaw" was not used as negatively in filmland as it would be later). The period between the two world wars was a light one for princesses, even with radio added to the media. The most memorable celluloid rescuer of white men during those years could have been the mystery rider with the singing arrows in Republic's fine serial *The Painted Stallion* (1937). The first surprise of that chapter play was that the rider was female. The second (missed by those who did not see the final episode) was that she was really a white girl.

By reason of default, therefore, the Golden Bow and Arrow Award for "helping ease the white man's burden in broadcast or film between the world wars" will have to be divided between a movie Pocahontas (in *Jamestown*, 1923) and a radio Sacagawea, whom Ireene Wicker, "The Singing Lady," brought to life in a series of story hours on NBC in the mid-1930s. For garish eye appeal, however, one should not overlook the dancing choruses of suitably unclad maidens in early Hollywood musicals, including one singing Western with a cowgirl protagonist. The reader may also wish to award musical honors to the Busby Berkeley dance ensembles of *Whoopee* and other screen frolics, or to the Jeanette MacDonald–Nelson Eddy gem *Rose Marie*, with its elaborately choreographed woodland number, "Totem-Tom-Tom."

During the 1940s and 1950s the princesses (including Pocahontas herself) came back in full form (pun accidental) and lingered into the 1970s and 1980s. They bathed in waterfall or stream: Yvonne de Carlo (*The Deerslayer*, 1943), Elsa Martinelli (*Indian Fighter*, 1955). They were thwarted in their love for white men: Linda Darnell (*Buffalo Bill,* 1943), Marisa Pavan (*Drum Beat,* 1954). They won their white men, but died tragically: Debra Paget (*Broken Arrow,* 1950), Marie Elena Marques (*Across the Wide Missouri,* 1951). And, above all, they served the white man—usually at the cost of either their lives or their pride.

In *The Far Horizons,* Donna Reed, as Sacagawea, smoothed the way for Charlton Heston and Fred MacMurray (Lewis and Clark) halfway across the continent. But in the White House (yes, Hollywood took her there) the Bird Woman felt out of place. With aching heart she gave up a lover she never in fact had, then returned to her homeland, where her brother was now the chief. *The Far Horizon's* self-effacing Indian guide, who knew her place and was Hollywood-glamorous beyond belief, represented a particularly low point of the movieland princess. Not only was history distorted—for Sacagawea was the purchased wife of the expedition's generally worthless French scout and the mother of a child born on the journey to her former Shoshoni home—but, in addition, the achievements of a woman truly important to western exploration were twisted and subverted into a phony bittersweet romance for the convenience of a forced farewell scene with Clark . . . or was it Lewis? Does it matter?

Lest by concentrating upon the Indian-princess manifestations of theater and film I suggest that fiction, recent fiction at least, has ignored the doeskin dress, let it be said that the princessmaiden still appears regularly in printed literature employing Indian themes. Son-seeahray of Elliott Arnold's *Blood Brother* (*Broken Arrow,* as a film) probably comes to mind most readily from among the post-World War II novels. Her description as the consecrated White Painted Lady of the Chiricahuas follows traditional lines. More reflective of the princess-bountiful theme, however, is her postbath self-evaluation revealing her desire to give pleasure to her white husband-to-be, Tom Jeffords:

> She looked at her body and was happy that it was beautiful. She looked at her hands and feet and was happy that they were well shaped. She looked at her breasts, cupping them in her hands, and she was happy they were round and firm and did not hang and that the nipples were small. She looked at her waist and was happy it was slender. She put her hands under her hips and was happy they were not broad. She lifted her legs from the water and was happy they were round. She looked at her thighs and saw they were soft and not fat and she was happy. She

29

thought of her body as something to give to him and she was almost impersonal in her survey and she thanked Yusn that what she had to give him was good and desirable and she hoped he would think it was beautiful.

Later she would die from a soldier's bullet, hoping only that Jeffords would not be angry with her.

Since Sonseeahray's appearance in 1947 there have been dozens of princesses in print. Even Pocahontas and Sacagawea still pop up as subjects of hardcover fiction. Here is the young Matoaka in John Clarke Bowman's 1973 novel, *Powhatan's Daughter:* "Her body was painted crimson with puccoon juice. She wore pearls in her ears, and a necklace of pearls wrapped three times around her neck hung down between her developing breasts." Later Bowman paraphrases a spicy John Smith recollection (J. N. Barker's offstage bacchanal)—with a bit of goddess mythology thrown in:

> . . . a troupe of thirty damsels came naked out of the woods, their only covering before and behind being a few green leaves. Their bodies were painted, some red, some blue, some yellow, and some parti-colored. Pocahontas led them, a pair of antlers on her head and otters' skins dangling from her girdle and her arm. A quiver of arrows made of cat's fur was across her shoulder, and in her hand a bow. Smith looked at her with amusement and perturbation. A veritable Diana.

Yet for sheer adoration in La Belle Sauvage tradition, however, one could scarcely find a better example than that of Will Henry's half-French, half-Pawnee narrator in the 1963 Random House novel *The Gates of the Mountains:*

> Sacajawea was not shy, but appealingly soft of speech and manner. And she was gracefully feminine beyond any woman I had seen. . . . Her head was not elongated, as so many of the Indians, but rather small and round, Caucasian in shape. So, too, were her features Caucasian. Small ears lay flat to her head. The short straight nose was neither flatly Mongol like the river Indians, nor high-bridged as with the horse Indians. Her mouth . . . had a form and softness not at all Indian. The teeth, of course, were perfect. . . . But her eyes remained the most startling thing about her.

Even more startling than the "rare dark auburn color of her hair"?

> They were not black or even dark or light brown. . . . They were gray. They were gray as my own eyes, although far, far darker, with that

certain hint of green-blue seen in deep clear water, or in a rain-washed prairie sky of a cloudless sunset; and the lashes which framed them were thick as broomstem grasses.

Her skin?

... a tigerish color, so light in tone that each blush was to be seen in Sacajawea's face as vividly as in the face of the fairest French or American girl. Yet with all this strange beauty, she was always the purest of pure Indians.

Do you not exaggerate, François Rivet?

One may say that being French and very young I add qualities to the Shoshone girl which no Indian maiden ever knew. The charge is fair but not true. Sacajawea was not only an uncommonly pretty young girl, she was a regal woman by any standard of any race. No man who ever knew her, was quite the same again.

And, *en fin?*

Grace was hers, and good manners. Intelligence she had, and a quick and lively tongue. Dignity covered her every move. She could look like a queen while gutting an elk. . . . She had no crown but her auburn hair. . . . But Sacajawea was a ruler of men's hearts by God's will.[5]

After that what can be said? John Barth did his best to make Pocahontas a ribald figure in *The Sot-Weed Factor* (1960). And television's Cher, in revealing doeskin fringes, brought forth a garish princess with no effort at all. But, still, the inviting echoes of the ancient forest maiden sounded strongly about the land—when James Michener's *Centennial* reached the television screen late in the 1970s; when Avon Books released a 1,359-page paperback original, Anna Lee Waldo's *Sacajawea,* in 1979; when McGraw-Hill put on its 1979 list Jane Lewis Brandt's *La Chingada,* the story of Cortés's "brilliant and beautiful Indian princess"; when CBS aired *The Chisolms* in the 1980s.

Did Marlon Brando, when he let the body of that lovely lass in her long braids shield him from the blows of a hostile audience, choose the most irresistible of all Indian images? Is the grass that grows beside the river green?

[5]Will Henry apparently is given to rapturous descriptions of Indian princesses. See his *No Survivors.*

The princess legend did not begin with Pocahontas but with the mythical representative of the New World called America. Here, in a facsimile of a late sixteenth-century illustration by Stradanus, the lightly clad maiden rises from her hammock to greet Americus Vespucci.

America's means of transportation were anything but orthodox, armadillos and such being the favored beasts of burden, as in the illustration of 1644, above left, or the sketch of 1594, above right. The amazon with spear and severed head dates from 1581.

De Soto was honored by a distinguished "Indian queen" (as shown in the Edith Duggan painting for A Nursery History of the United States, *left). In exchange for her pearl beads, however, she received shackles. The Pocahontas rescue of John Smith (illustrated in his* Generall Historie, *1644) became one of the set pieces of American culture.*

King Powhatan comands C: Smith to be slayne, his daughter Pokahontas beggs his life his thankfullnes and how he subiected 39 of their kings. reade the history.

Ætatis suæ 21. Aº 1616.

Matoaks als Rebecka daughter to the mighty Prince
Powhatan Emperour of Attanoughkomouck als Virginia
converted and baptized in the Christian faith, and
Wife to the worll Mr Tho: Rolff.

The formal portrait of Pocahontas as Lady Rebecca (page 35) contrasts with the folk painting of an open-air rescue of Smith below it. Still, the serene countenance of America's nonpareil can be seen in both paintings—and in the John Alcorn illustration for Jan Wahl's Pocahontas in London, *above.*

Artists were unrestrained in depicting the Pocahontas-Rolfe wedding. The sketch above is among the least fanciful. RIGHT: John Brougham's lampoon, Po-ca-hon-tas *(1855), just about finished John Smith's friend as a serious character of drama. With Brougham is Georgina Hodson.*

Burlesques notwithstanding, Pocahontas (or her substitutes) continued to inspire artists. This painting is A Trapper's Bride *by Alfred Jacob Miller.*

Opposite: *Pocahontas's Mexican counterpart, Marina, is surrounded by a Bantam Books standby of 1950–51. "Princess Ubiquitous."*

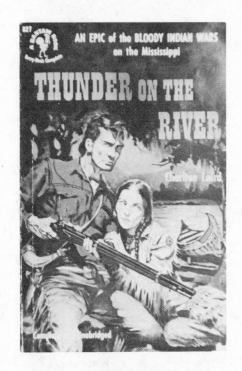

AN EPIC of the BLOODY INDIAN WARS
on the Mississippi

THUNDER ON THE RIVER

Charlton Laird

A BANTAM GIANT

Elliott Arnold

BLOOD BROTHER

EPIC NOVEL OF THE
GREAT APACHE WARS

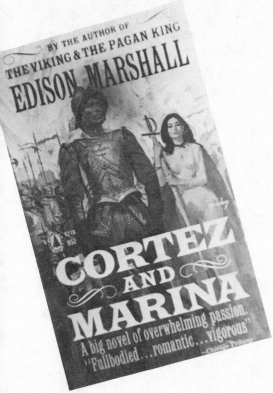

BY THE AUTHOR OF
THE VIKING & THE PAGAN KING
EDISON MARSHALL

CORTEZ AND MARINA

A big novel of overwhelming passion.
"Fullbodied...romantic...vigorous"

Smashing saga of the fight for the West—
AND OF ONE MAN'S HEROIC DECISION

NO SURVIVORS

WILL HENRY

Complete
Unabridged

39

Broadway had a latter-day Poca-
hontas in Fawn Afraid (Kather-
ine Florence) of The Girl I Left
Behind Me *(1893). Theodore*
Roberts played her father, Scar
Brow. The poster shows her fate.

Opposite: *Buffalo Bill's "Ar-*
row-head" (1908) and Marlon
Brando's Sacheen Littlefeather
(1973).

3

MEN FRIDAY

THEY would make ideal servants, of that Columbus was certain. The Taino Indians whom he encountered during his first sweep through the Caribbean were blessed with good physiques and docile natures. What more could a European gentleman wish in the way of physical support for his ventures into colonization and conquest? The admiral's optimism, in fact, was clouded only by one observation, which he candidly set down on paper: the women, from what he could see, did more work than the men.

Creators of popular fiction never made much of Columbus's suggestion of a sexual imbalance in Indian job performance, probably because, by the time most of them had taken up their pens, the explorer's Indians were gone. Within a few decades the Tainos and their neighbors, female as well as male, had been eliminated by the hundreds of thousands in Spanish endeavors to turn them into servile Christians (read "slaves"). Unaccustomed to much labor of any kind in their bountiful islands, they were rapidly replaced as the New World's bonded class by blacks from Africa, and popular literature would reflect that change. When the "busy female–lazy male" foolishness finally was tapped by portrayers of American milieus, the victim was not the Indian but the Negro. Thus, in thousands of American books and movies, dependable "mammies" carried out most of the productive activities in or about the white folks' residences while their

42

male counterparts dropped luggage, catnapped on duty, and (when confronted by danger) stuttered, "Feet, do your stuff!" It was one bit of stereotyping largely denied the Indian.[1]

Yet if fiction makers left undeveloped the gender contrasts in Indian servitude suggested by Columbus, they did make money with the manservant alone, pressing him into service all the way to the prairies of Tonto and his brothers. Caliban, that aboriginal composite in Shakespeare's *The Tempest*, stands as one of literature's classic servant problems. He just would not knuckle under. Moreover, he was resentful and given to drinking. But Caliban will have his time on the stage later on.

By far the most suitable of the early Indian servants was Robinson Crusoe's Man Friday. Indeed, he performed his duties so well and comported himself so humbly that, as the generations passed and the enslavement of the peoples of the Indies became a historical footnote, poor Friday lost his Indian identity in some versions of *Robinson Crusoe* and was transformed into the faithful black slave which the world had grown accustomed to encountering in fiction. The motion-picture industry would follow the same happenstance pattern: *here* making Friday a true Indian in the carefully made Luis Bunuel feature of 1954, *there* putting a black actor into a fright wig for a mid-1970s movie for television, and *over there* going the pure-black route for a 1975 British feature film emphasizing the social-moral struggle inherent in the story. Obviously, to some purveyors of popular culture—publishers, illustrators, screenplay writers, directors—one sorry native was very much like another, so what did it matter? Such indifference notwithstanding, however, a young person's image of Friday is obviously dependent upon which movie or book illustration or comic book he or she happens to come upon first.[2]

Few nowadays actually bother picking up the classic novel which everyone *knows* but not many have read. Were it to be read, Daniel

[1]So that the reader will not be misled, even a trifle, it must be stated that some authors have employed the sexual stereotyping. A recent example would be Jessamyn West in her novel *The Massacre at Fall Creek* (1975). On the first page of text the exposition reflects an Indian hater's estimate that "if Indian men had been half as industrious as their women, the whole country would have been cleared, planted, and built up long ago."

[2]Aside from the countless abridgments, translations, condensations, and retellings of *Robinson Crusoe* itself, bookstalls also displayed through the years the unconcealed imitations of Defoe's work known as Robinsonnades. The best known, of course, was *The Swiss Family Robinson,* but the list also includes the *Adventures of Philip Quarrl, Adventures of Peter Wilkins, Masterman Ready,* Jules Verne's *Mysterious Island,* and scores of other works.

Defoe's description of Crusoe's servant would dispel the short, kinky hair, large lips, dark-visaged Sambo image which is as demeaning to one race as it is unmindful of Defoe's description of another. Here is how readers saw, and still can see, Friday in legitimate editions of the book:

> He was a comely fellow, perfectly well made, with straight strong limbs, not too large, tall and well shap'd, and, as I reckon, about twenty six years of age. He had a very good countenance, not a fierce and surly aspect, but seem'd to have something very manly in his face; and yet he had all the sweetness and softness of an European in his countenance too, especially when he smiled.

Now some particulars for illustrators or film producers:

> His hair was long and black, not curl'd like wool; his forehead very high, and large, and a great vivacity and sparkling sharpness in his eyes. The colour of his skin was . . . a bright kind of dun olive . . . that had in it something very agreeable, tho not very easy to describe. His face was round and plump; his nose small, not flat like the Negroes; a very good mouth, thin lips, and his fine teeth well set, and white as ivory.

Robinson Crusoe's well-formed, long-haired, thin-lipped, small-nosed, dun-olive native—by the narrator's own words not a Negro—was one of those inhabitants of the New World observed and described frequently from the time of Columbus. He was an "Indian" of the Caribbean.

Where did he come from? Not from anywhere around the goat-filled Juan Fernández Islands, off the west coast of South America, where Alexander Selkirk, Defoe's inspiration for Robinson Crusoe, lived alone for several years. It is no secret that Defoe knew Selkirk's story well, but he placed Robinson's shipwreck on a different shore. Crusoe's island lay near the mouth of the Orinoco River, off the coast of what is now Venezuela. Just before describing the shipwreck, Defoe clearly plots the northward course of Crusoe's vessel along the Brazilian shore" past Fernando de Noronha . . . across the Equator" and to its "last Observation in 7 Degrees 22 Min. Northern Latitude." That is just about the latitude of the mouth of the Orinoco. Later in the story Crusoe learns that the "land which I perceiv'd to the W. and N.W. [of his island] was the great Island of *Trinidad.*"

So, although shipwreck stories would eventually be played out more often in Pacific isles than in the West Indies, the best of them all was a Caribbean adventure, and Friday a resident of that region. Can we, then, pinpoint his people? Yes. When Crusoe asked Friday to name them, he "could get no other name than *Caribs.*" Actually, that was enough. Robinson readily identified Friday's people as the "Caribees," whom his maps had placed "from the mouth of the River *Oroonooko* to *Guiana,* and onwards to St. Martha [in Colombia]." Christopher Columbus had met those fellows. In fact, he had done battle with them—as had the Tainos, the first Indians whom the admiral had encountered. The Caribs were formidable opponents, adding a touch of terror to their commando raids and internecine slaughters through a penchant for cannibalism. Alas, the stigma of that practice remained with them long after the surviving Caribs had abandoned it, for just as one Spanish approximation of their name, "Caribe," brought them geographic immortality through the sea which bears their name, another Spanish approximation, "Canibales," brought them linguistic infamy.

Friday himself was a cannibal at the time Crusoe rescued him and would have continued in the habit had not his tutor and Christianizer dissuaded him. That gastronomic aberration was just one more underlining of his Carib identity. It did, however, lead to some latter-day confusion about Friday's ethnic origins, for, like the now-familiar shipwreck premise, the cannibal device of plot during the nineteenth century became associated with African and Melanesian locales. It was yet another reason that Friday, the cannibal-turned-perfect-servant, sometimes was perceived as a black man, especially in a nation for whose citizens the words "slave" and "Negro" were virtually interchangeable until 1865. Abolitionists, to be sure, welcomed the idea of a black Friday who embodied the innocent virtues earlier ascribed to the Indian. Crusoe's man had readily turned aside from cannibalism, after all.

But physically, geographically, nominatively, and socially Friday was an island Indian, specifically a Carib. That is the way the original readers of *Robinson Crusoe* knew him (however imprecisely Europeans as a whole perceived Indian-ness). In 1719, when the book first appeared, the image of the noble Indian was ready for its fullest literary blossom. Until editors, illustrators, and literary pirates commenced playing fast and loose with the Defoe narration, readers by the tens of thousands—including, not incidentally, a host of later authors—had formed close ties with Robinson Crusoe and the "old trusty servant and companion" who had been at his side through danger, battle, and

45

amusement. One of those devoted readers was Jean-Jacques Rousseau, who was five years old when the book first appeared in print. In *Émile* (1762), Rousseau set forth *Robinson Crusoe* as the first, and always the preeminent, book in an ideal education. Johann Wolfgang von Goethe, born in 1749, was another acknowledged admirer of *Robinson Crusoe*. He read it as a child (and not in Joachim Heinrich Campe's retelling for children (1779), which, in continental Europe particularly, almost supplanted Defoe's work).

We can wonder what age James Fenimore Cooper (1789–1851) had reached when he too encountered Crusoe and his Man Friday. That Cooper knew the book well we can be sure because of its relationship to his shipwreck allegory of 1847, *The Crater*. A more significant literary corridor, however, connects Defoe's *Crusoe* (and its sequels) and Cooper's Leatherstocking tales. It is the one we must examine when relating a Man Friday of the eighteenth century to a Tonto of the twentieth.

Both Daniel Defoe and Fenimore Cooper drew lasting portraits of solitary white men, Christians, who are content and comfortable in what to others might be a wilderness. Eventually, however, the paths of the white men join those of admirable male Indians (Friday and Chingackgook), who become their staunch allies in adversity, their partners in isolation, their comrades in travel. There are other parallels. The prolonged battle of Crusoe and Friday against nineteen cannibals, with its careful inclusion of detail and its midaction rescue of a white captive, could be transposed with little alteration to *The Deerslayer*—Friday's exploits perhaps being vulnerable to the same kind of literary skepticism which an uncharacteristically severe Mark Twain directed at Cooper. And although the Leatherstocking series moves back and forth chronologically, Cooper lets Chingachgook (Sagamore), the Mohican, meet his death in tragic and undignified manner, just as Defoe had Friday, the Carib, die. Hawkeye's old friend, however, is at least given something of a death scene, while poor Friday is, in the manner of a present-day daytime-serial character, abruptly written out of the story. Both faithful Indians end their days as Christians, Friday an eager, if puzzled one, Chingachgook (now John Mohegan) a belated accepter of society's conventions.

Still, for all the Crusoe-Leatherstocking parallels, evolution (or conscience) seemed to have been at work with Cooper. Hawkeye, the unspoiled woodsman, unlike Crusoe, the shipwrecked slave trader, is content to leave Chingachgook to his Indian mode of worship. Also unlike Crusoe, Hawkeye seeks neither slave nor servant. Cooper would make no effort to replicate the master-and-servant motif that modern readers find either illuminating or obnoxious in *Robinson Crusoe*—though, on the other hand, it is apparent that the white man and the Mohican are not the same sort of person. In fairness to Defoe, incidentally, Friday does gain a bit of stature in the little-known later adventures of Robinson Crusoe, in which the two men finally return to America, only to have Friday slain by an arrow fusillade dispatched by canoe-borne Indians who seem to be his own people. "And so," Crusoe tells us, "ended the life of the most grateful, faithful, honest, and most affectionate servant that man ever had."

Yet, graceful as these sentiments are, Crusoe hardly bats an eye before going on to his next piece of business. What is more, the faithful Friday's death is made almost ludicrous by the obscene mass posturing of the canoemen who brought him down—an early example of what is now known as "mooning." No, Friday was reliable, cheerful, honest, and all the rest, yet he was a second-class citizen, not only in the eyes of the world but in the eyes of the white man who demanded he call him Master.

Not so Chingachgook. Hawkeye's friend, the loyal Mohican, may have been an American mythologizing of the noble savage. He may, moreover, have ended his days in Christianized squalor. Still, to his white companion at least, he was a social equal. Hawkeye, or Natty Bumppo, followed trails with a man whom he respected in *The Deerslayer* (1841), *The Last of the Mohicans* (1826), and *The Pathfinder* (1840). They were joint victims of the white man's civilization in *The Pioneers* (1823). And the aged Natty Bumppo strongly recalled his departed companion in *The Prairie* (1827; as mentioned earlier, while the Leatherstocking tales carry Bumppo from his early twenties, in the 1740s, to his eighties, in 1804, the novels did not appear in chronological sequence).

In a young nation in which there was already a visible strain of remorse among intellectuals over the displacement of the continent's first inhabitants—not to mention a developing tide of abolitionism—Cooper's ennobling picture of Chingachgook was generous and humane, perhaps, but not startling. The author, after all, as an educated person, would have encountered not just Defoe's Friday but the noble-savage images generated by Montaigne or Rousseau or Chateaubriand on the Continent and, likely enough, the American-based portraits of John Bartram or Philip Freneau or St. John de Crèvecoeur.

47

In the absence of some well-drawn counterimages to the noble creatures of fantasy whom he met in books, Cooper could readily enough embrace the fantasy—for his favored Mohicans at least.

To put it simply, Cooper knew the sea and the northern New York landscape, but he knew Indians hardly at all. The Cooperstown country in his lifetime was a Glimmerglass land from which all the original residents had long departed. Writing a half-dozen books about a people he had not known, however, bothered him no more than did writing a single one about a prairie he had not seen. Until the brief period in which he made a point to seek out some journeying Sioux and Pawnees (after the Leatherstocking series had been launched), Cooper's primary knowledge regarding the American Indian came from a book of history and recollections published in 1818 by the Reverend John Heckewelder, a long-term pastor to those Christianized Pennsylvania Indians known as Moravians. At almost any point in the Leatherstocking tales in which Cooper touches upon the philosophy, customs, religion, habits, loyalty, or attitudes of Algonquin or Iroquois, it is Pastor Heckewelder who is guiding his hand. Cooper even gave his hero in *The Deerslayer* an unstated connection with the understanding preacher by telling the reader that, after young Bumppo lost his mother and was adopted by Delawares, his formal education, brief as it was, came through Moravian missionaries.

In Heckewelder's *History, Manners, and Customs of the Indian Nations* Cooper could have found rich background material for many scenes or situations. The pastor's observations or the Indian's special consideration of the insane would have served the author well when he projected the capture sequences involving David Gamut, the eccentric psalm singer of *The Last of the Mohicans,* or Hetty Hutter, the retarded sister in *The Deerslayer.* Chapters on oratory and metaphor in Heckewelder's book were primers for Indian dialogue—though nothing seemed to help Cooper much where conversation was concerned. Readers who know the Leatherstocking tales would readily recognize how much the novels' creator could have gleaned from chapters entitled "Marriage and Treatment of Their Wives," "Respect for the Aged," "Pride and Greatness of Mind," "Peace Messengers," "Treaties," "Scalping—Whoops or Yells—Prisoners," "Superstition," "Drunkenness," "Funerals," and "Preachers and Prophets." Considering how many authors patterned their frontier epics upon Cooper's, the Heckewelder inspiration is doubly significant.

48

Most pertinent to us here, however, is John Heckewelder's impassioned chapter titled "Friendship." Reading it, one can discover why Cooper's Chingachgook stands so far above Defoe's Friday in the eyes of his white companion. Here is a Heckewelder sampler:

> Those who believe that no faith is to be placed in the friendship of an Indian are egregiously mistaken, and know very little of the character of those men of nature.
>
> . . . I could fill many pages with examples of Indian friendship and fidelity, not only to each other, but to men of other nations and of different color than themselves.
>
> . . . I believe it will be difficult to find a single case in which they betrayed a real friend or abandoned him in the hour of danger . . . [rather] he will stand in his defence at the hazard of his own life.

In all these sentiments Mr Robinson Crusoe might have concurred insofar as his special Indian, Friday, was concerned. But what would he have thought of the Heckewelder basis for the Hawkeye-Chingachgook relationship: "indeed, the friendship of an Indian is easily acquired, provided it is sought in good faith. But whoever chooses to obtain it must be sure to treat them on a footing of perfect equality."

The very thought of Indian-white equality would have staggered old Robinson, who never even referred to Friday as a man but called him "the creature" or "the savage." What would his reaction have been to the continuation of Heckewelder's analysis: "They are very jealous of the whites, who they think affect to consider themselves as beings of a superior nature and too often treat them [the Indians] with rude and undeserved contempt. This they seldom forgive."

Needless to say, Robinson Crusoe, who was on his way to Africa for slaves when he was shipwrecked—and who earlier had sold into slavery a Moorish boy through whose kindness he had escaped pirates—would have thought Pastor Heckewelder mad. Possibly Daniel Defoe would have too. But James Fenimore Cooper did not, and his writings, for all their circumlocutions and brushes with patronizing, reflect that fact. Cooper may have idealized. And he may have patronized (did not Heckewelder say that Indians "feel flattered when a white man does not disdain to treat them as children of the same creator"?). Yet where in literature—or film—or television—would there again be a frontier companion to match Chingachgook? Surely not in the best-known twentieth-century manifestation, Tonto. How could it be Tonto with his Friday English and his satirized willingness to do the Lone Ranger's dirty work? How could it be Tonto, who was created after the famed radio series began so that the masked rider of the plains would have someone to talk with other than his horse? Trustworthy, warmhearted, courageous as he was, Tonto ("fool" in Spanish) remained a surface character, his inner dimensions as masked as the Lone Ranger's visage, his longings much less known than Friday's, let alone Chingachgook's.[3]

These comparisons with Friday and Tonto are not meant to imply that Chingachgook was Hawkeye's heroic match—no one was—but he came close. Natty Bumppo, remember, was himself a greater-than-life figure. When only Bumppo's spirit lingers in the fictional Templeton (Cooperstown), a character in Cooper's little-known *Home as Found* (1838) eulogizes Hawkeye as one who possessed "the simplicity of a woodsman, the heroism of a savage, the faith of a Christian, and the feelings of a poet." It scarcely was necessary for the eulogizer to add that "a better man than he, after his fashion, seldom lived."

Seldom lived? Such a Promethean frontiersman *never* lived—except in Cooper's fiction, and the thousands of story-paper, dime-novel, stage-melodrama, and broadcasting and film imitations of Hawkeye who wandered primeval forests in coonskin caps or roamed the endless prairies in ten-gallon Stetsons. To walk or ride beside a giant and not be lost in his shadow required a richness of character which Cooper supplied to Chingachgook and that imitators, concentrating on externals, failed to deliver. The decades which saw the frontier hero step out of moccasins and into cowboy boots saw also his sidekick (even if he still carried bow and arrow) slip into a two-

[3]Tonto did have some moments of free expression, but they were fleeting. In the juvenile novel of 1936 spurred by the new radio series, the Lone Ranger's companion uses the ludicrous English yet is not afraid to reverse a practical joke played by the Ranger—who himself is more relaxed in both demeanor and speech than he is in the book's sequel, when his dramatized character has become fixed in a state of dignity broken only by his ventures into disguise. Late in the Lone Ranger television series, Tonto (no doubt because of the protests of his Indian portrayer, Jay Silverheels, and a glint of awareness shown by the producers) gently bemoans the numberless lumps on his head and asks the Lone Ranger why *he* does not bell the cat sometimes. Such moments stand out for their rarity, however, and without delineating his character merely reinforce Tonto's decades of uncomplaining acceptance of his comrade-organized life. The only solo adventures the Indian could treasure in his old age came in some *Tonto* comics of the 1950s and in garish, horror-oriented TV-animation series of the late 1960s in which Tonto, gibberish and all, was given five-minute entr'actes.

dimensional aspect one would more logically expect to find in a faithful horse or dog. Skilled he could be, stolid he could be, even comic
he could be, but never inner-directed. Never was a latter-day Indian
companion concerned with self—except as his own fate affected that
of the man he served. What, for example, do we know of Tonto that
is not a function of his relationship to the Lone Ranger? Riding beside
a driven wrong-righter, did he have any aspiration but that of following? Did he ever long to see his homeland? Was there a lost love? Did
he revere a father? Did he ever wish to suggest the next trail? Did he
despair of his hopeless grammar?

Chingachgook, on the other hand, felt and expressed emotions
respecting his own life and the life of his people. Cooper gave him a
woman to love and a son to protect, and later to mourn. Bumppo (as
the Deerslayer) would take the trail to support Chingachgook in his
courtship of the lovely Hist. Later he would share the Mohican's
pleasure in watching Uncas, the son whom Hist bore, grow to vital
manhood. Then at the heroic death of that son, hearing Chingachgook wail, "I am alone," Hawkeye would put a seal on their closeness:

". . . no, Sagamore, not alone. The gifts of our colors may be different,
but God has so placed us as to journey on the same path. I have no kin,
and I may also say, like you, no people. He was your son, and a red-skin
by nature; and it may be that your blood was nearer—but, if ever I forget
the lad who has so often fou't at my side in war, and slept at my side
in peace, may He who made us all, whatever be our color or our gift,
forget me! The boy has left us for a time; but Sagamore, you are not
alone.

Words a hundred years in time and understanding beyond those
Robinson Crusoe could express. Words that might have pointed the
way to ones of equal or greater understanding a century later. Yet
words that thus far in the realm of frontier adventure have represented
not a milestone on the journey upward but the highest point of ascent.

Down a few fictional trails the Indian and the white man walked side by side. Pictured are Chingachgook and Hawkeye in The Last of the Mohicans.

The Carib Friday shows his respect for Robinson Crusoe in two book illustrations of the 1800s.

Above: *Tonto, the Lone Ranger's Friday, in shadow and profile.* Below Left: *Clayton Moore and Jay Silverheels in the "cactus-ex-Stetson" still from the television series.* Below Right: *Lee Powell and Chief Thundercloud in the first Lone Ranger serial (1938).*

Above Left: *Pahoo (X Brands), the silent companion of television's* Yancy Derringer *(Jock Mahoney).* Above Right: *Chingachgook (Robert Barrat) and Hawkeye (Randolph Scott) in 1936.* Below: *Wild Bill Elliott aided by Iron Eyes Cody in* Overland with Kit Carson *(1939).*

Two actors known for their portrayals of Cochise: Jeff Chandler, with bow and knife, in Broken Arrow *(1950) and Michael Ansara, with John Lupton, in the television version.* Below left: *Edwin Forrest, whose Metamora inspired the Chandler-Cochise persona.*

Tonto with a sense of humor—Little Beaver of **Red Ryder.** *Robert Blake played in the film series alongside Allan Lane.*

ENGLISHMAN: *S'blood! Joseph [Yannhoontough] I hardly know what to say. You seem to talk fluently. Perhaps I have been too much prejudiced against the Indians.*

Professor John Smith of Dartmouth,
A Dialogue Between an Englishman and an Indian, 1779

4

INDIAN TALK

WHEN Hawkeye and Chingachgook, much as James Fenimore Cooper had drawn them, reached American television sets in 1972—as part of a British serialization of *The Last of the Mohicans*—an old and inherently plaguing question came to light again: How should an Indian talk? To hear a Hawkeye sprinkling his frontier bons mots with more than a trace of English accent was unsettling enough for an audience used to the John Wayne–Gary Cooper twang. To hear a Chingachgook unblinkingly enunciating complete sentences with scarcely a grunt was almost beyond comprehension.

Hawkeye's accent could be explained away by the possibility that his parents had emigrated from England (that is what the serial's director proposed, at least). How, though, could one adjust to Mohicans and Delawares and Hurons issuing forth in Oxonian or Shakespearean tones and tints? Simply by letting time do its handiwork, concluded many Americans, as their ears grew accustomed to the sounds of the weekly serial. It had been through a similar process, after all, that other modes of representing the American Indian had come and gone over the centuries. In stiff-backed early American literature and theater (as later in colloquialized dime novel, broadcast drama, and film drama), initial impression was important to the acceptance of Indian talk. Thereafter, repetition dulled perception. True,

58

after the Lone Ranger broadcasts and telecasts of the 1930s, 1940s, and 1950s had entered the realms of nostalgia, the more culturally sensitive onetime followers of the masked man's adventures may have recognized that the faithful Tonto's mode of speech was demeaning to a people—no matter how good and intelligent Tonto himself was. Yet when those adventure dramas were in flower, did "Gettum-up, Scout!" seem less-natural Indian argot to its hearers than the flowing words of a Cooper Indian had seemed to book readers of the century before—or the "Why, you angry mad with Friday, what me done?" of Daniel Defoe's native the century before that?

In the popular media, especially, Americans have too long been comfortable with what, through a haphazard union of theatrical rhetoric and Wild West jargon, became established as suitable Indian talk, from vocal pattern to sentence structure. Only after decades of relaxed acceptance of a parlance that never was did a dramatization brought from foreign shores evoke a disquieting note in the choral section. The initial reaction was that the BBC had blundered with its odd Mohican sounds of the Cooper serial. Possibly. Yet who at the time could recognize the proper note?

The truth is that, for anyone trying to bring a touch of verisimilitude to fiction or drama, the talking Indian has always been a terrible problem. If he speaks only his native tongue, how does the reader or audience discover what he is saying? If he speaks the white man's language, how well should he be able to speak it?

Attempts to circumvent the difficulty have proved fascinating, especially during the mass-media era. For television's first *Daniel Boone* series Boone's pal, Mingo (Ed Ames) was provided with an Oxford education. For her novel of 1979 about Indian culture, *Hanta Yo,* Ruth Beebe Hill, aided by a Dakota named Chunksa Yuha, translated her original manuscript into an early form of the Dakota tongue (with some variants of Lakota dialect). Then the book was remodeled conceptually and returned to English. Even with this ambitious, if somewhat puzzling, approach, the author found difficulty in reflecting her characters' style of speaking, as she explained in the preface:

> Any attempt to mold English into a Dakotah (Siouan) form results in a pidgin Indian, and an attempt to reverse the process results in pidgin English. And so I have observed Indian idiom as closely as possible in mood, tense, and definition whenever the English equivalent would limit the Dakotah concept.

Here is how one of Hill's Dakotas sounds when speaking of bravery: "Your brother proves himself brave against the enemy. Facing someone who will kill you, wound you, takes courage. But facing someone who will heal you perhaps takes more courage."

In shorter phrases Hill sometimes included both the Dakota expression and the English translation, as writers before her had done. Neil H. Swanson was one. In *Unconquered* he had his Senecas say things like "Ieinsdon'gwa! Sgaga'di! Dedji'aon'gwa!" An English translation followed, set off by brackets. More recently Richard Sale employed a similar technique, without the brackets, for *The White Buffalo* (1975). In film or television (where technical versatility has led to occasional use of the trick) the translation can be instant. Subtitles in English are stretched across the bottom of the screen, while warriors on horseback rattle off their attack plan in language presumably—but not necessarily—Dakota or Cheyenne. This "what-is-the-enemy-planning?" device (which is more awkward than effective) has also been employed for cinematic reconstructions of World War II, German or Japanese "gutturals" receiving translation in place of those assumed to characterize Dakota or Cheyenne.

In some motion pictures Indian languages have been disregarded entirely by having frontier parleys take place in French or Spanish, a weathered trapper or ranchero serving as translator. Not surprisingly, sign language has received a good workout on the screen, sometimes most appropriately, sometimes when a lingua franca is unnecessary or illogical. In his cowboy pictures, Colonel Tim McCoy, who knew both the oral and the visual aspects of one of the plains dialects, could bring off a horseback summit meeting with true finesse. Less grounded performers, in contrast, limited their arm-and-hand vocabulary to faintly recollected elocution gestures or prudently left the heavy communication to palm-and-larynx specialists hired for minor roles. The latter contrivance, incidentally, goes back to the legitimate theater, where, for instance, Edwin Milton Royle cast a mature Ute as Baco White for his play of 1905, *The Squaw Man,* so that the fellow could act as a fictional interpreter and at the same time ensure the correct pronunciation of Ute dialect by other players.

Always available to filmmakers (and playwrights) has been the too-familiar silent (or grunting) brave in a blanket, seen in every kind of movie from comedy—Joe E. Brown's *Broadminded* (1931), for instance—to epic drama—*Drums Along the Mohawk* (1939). Television carried the taciturnity device to an extreme with the Pawnee Pahoo

60

(played by X Brands), a mute Tonto of the *Yancy Derringer* series. With his opulent pointing, Pahoo could have put to shame Charles Dickens's silently cogent Ghost of Christmas Yet to Come.

Long before there were television dramas and motion pictures, however, Cooper, while not having to worry about spoken words in actors mouths, fell back upon the device used in the theater during his era. He had Chingachgook chat with Hawkeye in English—after telling the reader that their conversations were actually "free translations" from the Delaware tongue in which he endeavored "to preserve some of the peculiarities, both of the individual and of the language." Cooper explained that an Indian's language had the "richness and sententious fullness of the Chinese." An Indian, added Cooper, could "express a phrase in a word—qualify the meaning of an entire sentence by a syllable—and even convey different significations by the simplest inflections of the voice." Thus, while sitting on a log near a stream, Chingachgook would say something to Hawkeye that Cooper would freely translate as:

> "We came from the place where the sun is hid at night, over great plains where the buffaloes live, until we reached the great river. There we fought the Alligewi, till the ground was red with their blood. From the banks of the big river to the shores of the salt lake, there was none to meet us. The Maquas followed at a distance."

Hawkeye's replies in philosophical conversations like these were equally formal and often deferential. When he was speaking English, however, the frontiersman bounced from parliamentary elegance to buckskin lingo at the change of a paragraph.[1] Chingachgook's rare remarks in English (or were they too in Delaware?) came down to "Hugh. . . . Hugh"—which modern readers eventually realize is not a first name but Cooper's way of freely translating the more familiar "Ugh!"

[1]Mark Twain derided Bumppo's dialogue, but Anthony Burgess reminded later readers that "it takes a long time for a national fiction to learn how to talk." "Said Mr. Cooper to His Wife: 'You Know, I Could Write Something Better than That," *New York Times Magazine*, May 7, 1972.

Oliver La Farge's Pulitzer Prize–winning *Laughing Boy* (1929) would seem to extend Burgess's argument to "translated" Indian dialogue. When the book's characters are supposed to be speaking Navajo (and they do so almost exclusively), their phrases, though definitely not of the English pattern, seem more natural than Cooper's simulated Mohican. When La Farge's principal woman character changes over to English, however, one thinks of both *Robinson Crusoe* and Remedial Communication 101: "I can' do it. It ain't I don' want to, George. I can' dat's all. . . . You know dat."

When up against prolonged Indian-white conversations, sans ughs, moviemakers have preferred the Cooper compromise, usually forgoing explanation but sometimes, as in *Broken Arrow*, letting the narrator (James Stewart) tell the audience that "when the Apaches speak, they will speak in our language." Still, without falling back upon dramatic license, writers have long had another, albeit condescending, device for letting people understand what an Indian has to say. Daniel Defoe, founder of the Tonto Institute for Communication, demonstrated the solution by having Robinson Crusoe teach English to Friday so that they might converse in a language convenient for both Robinson and the reader. Presumably the disjointed outcome of the instruction was as much the fault of the teacher as the pupil, but Crusoe insisted otherwise. Deviation such as resistance to plural endings, said that amateur pedagogue, was nothing more than a fact of nature, much like the native's weakness with verb endings:

> Here it is to be observed that all these natives, as also those of Africa, when they learn English, always add two e's at the ends of words where we use one, and they place the accent upon them, as makee, takee, and the like, and we could not break them of it; nay I could hardly make Friday leave it off, though at last he did.

Those actual scholars of language and folklore the brothers Grimm no doubt could have explained how the "makees" and "takees" of the tropical Indian of fiction were diffused into the "makems" and "takems" of Tontoland on the north. What, we can wonder, was the route of permutation? Was there a Grimm's law for Indian consonants? For definite articles? For pronouns? And why cannot an absurdly artificial dialect be put to rest when it serves only to demean? That, of course, is the critical question because, even though thus far we have been focusing upon the mechanical problems of making an Indian understood within a framework of literary or theatrical conventions, the means by which an audience is made to understand an Indian is sociologically less important than the image formed when he speaks.

This country's early writers—those who wished to do some reading on the subject, anyway—could have turned to some rather prominent observers or commentators on Indian speech. Thomas Jefferson, for instance, ruefully expressed the wish that the orators of Congress would do just half as well as those of the Indian nations. Much earlier, William Penn, who made it his business to learn the language of the Lenni Lenape (Delawares) so that he "might not want an Interpreter on any occasion," had called that language "lofty, yet narrow." He knew no "Language spoken in Europe, that hath words of more sweetness or greatness, in Accent and Emphasis, than theirs." Penn also spotted a shorthand quality in the language he studied—"one word serveth in the place of three, and the rest are supplied by the Understanding of the Hearer." The Quaker, writing in 1683, saw his newly learned language as different in structure from—but not inferior to—English.

William Penn's enthusiasm for the Lenni Lenape tongue may have led him to endorse a curious theory that the Indian dialects were related to Hebrew. In that misapprehension Penn was far from alone. As late as 1775, historian James Adair, an Indian agent and trader under George III, was extending it to the languages of the southern Indians, which he called "copious and very expressive." Linguistic blind alleys notwithstanding, Adair patiently examined by first hand experience the southern tongues for noun declensions and cases (he found none) and for verb patterns (what Adair called the preterperfect, "Yesterday I went and saw," sometimes replaced the present indicative, "Now I go and see"). Although adjectives had to stumble along without comparative or superlative degrees, Adair caught a colorful manner of comparison in which opposites were placed alongside each other, Cole Porter style: "You're the top . . . I'm the bottom." Additionally, adjectives could be doubled, and adverbs meaning "much" or "little" could be placed before other words, as in "much brave"—a basis, perhaps, of the "heap big Indian" conceit of indifferent authors. In all, Adair praised a group of languages which were "concise, emphatical, sonorous, and bold."

A recognized philologist, Pierre Étienne Du Ponceau, examined North American Indian grammars in the 1830s. While he may not have been flattering when he refused to speculate on whether "savages" could boast of many ideas, he was open in saying that "if their ideas are few, their words to express them are many." Du Ponceau continued, "I am lost in astonishment at the copiousness and admirable structure of the American languages." In 1819, Pastor John Heckewelder, Cooper's historical guide, while decrying the skepticism about Indian oratorical abilities which had resulted from prejudice, called the native eloquence both "natural and simple" . . . and "forcible and impressive." If Indian argument was few in points, it was rich in metaphor, contended Heckewelder, who supported his argument with a string of pithy expressions, from "Bury the hatchet" and "Speak from the heart" to "We have concluded a peace, which is to

last as long as the sun shall shine, and the rivers flow with water."
Henry David Thoreau admired the richness and variety of Indian
terminology for things of nature. For abstract matters, though, thoreau perceived a narrower range of expression.

Allowing, then, for biases, partial errors of judgment, scholarly
tangents, and the like, one could say that at the time American writers
began turning to the Indian for subject matter there was ample educated opinion to suggest that he was not a verbal cripple. And it would
be correspondingly fair to state that until the second half of the 1800s
most authors and playwrights gave him his rhetorical due—and then
some. We have already looked at the ten-dollar language of Cooper
in *The Last of the Mohicans,* but, by standards of conversational elegance
prevailing in the theater of his day, Cooper was among the plain and
simple people. Here is just a fraction of a speech by Pocahontas in
James N. Barker's popular *The Indian Princess; or La Belle Sauvage,* "an
operatic melo-drame" first acted in 1808:

O my love!

Guided by thee, has not my daring soul,
O'ertopt the far off mountains of the east,
Where, as our fathers' fable, shad'wy hunters
Pursue the deer, or clasp the melting maid,
Mid ever blooming spring? Thence, soaring high
From the deep vale of legendary fiction,
Hast though not heaven-ward turn'd my dazzled sight,
Where sing the spirits of the blessed good
Around the bright throne of the Holy One?

Barker, it should be noted, employed the blank verse primarily in the
love scene between Pocahontas and John Rolfe, but none of his Indian
(or English) characters is a piker with words, and "thou's" and "thy's"
abound in this prototype of the princess plays.

Closer to reality in suggestion of English as spoken by the Indian
was Major Robert Rogers in his "lost" play, *Ponteach* (published in
1766). If any writer could have been expected to downgrade the
Indian by putting infantile sounds in his mouth, it was the famed
Indian fighter who had commanded Rogers' Rangers and had done
battle against Pontiac's forces. Yet Rogers, feeling sympathy for his
adversary, produced a pioneer American problem play (which may or
may not have been performed during his lifetime). This is how some
of his Indian characters spoke in a fur-trading interlude:

1ST INDIAN
So, what you trade with Indians here to-day?

M'DOLE
Yes, if my goods will suit, and we agree.

2ND INDIAN
'tis Rum we want, we're tired, hot, and thirsty.

3RD INDIAN
You, Mr. Englishman, have you got Rum?

Since McDole has already told a pal that "it's no Crime to cheat and gull an Indian," the reader can assume the result of the exchange. Pontiac later reacts this way:

> Indians a'nt Fools, if White Men think us so;
> We see, we hear, we think as well as you;
> We know they're [*sic*] Lies and Mischiefs in the World;
> We don't know whom to trust, nor when to fear;
> Men are uncertain, changing as the Wind . . .
> But I call no man bad, till such he's found.

A century and three-quarters after the *Ponteach* furs-for-rum scene was written, a band of drunken Sioux staggered into an advance camp in the film *Western Union* (1941). How did the leader put things?

> Me want whiskey!

Pronoun trouble, an Indian disease dormant in the era of Rogers' Rangers.

Always in possession of his pronouns, however, was the theater's Edwin Forrest, America's foremost portrayer of noble Indians. Playing a chief in the New York company of M. M. Noah's *She Would Be a Soldier, or, The Plains of Chippewa* (1819), Forrest could declaim to Captain Pendragon:

> Young man, the Indian warrior knows no master but the Great Spirit, whose voice is heard in thunder, and whose eye is seen in the lightning's flash; free as air, we bow the knee to no man; our forests are our home, our defence is our arms, our sustenance the deer and the elk, which we run down. White men encroach upon our borders, and drive us into war; we raise the tomahawk against your enemies, because your king has promised as protection and supplies. We fight for freedom, and in that cause, the great king and the poor Indian start upon equal terms.

To readers of the Tonto era, the elegance of the chief's language may appear even more remarkable when contrasted with Noah's unhappy simulation of the French accent of Pendragon's valet:

Parbleu, he is von very sensible sauvage; vill you take von pinch snuff.

To which the stately Indian responds:

Pshaw!

Edwin Forrest's most memorable, and most elegant, Indian was the title character in *Metamora* (1829), a play tailored for the actor by John Augustus Stone with an energy that put it a cut above most other Indian vehicles. Indeed, it had been selected in a writing competition by a panel of judges that included William Cullen Bryant. Nonetheless, by today's standards the dialogue is sometimes overblown. This weakness is concealed somewhat when Metamora confronts the English: "Metamora has been the friend of the white man; yet if the flint be smitten too hard it will show that in its heart is fire."

Pomposity emerges, however, in the lofty chief's domestic dialogue. Here is the way Metamora answers his wife when she asks whether he will be home in time for dinner: ". . . before the otter has tasted his midday food on the bank of the stream, his skin shall make a garment for Nahmeokee when the snow whitens the hunting grounds and the cold wind whistles through the trees. . . ."

Although both whites and Indians lapsed into such ludicrous descriptions in *Metamora,* audiences came out to see Edwin Forrest play the role through four decades and wept at a still-effective death scene.

Forrest, ironically, was apprehensive before the initial presentation of the heralded prize-winning play, built, as the contest required, upon a native theme. Nonetheless, the athletic actor's bravura performance alone probably would have carried the day. Forrest's voice, reported one awed critic, "surged and roared like the angry sea; as it reached its boiling, seething climax, in which the serpent hiss of hate was heard, at intervals . . . like the falls of Niagara." Said another reviewer about the actor's personification of one of nature's noblemen, "Forrest caught the very manner of their breathing." The press, in other words, could match a playwright in metaphor during that era, a point worth remembering when putting nineteenth-century theatrical dialogue into perspective.

When the stage began to burlesque popular dramatic genres in the mid-1800s, it was inevitable that the Indian play would be included in the festivities, primarily through John Brougham's spoof of all Noble Savage dramas, *Po-Ca-Hon-Tas; or, the Gentle Savage.* Nonetheless, the flamboyance of Edwin Forrest and lesser purveyors of woodland majesty and bombast was the primary target of Brougham's humor, not the American Indian himself, or his speech. Whites and Indians are indistinguishable in grammar and phrasing in Brougham's popular burlesque, and both groups show equal weakness for the pun.

It was not theatrical burlesque which brought down Indian rhetoric; it was something much more serious. When the vogue of the Noble Savage waned in the middle years of the nineteenth century and a harsher racial concept expanded to fill the growing vacuum, a matching style of Indian talk accompanied the change. Playing no small role in the transformation was Robert Montgomery Bird's *Nick of the Woods; or, The Jibbenainosay* (1837). Today one of those literary landmarks that are studied more than read, *Nick of the Woods* was the most successful "bad Indian" novel of its era, and possibly of all time. Bird himself, in the preface to the first edition, confessed to having placed "around the Indian portraits in our picture . . . hues darker than are usually employed by the painters of such figures." That was because, explained the author, "the North American savage has never appeared to us the gallant and heroic personage he seems to others." Those others, of course, included Chateaubriand and, more significantly, Cooper. Rejecting the stereotype of the "beau ideal," Bird attempted to portray the undomesticated Indian in a style "as correct and true to nature as he could." Where an Indian had not been "softened by cultivation," Bird felt compelled to draw him as "ignorant, violent, debased, brutal."

Now Bird was an author whom scholars recognize as a pioneer in simulating dialect (albeit without uniform success). His Quaker and his New Englander are clearly distinguishable from his Kentuckians. And his ring-tailed roarer, Ralph Stackpole, became a literary prototype, for all his weaknesses of character and sensitivity:

Tarnal death to me . . . if that don't make me eat a niggur, may I be totaciously chawed up myself.

Bird's black slave also is easily differentiated by his speech, though the author's degree of original inspiration can be questioned:

67

"... don't be afraid, Missie Edie; nebber mind; - ole Emperor will fight and die for missie, old Massa John's daughter."

It is only Bird's nominal hero, and his lady, who declaim in archaic fashion lines like "Away with you, you scoundrel and jackanapes. . . . We will have none of your base company."

In light of Bird's attention to the different flavors of spoken language (both real and artificial), it would have been absolutely in character to generate a lingo appropriate to what he considered ignorant or debased Indians. Consciously, or unconsciously, he did so. Thus one of his feathered characters in a "guttural" voice muttered:

> "Long knife no move; see how Piankeshaw kill long-knife's brudders!
> —Piankeshaw great fighting man!"

Later in the novel Quaker Nathan Slaughter (who after the slaying of his family became an Indian-hating avenger known as the Jibbenainosay) comes face-to-face with archvillain Wenonga, a Shawnee. Get ready for the faulty pronoun syndrome:

> "Me Injun-man!" said the chief, addressing his words to the prisoner, and therefore in the prisoner's language,—"Me kill all white-man! Me Wenonga: me drink white-man's blood; me no heart!"

No resemblance there to the Noble Savage.

Nick of the Woods, livelier reading than the dialogue of some of its characters would suggest, went through multiple printings and several times was converted to play form by other writers (notably Louisa Medina, whose 1838 dramatization was still being performed in the 1870s). Cooper surely would have encountered the novel, and while he may have taken comfort from the attacks on Bird by those favoring a less barbarous delineation of the Indian, he may also have decided to make an adjustment or two in his own styling of Indian dialect. Here, for example, is the way Magua, the Indian heavy, executed his "imperfect English" in *The Last of the Mohicans,* published eleven years before *Nick of the Woods:*

> "When Magua left his people, his wife was given to another chief; he has now made friends with the Hurons, and he will go back to the graves of his tribe, on the shores of the great lake. Let the daughter of the English chief follow, and live in his wigwam forever.

Contrast that formal declamation of Magua with the dialogue of another Cooper Indian (who, like Magua, had for a time lived with white people). Hist, Chingachgook's bride-to-be in *The Deerslayer,* 1841)—written after *Nick of the Woods*—talks to Hetty Hutter in almost comic-Indian fashion:

> "No t'ink more of him—no say more of scalp . . . you pale-face, I redskin; we bring up different fashion. . . . Better not talk of any but fader and Hurry; Mingo understand *dat;* he no understand *t'udder.* Promise you no talk about what you no understand."

Cooper, however influenced he may have been by the changing Indian image or by Bird's styling of it, let his Indians remain human beings when he began altering their dialogue, and usually he kept them out of personal-pronoun trouble (though Hist did call herself "him" at times). But other authors leaped on the "me Injun-man" bandwagon to such an extent that for a hundred years and more Indians who did not speak in the elegant metaphors soon reserved for stately chief or lovely princess were locked into the Friday Tonto speech of "me's" and "him's," of "ughs" and "heap bigs," of "hows" and verbs ending in " 'um."

For the reader's edification, here is a cavalcade of Indian-speak. Gettum ready!

Dakotas responding to a campfire tale:

> "How! how!"
> [more speech by white man]
> "How! how! how!"
> [speech continues]
> "How?"
> [speech continues]
> "how! how! how!
> [speech concludes]
> "How! how! how! how!"   Francis Parkman, *The Oregon Trail,* 1847

Many Bears studies a scouting report:

> "Ugh! More blue-Coats. Great many,
> No use follow. Get all killed. Big guns.
> Indians no like 'em. Ugh!"
> William O. Stoddard, *The Talking Leaves,* 1882

Winnetou concludes an address, and Apache warriors respond:

"Howgh. Ich habe gesprechen."
"Uff, uff!"

Karl May, Winnetou, 1892

Awonusk (an "old squaw") to young captives:

"No, no, no, . . . Indians no kill
Chon [John]. Make Chon a great brave. . . .
Big magic, . . . Pow-wow. Tell about
Great White Spirit who lives in sky, up, up."

Mary P. Wells Smith, The Young Puritans in Captivity, 1899

An Indian captor to some youngsters:

"Young Long-Knife heap big fool!"

James A. Braden, Captives Three, 1904

A ranch Indian, Buck Tooth, to the boy heroes:

"Ugh. . . . Me after 'em too—Yaquis! . . . Me catchum an' shootum same like um shoot me!"

Willard F. Baker, The Boy Ranchers Among the Indians, 1922

Slim Girl to her white admirer:

"You tink lak dat about me! You tink I forget everything! What for you tink dose tings, hey?"

Oliver La Farge, Laughing Boy, 1929

Ruby Big Elk to a white woman:

"Teach um song."

Joe Yellow Eyes to a white woman:

"Sure take um home."

Short Tooth to a white man:

"How! . . . Want um paper."

Edna Ferber, Cimarron, 1930

Harka to Bobby Benson on a radio program of the 1930s:

Ho, Bobby Boy, You tired huh? . . . Me know. [Airplane motors] get me too. Be glad to be back on Ranch and hear no noise, only coyote howl and tecolate hoot.

Bobby Benson and the H-Bar-O Rangers

Blue Back, the friendly Indian:

"Like you. Fine friends. Me, you. Fine." [and later in the book] "Sure. Fine. . . . You watch'm woods close. . . . They come some more. They mad. . . . You watch'm woods."

Walter D. Edmonds, *Drums Along the Mohawk,* 1936

Indian scout, Konkapot, in drunken hymn-singing rhapsodies:

"Moe [More] . . . Moe . . . Moe. . . . You know Dusty Fiddles [Adeste Fideles]? . . . You my sweet bludda!"

Kenneth Roberts, *Northwest Passage,* 1937

Four consecutive lines by the radio Tonto:

Who you?
Ugh.
You see-um him?
Me want-um him.

Fran Striker, *The Lone Ranger,* June 30, 1939

Little Beaver, a juvenile, to a rescued older pal:

"Needum shave, Red Ryder. Don't you kissum me!"

R. R. Winterbotham (using Fred
Harman characters for) *Red Ryder and The
Mystery of Whispering Walls,* 1941

Some "delighted savages" before dinner:

"Ho! Ho! Ho!"

Sterling North, *Captured by the Mohawks,* 1960

Pawnees between swallows of coffee and biscuits:

"How, how."   Thomas Berger, *Little Big Man,* 1964

Reader gettum sick? Have-um enough?

The talking Indian of fiction has been if not drowned then at least engulfed by a sea of confusions. His first words to white men, in whatever area or dialect, were recorded by untrained ears—sometimes by ears listening for special clues to lands of riches like "Cathay." Often those words traveled circuitous routes—even through several European tongues—to the English dictionary (or frontier equivalent). Some of an Indian's sounds did not exist in the language of his hearers and were lost entirely or were turned in to grunted approximations (in books beyond count Indian speech is described as "guttural"). Then came the generalizations, based upon the miscon-

71

ception that all the nations spoke something called "Indian." Thus "How!" (an approximation of Sioux or Osage words of greeting) was put into the mouth of every Indian from Canada to Mexico, and beyond; "squaw" was applied to all Indian women, though the term was an approximation of regional Algonquin; and so on. Respected writers, for example Francis Parkman, did not help the generalization problem by calling "How!" "a monosyllable by which an Indian contrives to express half the emotions of which he is susceptible." Ernest Thompson Seton assumed universal affirmatives and negatives and in his well-intentioned *Rolf of the Woods* (1911) misled young readers by stating that "ugh (yes) and wah (no) are Indianisms that continue no matter how well the English has been acquired."[2]

Compounding generalization was imitation. One "heap big" (whatever its slight foundation in forest grammar) was followed by thousands of "heap bigs." One ancient contraction of the English "him"—as in "Make'm drunk"—was in some lost decade mindlessly converted into a verbal ending sans pronoun—"See-um clouds"—and generations of lazy authors followed suit. Abundant imitation came also on the heels of supposedly direct translations of imagery: "Great White Father," "Happy Hunting Grounds," "squawman." These phrases, along with "heap big chief," suggested H. L. Mencken in *The American Language,* "owed more to the imagination of the pioneers than to the actual usage of the Indians." Yet how many novelists or screenplay writers would get through an Indian story without them?

Some have tried. Willa Cather chose to simulate English as a second language for an old Navajo in *Death Comes for the Archbishop* (1926). When Eusabio visits his dying clergyman friend, he speaks in a kind of shorthand, but something of his character and feeling comes through:

> "I come on the cars [railway], Padre I get on the cars at Gallup, and the same day I am here. You remember when we come together once to Santa Fe from my country? How long it take us? Two weeks pretty near. Men travel faster now, but I do not know if they go to better things."

Many readers would find no racial slur in the Cather dialogue, suggesting as it does a vocal pattern. Other readers would counter that no approximation of Indian conversation in English which smacks

---

[2]The meaning of "ugh" we can leave to heaven. Seton's "wah" might be an old Sioux expletive standing somewhere between "bah" and "phooey." Even so, the author used it with the wrong Indians.

even remotely of *Robinson Crusoe* and *The Lone Ranger* can be acceptable until time has made the stereotyping disappear. If the Indian must speak English in a frontier setting, these readers would say, let it be in simple and direct sentences, without metaphors and without clichés. Aside from being less insulting than much imaginary Indian talk, this approach would be no less authentic historically than the conventional palaver.[3] Comfort with a style of speech never used by an Indian in real life should not be mistaken for authenticity—not even by Indian performers, who sometimes fall into artificial patterns of speech in the same way that they put on Sioux headdresses because that is the way "everyone" assumes Indians dress.

The time has passed for fully reconstructing the actual manner in which Indians handled English conversation in the days before the mass-media era colored all language. We have only recollections and rough transcriptions of spoken exchanges in colonial and frontier days —by persons whose own English phrasing and pronunciation would be far from the standard American of radio and television. Still, if we do not know precisely how to treat Indian dialogue, we know, most assuredly, how not to. The oldtime Indian talk is wrong, dead wrong. Someday even writers for the popular media will realize that fact. Someday.

[3]George Philip Krapp, who found a few of the rare examples of early American efforts to record the English of Indians and included them in *The English Language in America* (1925), believed that no authentic Indian English pattern ever developed. Why not? Because Indians who learned English learned it so well that special colorations were not apparent. Those who did not learn English, Krapp explained, remained silent in the presence of white men to avoid appearing ridiculous—thus drawing the "sullen, morose and impassive" reputation not characteristic of the "Indian in his natural surroundings."

5

LUST BETWEEN THE BOOKENDS

O<small>N THE TENTH</small> of February . . . came the Indians with great
numbers upon Lancaster: their first coming was about sunris-
ing. The words were those of a seventeenth-century home-
maker, Mary Rowlandson. Her husband was Lancaster's pastor,
absent from his home on a special mission. The dawn attack made
Lancaster one of the many village battlegrounds in a tortuous frontier
struggle which came to be known as King Philip's War.

Surrounded by colonists, annoyed by religious proselytizers, confused by bureaucrats, betrayed by charlatans, the Indians of New
England—the Wampanoags, the Nipmucs, the Pennacooks, the Narra-
gansets, the Abnakis—rose in frustration and revenge under Metacomet (King Philip) exactly a century before the outbreak of the
American Revolution. The village of Swansea took the first attack, on
Sunday, June 24, 1675 (before Metacomet was quite ready to launch
his long-planned uprising, say some historians). Then came raids on
Taunton, Middleborough, Dartmouth, Hadley, Deerfield, Braintree,
and other communities. Throughout the New England frontier farm-
ers and tradesmen lay anxiously abed, wondering whether first light
would find them fighting for their lives and those of their loved ones.
After a seeming lull in the fighting, the dreaded war cries came to
Lancaster on a wintry morning.

The attack, devastating as it was, carried no particular strategic or historical significance. It made its mark on the public because one woman, Mary Rowlandson, set down a vivid account of that raid and her capture in it. Written shortly after her release, it was America's first significant narrative of the white female in the hands of Indians and was by far the most successful. A second edition—the first has never been found—issued from a printing press in Cambridge, Massachusetts, in 1682, four years after Mrs. Rowlandson's death. Subsequent editions flowed from many presses thereafter. Before its senescent language dated the narrative, Mrs. Rowlandson's story established itself as an early-day bestseller. Moreover, it became the book for subsequent writers to build captivity stories upon (or for readers to compare them with). Even after it had vanished from bookshops, one can fairly surmise that authors of later "captivities" had discovered the Rowlandson book, or an imitation thereof, in library or attic.

Mrs. Rowlandson's purpose in writing about her eleven weeks and five days in the world of the Narragansetts was revealed in the title: *The Sovereignty & Goodness of God, Together with the Faithfulness of His Promises Displayed: Being a Narrative of the Captivity and Restoration of Mrs. Mary Rowlandson. . . .* The author's intention, after the Puritan mode, was didactic, not sensational. She wanted to impart a message concerning religious obligation in a wilderness world. Yet even today the work is sometimes described by literary critics as hair-raising. How much more unsettling it must have been when the depicted menaces were still only a night's march away from frontier cabins. It is well to remember that for two centuries and more the Rowlandson capture reflected elements of actual threat to many Americans—and a convenient excuse for land grabbing and Indian damning to others. That is a long time for a peril (or an excuse) to bounce around in fact and fiction. And bounce it did, first in clergy-supported, or contorted, narratives not matched in circulation until the appearance of the American novel in the 1800s and then in the acknowledged fiction of theater, novel, and mass media. Almost a century after genuine danger of surprise raid had passed, the literary or dramatic portrayal of a white woman in the hands of Indians would remain profitable to its creators, with no sign that the genre would cease to attract readers.

The scenes of horror or privation that Mary Rowlandson bequeathed to her successors rebound today from printed page or theater screen or picture tube: a shrieking attack on an anxious compound, terrified settlers dragged from their isolated cabins, a brave defense of a fortified building until flaming arrows force the outnumbered defenders out of the burning refuge and into the hands of the attackers. In the Lancaster of Mary Rowlandson's narrative one by one the now-familiar scenes unfold. Before the battle is over, Mary's sister and many of her friends die by knife, club, or musket. For the two-dozen colonists who survive, an anguished northward march begins, with Mary holding Sarah, her wounded child, in her arms, while her two older children walk at her side until they are carried off in another direction.

At that point the Rowlandson narrative becomes the story of an individual captive, for the tiny Sarah dies of her wounds in a few days and Mary feels even more alone (oddly, Sarah's death brings the first sympathetic act of the captors: they bury the child for the suffering mother). On the trail north Mary learns to choke down Indian food. She is taunted by women of the tribe, receives an occasional kindness, and witnesses the effects of torture upon less-fortunate whites. By tranquil demeanor Mary escapes the fate of one complaining female captive, who is tied naked to a stake and killed by stone and arrow, an infant child in her arms, an unborn one in her womb.

Mary Rowlandson's eventual rescue—actually a ransoming—is more prosaic than pulsating, a missed opportunity for derring-do that later more commercially oriented writers generally would rectify (discarding, necessarily, the formula of the Puritan clergy, who, in shaping "true captivities," emphasized redemption by grace alone from temptations such as intermarriage, false religion, and cannibalism). In works of fiction heroic deliverances by Daniel Boones would become commonplace; Cooper and his successors delighted in them. Few imaginary liberators, however, and even fewer Mary Rowlandsons, would match in panache the affirmative action of the real-life Hannah Dustin. Instead of waiting for a Lancelot, she axed her sleeping captors, then took their scalps for bounty, thus winning a place in both history and literature. In 1787 an anonymous author appropriated Hannah's escape technique to let his fictional heroine escape the sexual advances of an Indian captor of "gigantic figure" in the erotic *Panther Captivity,* while, in more serious literature, Cotton Mather, Nathaniel Hawthorne, and Henry David Thoreau (to different ends) also took up the Dustin story. Eventually tourists were able to gaze at a statue of Old Mother Dustin in Haverhill, Massachusetts—or to inspect the very apple tree against which (in Thoreau's geographical

76

reconstruction of the 1697 event) the head of Hannah's infant son was bashed.[1]

But let us now redeem Mary Rowlandson. After a colorful audience with King Philip himself, Mary can do no more than stand by prayerfully while her ransom value is established, the formal bargaining accompanied by general goodwill and various amenities. At last a ransomed Mary is reunited with her husband and surviving children. Now her period of physical suffering gives way to one of psychological recovery—helped not at all, we can be sure, by curiosity unspoken.

During her captivity Mary Rowlandson had been given to an Indian named Quannopin. Did he or some other captor violate her? Here is the woman's answer: "I have been in the midst of those roaring lions and savage bears that feared neither God nor man, nor the devil, by night and day, alone and in company, sleeping all sorts together." The opportunity was there, obviously, but Mrs. Rowlandson continues: ". . . not one of them ever offered the least abuse of unchastity to me in word or action." Anticipating the universal skeptics, the ransomed captive added: "Though some are ready to say I speak it to my own credit; but I speak it in the presence of God, and to his glory."

Thus the Indians who had carried off Mary Rowlandson and her tiny child were portrayed in an influential captivity tale as looters and burners and cruel killers but not as rapists. They could knock a suckling child on the head or strip a wounded man and "split open his bowels"—Mrs. Rowlandson did not spare the reader any details of massacre—yet once the battle was over, these literary prototypes were seen as severe or callous rather than lecherous, a bit of comparative generosity that would rarely be extended thereafter.[2]

---

[1] The crushing of infant skulls by Indian raiders, an oddly enduring action in American literature, occurs in many other captivity tales, as well as in Anna Eliza Bleeker's novel of 1797 *The History of Marie Kittle.* It turns up in Robert Penn Warren's narrative poem *Brother to Dragons* (1953), when Thomas Jefferson remarks that if some captive mother stops to feed her "brat" the Indian captor will "snatch its heels and snap the head against a tree trunk, like a whip." The head then "pops like an egg," says Jefferson.

[2] In that regard Puritan personal recollection differed from Puritan polemic, which, as Richard Slotkin observed, revealed a marked preference for incidents of sexual assault rather than of "voluntary marriage between white captives and Indians . . . despite the fact that because of their mores the eastern Indians almost never commited rape." Slotkin, *Regeneration Through Violence,* p. 125.

While it would be a mistake to assume universal psychosexual behavior patterns in all Indian groups, for insight into one society, the Ojibwa (Longfellow's Indians in *Hiawatha*), the reader might enjoy chap. 16 of A. Irving Hallowell's *Culture and Experience.* Many other aspects of Ojibwa life are included in this collection of Hallowell's writings.

In juvenile fiction and film the sexual menace to female captives would invariably be disregarded—as it would be in numberless Saturday-afternoon cowboy movies in which a white villain's henchmen would carry the heroine to an isolated cabin and there ignore her almost completely while barking at each other over endless games of cards. When Indian captivity was subject matter for adults, however, the sexual motif, even when unstated, always lay just beneath the surface of the action, camouflaged, perhaps, by the endless details of torture and bloodshed that historian Richard Drinnon, in regard to captivity tales, called "violence pornography." Although New Englanders of Mary Rowlandson's day had reason to know that eastern Indians rarely committed rape (despite what was charged in pulpits), Puritan leaders had brooded, not too abstrusely, and probably more convincingly, over the erotic threat of Indians. Moreover, liberal observers of the early American scene had intimated sensual pleasures of pagan groves, or of nonconformist settlements like Thomas Morton's Merrymount, in depicting Indian-white social blending. When it was a storyteller's wont, therefore, he or she had only to summon a strapping Indian abductor, undisciplined, almost naked, to activate the curiosity of a reader in crinoline, while at the same time vicariously threatening her innocence. The genteel tradition did not, of course, permit acknowledgment of the impact of a sleek male form upon the imagination of a sequestered female. But it was there all the time—down unto the days of the fictional sheiks of the 1920s, the ones realized on the silver screen by a Rudolph Valentino or a Ramon Novarro.

Sometimes impressions from the Indian lands (which moved farther and farther from most readers each decade) led authors in a less than romantic direction, especially while the western wars raged. Persons on the advancing frontier, persons who had talked with white captives, whispered stories. Newspaper accounts and published diaries contained their own reminders of forced marriage or sexual assault. Inevitably such material would be taken up by authors of general fiction—writing for both men and women—while, ironically, being virtually ignored by adventure spinners aiming primarily at male readers. Not until the mid-twentieth century, though, did authors, especially screenwriters, feel safe enough to flaunt the whispered actions, to depict the physical consummations only threatened in fiction such as the *Panther Captivity* or *The Last of the Mohicans*. So, almost a century after the last Indian had fought to protect his homeland, he was finally shown in action as a ravisher—of prodigious energy and accomplishment.

In light of such progress we can wonder whether things were not better for the Indian's *social* reputation in the early decades of the 1800s, when the Puritan libel of sexual depravity was muted, and the noble, if artificial, stage Indian was at his zenith; when parades of Pocahontases were wooed before the footlights by handsome Englishmen; when actor Edwin Forrest vivified the tender family life of a courageous chieftain in *Metamora;* when an Indian hero and a white woman forged a marital bond ended only by their deaths in the six-canto Eastburn and Sands poem *Yamoyden: A Tale of the Wars of King Philip;* yes, when in Lydia Francis Child's apprentice novel, *Hobomok: A Tale of Early Times,* an Indian gave up the white wife he loved in order that she and their son could have a better life with her white former fiancé (who had been presumed dead).

In 1829 even James Fenimore Cooper, not one to let his Indian and white characters lightly cross the miscegenation barrier, let two of them do so in his well-intentioned novel *The Wept of the Wish-ton-Wish.* Ruth Heathcote, carried off by Indians in 1666, remembers nothing of her Puritan childhood when reunited with her family a decade or so later during King Philip's War. Married happily, to Narragansett chief Conanchet, Ruth (or Narra-mattah) is an Indian in every way but birth. Nobler by far than the wily Puritan cleric who maneuvers them into the hands of their Indian enemies, she and Conanchet die together in the manner of Romeo and Juliet. Admitting that Cooper disliked Puritans and saw Indians as either good or bad (depending upon their tribes), *The Wept of the Wish-ton-Wish,* like some other works of its era, offers a picture of an Indian male–white female relationship that stands significantly above the spectacles of sexual degeneracy later to be displayed in novel and film—when most Americans were unaware that stories of loving marriages like Ruth's and Conanchet's had ever been published.

It is not unusual to overlook the almost staggering turnabout in literary and dramatic portrayal of the American Indian that began in the mid-1800s. As the frontier of Indian tales changed from colonial forest, with its bowmen on foot or in canoe, to distant West, with its rifle-carrying warriors on horseback; as the theatrical milieu changed from proscenium stage to Wild West show, then flickering screen; as romantic poets abandoned the Noble Savage and the publication milieu changed from gentlemanly publishing house to mass-market industry, so did the American Indian's reputation decline, hastened down the path by the brutal wars in the West. Although sexuality was exploited later than violence and sadism (its surrogates in early captivity tales) the erotic component of Indian-related fiction was eventually distorted just like every other element of content, though not necessarily in the text itself. Long before censorial restraint was pushed aside in the twentieth century, publishers had shown that they knew how to combine Puritan slanders with erotic fancies. When, in the 1940s, thrusting décolletage had become a standard for the dust jackets of historical romances, books with Indian subjects received special attention from artists skilled in reproducing leers and lusts. That injury which authors did not happen to inflict, illustrators did.

Of course, as areas of devastation for the moral image of the Indian male following World War II, the dust jackets of the female-oriented book clubs took second place to the covers of paperback novels. Not since the dime-novel era had the graphics been so vivid. Pocket Books, Inc., had revived the soft-cover publishing concept in 1939, and by the end of the next decade low-cost reprinting was a flourishing industry with many participants. As competition increased, so did the garishness and exaggeration of the cover material—the better to catch the eye scanning a drugstore display rack, naturally. No claim seemed too extravagant as long as some tiny nugget of fact could be found to support it. The Cartoonist Harvey Kurtzman was uncomfortably close to the very nonsense he was parodying for *Mad* magazine when he designed a few imaginary covers of literary classics. *Tom Sawyer*'s cover, for instance, showed a somewhat mature Tom gazing downward with popping eyes at a sensuously reclining Becky Thatcher. In capital letters was the legend "Trapped in a cave together they found strange excitements." Kurtzman's cover for *Moby Dick* ("A tale of incredible passion") depicted a hollow-eyed male taking his leave from a blonde in his bedroom. "Colossal Ahab," the cover proclaimed. "He left his bride to keep a rendezvous with the only one whose desires could match his own."

Real-life covers of Indian-related novels might have been just as mirthful had they not been so universally libelous and so indicative of the latter-day course of captivity fiction. Agitated battle sequences remained the stuff of cavalry-versus-Indians paperbacks, but carnal lust—bare-chested brave for white maiden—became the sustaining packaging apparatus for the twentieth-century captivity tale. In a nation that no longer needed literature to help it come to grips with the abduction of civilians on its frontiers (an Iranian hostage problem being unimaginable), the focus narrowed. Sexual menace became the captivity genre's lifeline—one reaching (minus concern for the captive's soul) all the way back to the Puritan object lessons of Cotton Mather and associates, who, as Richard Slotkin pointed out, "saw the Indian as insatiably lustful, a being of overbearing sexual power."[3] By the 1950s (except in pure shoot-'em-ups) savage lust was the one ingredient deemed necessary to the sale of captivity novels. For new books the authors knew what to deliver. For reissues the hurried distillation of a dram of pure-grained lasciviousness required considerable blurbal inventiveness.

A case in point could be a novel of 1934, *The Cold Journey,* by Grace Zaring Stone, author of an interracial romance, *The Bitter Tea of General Yen* (under the name Ethel Vance she later produced *Escape* and *Winter Meeting*). An episodic and sometimes meandering narrative, *The Cold Journey* described the northward trek and eventual ransom of colonists captured in the French and Indian raid on Deerfield, Massachusetts (called Redfield in the novel). With violent elements minimized and romantic interludes never exceeding the hand-patting stage, the book is of greatest value for its perceptive exchanges of metaphysical dialogue and for its examination of the mechanics of capture for ransom in the early eighteenth century.

What did the paperback publisher do to spice a sometimes philosophical novel for the postwar newsstand trade? It seized upon the relationship between schoolmaster Lygon's young wife and French captain Hertel LeMoyne, who, thinking Lygon dead, quietly negotiated her purchase from the incidental Indian character who happened to capture her. Over a dramatic illustration of a knife-wielding warrior jealously guarding a wistfully kneeling beauty from a rescuing French officer, yellow Letters blare:

The Red Man Owned her completely . . .
　he wanted her ALIVE

And so he did, if as a good businessman he was to collect the expected ransom. Yet had that matter-of-fact Indian bargainer been able somehow to step into the future and examine the Bantam Books edition of 1946, he would have been as confused as an ordinary reader in at-

[3]Slotkin, *Regeneration Through Violence,* p. 202.

tempting to locate the lurid front-cover confrontation anywhere within the pages of *The Cold Journey*.[4]

Only slightly more justified was the similar cover that Bantam used on Muriel Elwood's *Heritage of the River* a few years later. In that story of an earlier set of Indian captives a brave did possess red-haired Marguerite Boissart briefly (though not carnally), but the incident was a minor part of the romantic narrative in which amours were set against Canadian frontier hardships. At least the leering warrior on the paperback cover of *Heritage of the River* is clean-looking and hand-some. Much good it did his comrades, though. Inside the book Elwood treats the Indians as hopeless savages or unkempt pelt traders. While it is not unusual for the white characters in a novel about Indians to refer to their adversaries as redskins, it is dismaying when an author uses that terminology in expository sections. Muriel Elwood does so in *Heritage of the River*.

Not that the denigration prevented critics from praising the hard-cover edition of 1945. *Saturday Review,* for instance, reflected the fact that once again a storyteller had mixed the magic formula of the "wild-Indian" tale: "Marguerite's capitivity and her eventual escape from the Indian camp is a recital guaranteed to make the reader glance around him and jump at the snap of a twig outside the window." Indian-thriller buffs know all about twig snaps.

In describing the excesses of cover illustrations, one would be wrong to imply that all the pictured heroines were celibate. Once in a while the heroine of a pre-1960s Indian tale did get caught up in a bit of woodland activity. When she was portrayed as enjoying herself, however, her partner was, by near fiat, a white man (or a half-white like Joseph St. Castine in Margaret Widdemer's *The Golden Wildcat,* 1954). Indians rarely shared in the real campfire fun. When Guyasu-ta's Senecas pulled Abby Hale out of her clothes in Neil H. Swanson's *Unconquered* (1947), it was to string her between two trees for fire torture. When an almost-naked Seminole held an almost-naked Mary Grant above his head in Frank G. Slaughter's *Fort Everglades* (1951), it was to lure her white lover into individual combat. Fair maid in the wilds could indulge brave chief only if he was an Indian by preference or adoption, and not until a few hundred pages had been spent in

---

[4]It is perhaps encouraging that a paperback reissue of *The Cold Journey* (1970) was given a nonsalacious front cover. Then again, the illustration may simply have reflected one artist's good taste.

haughty resistance. Aroused by an "Indian," she could surrender to a white man.

Representative of the "proud-beauty-versus-handsome-near-Indian" format was *Wild Drums Beat,* a Pocket Books paperback of 1954 by F. Van Wyck Mason (an earlier version of the story had appeared in 1932 under the title *Captain Renegade*). Set during the War of 1812, *Wild Drums Beat* portrays in titillating fashion the romance of Greg Sheldon, disgraced naval officer turned Natty Bumppo, and flame-haired Stella Merchant, whom he helps to escape from the Frenchtown Massacre. Although an adopted leader of the Erie tribe, Sheldon (or Captain Bear) evinces little respect for Indians outside the Bear clan. On page four, for instance, occurs this throwback to the good Indian-dead Indian philosophy of the dime-novel and Phil Sheridan era:

> The man in buckskins [Sheldon] paid no attention to the man he had killed. Instead, he peered around, searching the snowy landscape for some sign of more Creeks who might be watching the result of the brief duel. . . .
> Reassured, he looked back at the fallen Indian. A thin, mirthless smile passed over his lips and disappeared.
> "One less," he told himself.

Sheldon's driving purpose at the time of the massacre is to get some needed gunpowder to his Erie warriors. His diversion, literally and figuratively, is the damsel he actually calls "Beauty" Merchant. On page after page Sheldon alternates deadly struggles against "foul-smelling" or "greasy" Sauks, Creeks, and Wyandots with visual or tactile assessments of Miss Marchant's bosom—the scope of which Mason cannot seem to keep in mind. When Sheldon bursts into the defiant Stella's bedroom during the massacre, this kind of nonsense interrupts:

> She trembled in his arms. It was then that he realized she wore nothing beyond a thin shift which he had torn from one shoulder in his grab at her. The pallid globe of a small and symmetrical breast shone above the arm he had flung about her. At the same time he felt the warmth of the body pressed so close to him.

That with the enemy at the very gates!

Soon it becomes necessary for Sheldon, or Captain Bear, to rap the proud beauty stoutly on the skull to calm her. Moments later his hand is inside the unconscious girl's riding habit "to feel the persistent beat of Stella Merchant's heart" (pallid globes permitting). Four paragraphs later Bear again is groping beneath the velvet and linen "to find a reassuring pulse beneath a gently rounded breast." After a quick struggle with "a Creek by the stink of him," Sheldon is once again playing doctor with his "rough hand." This time there is enough light to allow a visual evaluation as well, for "his exploration had bared her bosom sufficiently to render visible the division of firm and generous young breasts." Two pages later Stella sits up, her blouse falls open, and Greg cannot "move his eyes away from the expanse of white skin disclosed by the gaping cloth." He does, however, have to start moving toward home. So, disguised as a Creek, Sheldon drags Stella through Indian lines, leaving the open dress alone because "her exposed breast fitted the picture."

" 'Please my—my dress,' she whispered. 'I—I'm all exposed.' "

Not a speck of mercy from her keen-eyed escort. Then comes some relief from all the sneaky-peeky. Two drunken Wyandots appear. Acting more forthrightly than the girl's disguised protector, "one of the braves walked up to Stella Marchant and curiously fingered a ripe breast exposed to the icy wind." Wishing only to share some portion of Sheldon's "beautiful loot," the Wyandots are easily diverted to other spoils. When they are gone, Sheldon, his own lechery unmentioned, allows that " 'it must have been prodigious hard for you to have those savages—uh—touch you.' " " 'It's all right,' the girl replied in a weary voice. 'After all, I wasn't harmed.' "

Count one for the Wyandots . . . and, alas, for Mason, who clearly had his rhetorical eye in the right economic direction. As Leslie Fiedler observed in *The Return of the Vanishing Native,* the baring of female captives' breasts has always sold books. It has sold paintings too, for example, the pictorial death of Jane McCrea. Poet Joel Barlow (1754–1812) gave Jane the name "Lucinda" for an ode in the euphemistic tradition that reached the same absurdity as Beauty Merchant's "pallid globes" of the massacre sequence. Out of Lucinda's rent kerchief Barlow summoned nothing other than "globes of snow."

During the leering, gasping era of *Wild Drums Beat* and *Unconquered,* who would have expected that in the 1960s a popular author would reverse the voyeuristic roles of captive and captor and greatly increase the sexual participation by both? In *Scarlet Plume,* Frederick Manfred *(Lord Grizzly)* reworked the Cooper formula of good, bad, and neuter Indians, but with heavily amatory overtones—not to mention a visually curious *heroine,* who even in captivity found herself enjoying things.

Just to refresh the reader's memory, here is what a Cooper female (Cora in *The Last of the Mohicans*) had to say to her sister about a proposal from Magua, a representative of the *bad* Indian group: "He would have me," she continued, her accents sinking under a deep consciousness of the degradation of the proposal, "follow him to the wilderness; go to the habitations of the Hurons; to remain there; in short to become his wife." Two hundred pages later the dark-eyed Cora has not altered her viewpoint, Here is her reply to the observation of the ancient Tamenund (a *neuter* Indian) that, were she to let the great warrior take her to wife, the British race would not come to an end: "Better, a thousand times, it should," explained the horror-struck Cora, "than meet with such a degradation."

Actually, Cora was reacting not to marriage with an Indian but to marriage with the wrong Indian. Had the proposal come from the devoted and daring Uncas, a *good* Indian, her answer might have been different. The young Mohican, however, concealed his affection—except from Hawkeye, who noticed his nonchauvinistic behavior around Cora. Even unto his death in defense of the British girl he loved, Uncas remained silent. Was he (or Cooper) remembering the proprieties? (*The Wept of Wish-ton-Wish,* with its Indian male–white female marriage came several years after the Mohicans.) A further complication was Cora's background. The reader learns that she was the offspring of her father's marriage to a West Indian woman. Magua, thus, was turned aside by, and Uncas was in love with, a woman who in her era would have been called a mulatto. Perhaps a third blending of races was beyond literary consideration, with slavery still flourishing in the United States.

Whatever Uncas or Cora or Cooper thought, it is clear how Cora's bland sister, Alice, looked at not only the marriage proposal from Magua but the whole idea of union with an Indian, any Indian. When Cora reminds her that the acceptance of Magua's offer would at least be a way to save their small party from death, Alice answers: "Cora! Cora! You jest with our misery! Name not the horrid alternative again; the thought itself is worse than a thousand deaths."

From the days of the Oregon Trail onward, the Alices of Indian fiction would outnumber the Coras, those bride-of-the Indian poems and novels of the 1820s having produced no issue. Even allowing for

85

novels such as Mary Johnston's *The Great Valley* (1926), in which the captive Elizabeth submits to marriage with Long Thunder while plotting her eventual escape, it is not unlikely that until relatively recently a goodly number of readers accepted the death-before-dishonor response to an Indian brave's overture, as set forth in fiction.

In the real world Vine Deloria, Jr., discovered a singular reflection of that philosophy. During Deloria's tenure as excutive director of the National Congress of American Indians, it was, as he put it, a "rare" day when some white visitor did not announce to him that he or she had an Indian ancester. Deloria never tried to disabuse a pretender, but he did soon begin to notice that the claims had a curious aspect: almost always the alleged Indian descent came from a *female* forebear. Now, descent from a Cherokee great-great-grandmother perhaps added a touch of royalty to the fantasy—claimants using the same conceit that their white ancestors may have used in making princesses of Indian maidens. But aspirations to royalty aside, no white claimant to Indian heritage, as Deloria saw it, chose to place on the family tree a male ancestor with the "aura of the savage warrior, the unknown primitive, the instinctive animal."[5]

In *Scarlet Plume* (1964), nonetheless, Frederick Manfred defies tradition. Far from averting maidenly eyes from the long-familiar fate worse than death, the author of this violent captivity novel lets his heroine revel in it, to what advantage it is not easy to judge. One of the few writers of Westerns noticed by critics, Manfred earnestly classifies the instances of possible dishonor through almost ludicrous descriptions of what he likes to call "phalluses." Thus the snarling rapist Mad Bear, after cutting a fetus from a screaming woman, falls upon Judith Raveling with a phallus that resembles "the neck of a wild swan" (a sure sign of a bad Indian). In contrast, puffy old Chief Whitebone, to whom Judith is given as a wife, has, she discovers, a "gray-tinged pudendum" that lies "in a (milkwort) puddle between his thighs." That of his son, Two Two, calls to mind "three freshly popped mushrooms" (these unfortunates, obviously, are neuter Indians, neither good nor bad). Yet, mushrooms and all, Judith cannot resist "several furtive looks at both males. Lord, Lord. What she hadn't all seen in the space of one. day."[6]

---

[5]Vine Deloria, Jr., *Custer Died for Your Sins,* p. 3.

[6]And Judith would see more later on—every inch of every adult male in the Yankton band, including Bullhead, a foul-tempered rapist who finds religion when his testicles are "bit off" by a bolt of lightning. The reader, mercifully, is left in the dark about how much Judith

The title character of *Scarlet Plume* is Manfred's master specimen, handome enough for a liberated Judith Raveling to seduce in the forest—some pages after her appetite has been whetted by the sight of his "erect phallus" in an au naturel buffalo dance. Once Judith has ripped off his breechclout, his "copper knob" turns into a "wonderful cucumber of love for her." Yes, reader, it does: "She gasped at the engorged red color of it. . . . Stars rose. Stars fell. . . . She was a great plum about to burst."

Verily, Scarlet Plume is a good Indian, in a new meaning of the designation. The passive or engorged state of his goodness is diligently observed by the Raveling woman every few pages or so throughout the novel—during lovemaking, between acts, and even during the prelude, the main work, and the postlude of an early-morning battle with a puma: the noble instrument "awakened a little" while a nude Scarlet Plume awaited the deadly cat, stood "aroused" during the battle itself, and "gleamed with a silken purple sheen" in victory.

To the surprise of no reader who has hung on through the sexual climaxes to the literary climax of *Scarlet Plume,* the captive Judith chooses to live with her Yankton Sioux should it be possible. Yet, because of the Minnesota uprising of 1862, it is not. Scarlet Plume (now a Christ figure to Judith) is unfairly sentenced to be hanged with thirty-seven others and winds up a cadaver for anatomical study—this after a gratuitous severing of his "dangling copper phallus" while he was a prisoner. Once again curious eyes will state at him, or at what is left of him after neuterization. Judith departs from white society to go to a "place where all men were once one flesh, with black hair and dark skin."

Frederick Manfred may have started no bandwagon with *Scarlet Plume,* but only a modest amount of browsing among paperback racks during the years since its appearance would convince an observer that the portrayal of Indian male sexuality is, to say the least, more open than it was earlier—and not just in captivity tales. While no one has thus far matched Manfred in phallic metaphors, many readers might be startled by the Squanto encountered in Selwyn Anne Grames's

---

saw of teenagers Moldy Clothes, Large Organ, and In A Hurry To Become A Copulator. In a book in which white characters have elegant names like Theodosia and Mavis, all the Indian characters have descriptive ones appearing only in translation. Examples are Bone Gnawer, Squirts Milk, Plenty Lice, and Antheap.

Royal Savage. The Pilgrims' friend in that publication of 1980 may be a boudoir captivator rather than a forest captor, but the ladies of Old England must have been overwhelmed by the Indian prince, to judge from the Grames account. They longed to see his body unclothed, we are told more than once. What is more, they "contrived to free his throbbing phallus" from its restraining garments, "cursed the moon" for hiding it from view, explored his body till their hands found (depending upon the chapter) his "turgid" or "tumescent phallus," and (when the light was good enough) "gasped again at the sight of his now flaccid member, which, even in its state of temporary exhaustion, was large."[7]

Royal Savage, with its stupendous Squanto, may seem hyperbolic, but it is not unique among recent novels about Indians. By the 1980s the ladies of frontier romances were gawking with such zeal and earnestness at invariably impressive anatomical exhibits as to make almost passé the once proper reaction of a fictional female when confronted by offhanded Indian-male nakedness. Janice Holt Giles's *Hannah Fowler* (1956) contains an example of how things used to be. When after a river crossing a hoary Shawnee, to dry out, "slid the breechclout . . . to one side and made an obscene motion of wringing water from a part of his body which Hannah had been taught to ignore," the captive heroine, "embarrassed and ashamed, flung her arm across her eyes."

> It's all well and good, she thought indignantly, for Dannel Boone to say be pleasant and try to get along good with Indians. Being a man he could, but there are things, she told herself, no woman ought to be called upon to see.

[7]How author Grames came about the information concerning Squanto's intimate physiology one cannot imagine, though the roots of backfence gossip about Indian male anatomy go back to the first European explorers, especially the man for whom America was named. In *Mundus Novus* (1504–05), an influential ethnographic pamphlet, Americus Vespucci noted that the natives of Brazil had a custom "very shameful and beyond all human belief. For their women, being very lustful, cause the private parts of their husbands to swell up to such a huge size that they appear deformed and disgusting." The magnification, accomplished by using an unspecified device in conjunction with the "biting of certain poisonous animals," sometimes caused things to "break," producing eunuchs instead of colossi.

Tales like Vespucci's die hard. In a *Playboy* short story of 1981 the purveyor of a penis-enlarging secret is called Dr. Brazil. The key to the miracle is a tiny "statue of the god Mbigoné (pun no doubt intended), carved by one of the few South American sorcerers qualified to invoke the power of the ancient Indian gods." Central character Ben Oszchio (cf. Pinocchio) even has a lustful wife in the Vespucci mold who tries magic too. Walter Lowe, Jr., "Ben Oszchio," *Playboy,* July, 1981, pp. 143 ff.

Two decades after the Giles book, a reader was unlikely to run across a female character, captive or not, who would so much as turn away her eyes, let alone fling an arm across them. It is true that in *Emerald Fire* (Julie Grice, 1978) Wolf Dreamer of the Sioux relaxed Emerald Regan with a hallucinogen before "her eyes were drawn to his nakedness," but she really did not need much encouragement. Moments after "she saw his smooth, bronzed skin" her handsome captor's "hardness" was "pressing against her."

Beth Dowland of Lois Swann's favorably received *The Mists of Manittoo* (1976) knew how to get right to the point with Wakwa, her "Massachuseuck" protector:

"I love yourself and I would see you. Without this." Beth gingerly touched the front of his beaded arpon.

Observational privileges having been granted by the Indian in elaborate phraseology worthy of the early 1800s, the youthful Beth:

... pulled on the cord and Wakwa threw aside the apron and watched her face as she looked at the arching stalk of his phallus and then met his gaze.

"How perfect you are," Beth said later.

A more experienced woman assumed the initiative in Tom Ryan's *The Savage* (1979), built upon the life of a character identified as the son of Metacomet (King Phillip). Young Annawan, renamed Samuel Wardwell, Jr., is lying naked on his back after a swim:

"My, that looks inviting." The voice, followed by a laugh, caused him to turn his head to the bank. Charlotte [Roark] stood in the grass.

Annawan rolls onto his stomach, ignoring her:

"I see that I have to come to you, then. All right. . . . Don't you feel the slightest bit compromised by allowing a young lady to gaze upon your nakedness?"

Under the Roark woman's persistent fondling Annawan finally turns over and discovers the fire in her eyes:

She uttered a tiny moan as she saw what her caresses had erected. [*sic*]

So much for Wampanoag reserve in face of determined pursuit. Yet what could a reader have expected by way of restraint in inexperienced Annawan when, in a slightly earlier example of modern frontier fiction, a far more substantial historical figure, namely Pontiac, also had discovered how a disarming white woman and a woodland stream can combine to break down inhibitions. Although no match for the Grames Squanto, the Pontiac of Christine Savage's *Love's Wildest Fires* (1977) did enjoy a several-page dalliance with Elizabeth Gladwyn. It grew out of a naked postrescue swim during which this Beth "was not surprised to feel the burning spot where his mahnood rose to touch the small of her back." The grateful young woman's passion was not sufficient for permanent alliance with an Ottawa, however. Amphibious sex had been fun . . . "an almost unbearable ecstasy" . . . but when the moment was gone, Beth remembered that "she was English."

Maria Frame of Gayle Rogers's *The Second Kiss* was more enduringly enthusiastic. Although untouched by any man, she tried to lure her forbearing captor into a premarital relationship through visual and verbal enticements spread across a full two hundred pages. And at the end of the novel, though restored to white society, she chose to return to her Blackfoot paragon, who believed in doing things the proper way, for all Maria's pantings. The paperback publisher, trying in 1977 to imply more amatory explosiveness than the novel of 1972 contained, renamed the book *Nakoa's Woman.*

Did the abundance of Indian Lancelots in the late twentieth century's Indian fiction leave any room for less desirable figures, romantically speaking? It did, though possibly not as much as in former days. Nonetheless, in the eyes of some authors, knife-wielding, woman-torturing demons still possessed plot value. Like their fictional precursors, they could threaten or torment a heroine prior to the dramatic intervention of the hero—now often another Indian. Regrettably, however, many of the nouveau demons were doing, in textual detail, the unpleasant things that Puritans had alleged, and later-day paperback covers had luridly suggested, they were fond of doing. The only bow to contemporary sensibilities might be a statement in narration or dialogue that the perpetrator of some infamy was beyond the pale of even Indian morality, and possibly mentally unbalanced. Calvin Duggai, a Navajo of the modern era in John Ives's *Fear in a Handful of Dust* (1979), was actually dispatched to a mental institution. Escaping, this creature of fiction kidnapped (with what the Jove Publishing blurbist called "vicious cunning"), the experts whose testimony had resulted in his confinement. Cutting all the clothing from his bound-and-gagged captives, including lovely Shirley Painter, he leaves them "to perish in the blazing hell of an Arizona desert," says the back cover.

Although the advertising implies more, Duggai's vengeful pleasure comes from covertly watching his naked victims suffer. In contrast. Crazy Wolf, an aberrant Sioux lust-person of *The Tender and the Savage* (Paula Fairman, 1980), dogmatically denudes, abuses, and coerces Crimson Royal with anything but passive observation in mind. Entering the tipi where Crimson lies captive, Crazy Wolf "stares down at her, his eyes reflecting the red glow of the fires, his face looking *demonic* [italics mine] in the flickering light." Ignoring Crimson's obtuse questioning, Crazy Wolf frenziedly commences to cut off her clothes, "exposing her nudity to his cruel eyes." Then comes the inductive dawn:

Crimson realized that he intended to rape her!

The action progresses more rapidly than the twenty-two-year-old woman's ratiocination:

"Ahh," she heard Crazy Wolf say, then she felt his course hands on her body, roughly kneading a breast before trailing down to the junction of her legs and grabbing her.

What a cruel twist of fate, she thought, that the first man who would ever touch her there would be *a savage Indian* [italics again mine].

Crimson is saved, this time, by the hero, a white Indian, who whacks Crazy Wolf "just as Crimson felt him about to enter her." Later in the book, however, "the brute who would ravage" Crimson repeatedly has his way, having tortured the trussed-up woman into acquiescence.

Sometimes in frontier novels sexual misadventures only seem to happen. An ancient nightmare of Indian lust was elaborated in Constance Gluyas's *Rogue's Mistress* (1977) when young, ambitious Black Cloud fantasized about the nearby "golden-skinned maiden" with "the mouth that was like a ripe red fruit:"

He saw her lying on the soft skin of his bedding. Her legs were opened wide . . . opened to accommodate him. Naked, his loins hot and throbbing, he would stand over her, letting her admire the huge swollen length of his masculinity. She would lift her arms, crying out to him to enter her. Her fingers would reach hungrily, already curling as though she held the object of her desire between them.

And so it continues, fantasy stumbling over hyperbole in book after book, the phrasing so predictable, the direction so obvious, that if there is an affront to human decency therein, that affront is rooted not so much in prurience as in racist implication. It is not enough, apparently, to rip the last garment from the Indian male; he must be inspected and admired like a fine animal. He can be shown to be a surprisingly gentle or loving creature, even saintlike, yet, as if in response to ancient innuendoes, his manifest breeding credentials must nonetheless be displayed, measured, and shown to be in excellent working order—a condition rarely imposed upon the white heroes of frontier romances, especially those who, like Squanto or Pontiac, actually lived.

Will the late-twentieth-century stream of fiction continue to carry to a thus-far receptive audience a thriving school of unclad warriors and their adoring white women (whose wide-eyed admiration of their Apollos smacks more than a little of sexist writing in some novels)? Will the supernatural males anguished over by the Puritans seduce more and more readers by materializing in the stereotyped bodies of prodigiously good Indians? One probably should not wager against it, passing literary fancies, and my hopes for this chapter, notwithstanding.

One thing is certain. What one observer called "Indian sex" is not in the "deep freeze" to which that writer would have assigned it in 1975; nor did it cease to be a matter of profit or social concern following the birth of the Wild West show, despite what some essays might lead one to believe. Gary Jennings's bestselling novel *Aztec* contained so much sexual content that book club advertising of 1981 presented a rare warning to buyers. Ruth Hill's *Hanta Yo* raised the hackles of Sioux for (among other items) its graphic representation of nuptual practices that tribal councils said would have violated Lakota mores.

Well, then, what if sex, stereotyped or not, continues to sell books about Indians? What if the masculine embodiments of sexual delight multiply in print and catch the eyes of those filming movie romances? Might admiration, albeit leering, of the Indian's potential for romantic satisfaction improve his cultural image, if only by partially displacing the savage warrior one? That question, perhaps, should be answered by by a second one: Is the exchange of one distortion for another all that the Indian can hope for at the approach of the twenty-first century?

The sexual magnetism of the half-naked Indian is an attraction not lost to the mind of the artist or filmmaker. Although the Indian male often is presented as a threat to female virtue—a prospect that can either repel or entice—the prairie maid, in buckskin or buff, usually brings anxiety only to natural-born censors. The painting is by Alfred Jacob Miller.

Left: *The "Indian Women Bathing" are from* Our Native Land, *a travel book of 1882.* Right: *The pious cheesecake is part of a painting commemorating a treaty soon disregarded.*

Frances Dee poses as an Indian Princess, most of whose apparel has gone to her head. Now we're beginning to understand what it was that made the wild Indians wild!

"Princesses" of stage (Dorothy Knapp on horse), screen (Frances Dee on rug), and nightclub (Cher on mike). The larger the headdress, the smaller the remaining outfit.

CHIEF WAHOO

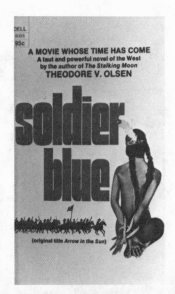

Starlight (below right) *of Garrett Price's* White Boy *seems overwhelmed by less decorous princesses, including Chief Wahoo's* Minnie Ha-Cha *and* Lil Abner's *Minnie Mustache—not to mention Yma Sumac (center) and the Seven Seas to Calais dancers (below left).*

Below: *Centuries apart, Indian males demonstrate their power over women. The Timucua* (left) *was limned by LeMoyne in the 1500s.* Above: *While a paperback heroine swoons, Alice and Cora admire Uncas in a Marvel Comics version of* The Last of the Mohicans.

Above: *A standing Douglas Fairbanks in* The Half Breed *(1916) and a kneeling Richard Dix in a publicity still for* The Vanishing American *(1925).*

Right: *Richard Dix sits cross-legged at the feet of teacher Lois Wilson in* The Vanishing American.

Cowboy star George O'Brien changes roles to demonstrate his oiled physique in The Golden West *(1932).*

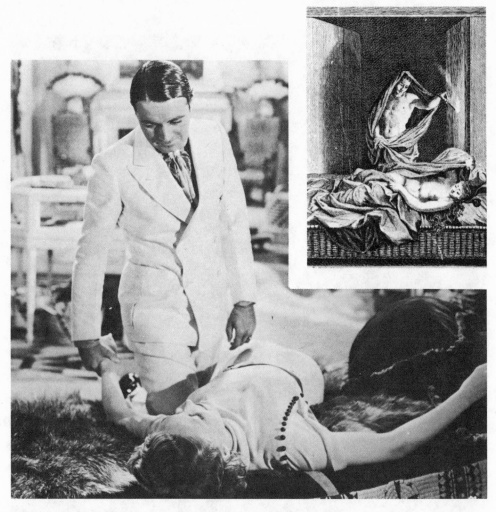

The approach of Richard Barthelmess to Claire Dodd in Massacre *(1934) echoes that of another Indian to his "maitresse" in a European print of the eighteenth century.*

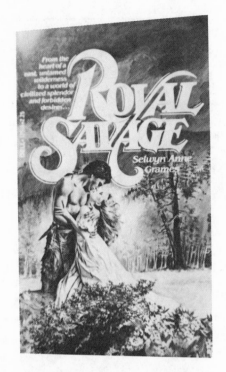

The ultimate title in this genre would have to be Savage Savage.

101

When openly amorous relationships are not in order, the Indian abductor is always there to be drawn upon.

A fierce Indian warrior,
a beautiful white captive—
An enthralling love story.
"Brutal...tender...impossible to forget!"
—San Rafael Independent Journal

Nakoa's Woman
(formerly *The Second Kiss*)
Gayle Rogers

The Mists of Manittoo
Lois Swann
THE HAUNTINGLY BEAUTIFUL STORY OF FORBIDDEN LOVE

Scarlet Plume

FREDERICK MANFRED
Author of *LORD GRIZZLY*
The passionate love of a frontierswoman
for the savage Sioux who captured her

APACHE GREED
(DESERT CAMPFIRE)

A Savage Indian...
A Noble White Woman...
A Tempestuous
Hunger...

WILLIAM HOPSON

Indian abductors tended to look alike in paperback art of the 1950s and 1960s. The subdued cover of The Cold Journey *appeared a generation after the one to its right.*

"Ay, Captain," said Bruce, "thar's the thing that
sticks most in the heart of them that live in the
wilderness and have wives and daughters;—to
think of *their* falling into the hands of the
brutes."

Robert Montgomery Bird, *Nick of the Woods,* 1837

6

AND YOU KNOW WHAT THEY DO TO WHITE WOMEN

I F A WHITE WOMAN in the hands of a painted Indian was commercially viable on the printed page, whould she not be even more so
when thrust into a motion picture? After all, the potential was there
for combining the moral dilemma of a New England captivity narrative
with the vivid pictorial material of a paperback cover. Hollywood,
however, exploited that potential in a manner that seldom offered
much on-screen temptation, let alone romance. Its oblique approach
was best reflected in one of the ubiquitous clichés of cinemaland.
Audiences began hearing it as soon as the movies started to talk, on
the eve of the Depression. And a half-century later, when Hollywood
was showing signs of embarrassment over the old-fashioned Indian
picture, that same cliché still came in handy. Actor James Whitmore,
for one, mouthed it in *Chato's Land.* As a saddle-weary scout, standing
passively as two white bullies rape an Apache woman, Whitmore restrained a sidekick with

Malachi, did you ever see what Indians do when they get a *white* woman?

That, of course, was the chestnut disguised, an elegant variation.
More often a film's frontier sage would put it straight out, with a
knowing arch of the eyebrow:

And you *know* what they do to white women.

In the Cecil B. DeMille epic of 1947, *Unconquered,* as a matter of fact, the well-traveled insinuation was inserted more than once, just to make certain that even a dozing moviegoer could anticipate what was in store for a torn-bodiced Paulette Goddard in the hands of Boris Karloff's Senecas, not one of whom was likely to be a Scarlet Plume. The frontier saga, cinema-style, seldom put forth sheiks in breechclouts. Its captor Indians offered mainly shame and terror.

Undoubtedly the film industry's self-protective cautions against miscegenation placed an invisible lid upon treatments of Indian male–white female amours, yet coincidences of history and geography combined to make such treatments unlikely had there been no constraints. As mentioned earlier, printed captivity fiction came into being and set its patterns with eastern Indians as the agents of abduction and Puritans as the fashioners of the thesis. It was not, then, the Indian rapist that the genre's creators really feared but the Indian seducer, the demon who would lure the children of God into the wilderness of Satan. That motif persisted, sometimes strongly, sometimes faintly, in printed works (whatever their locales) after Puritan influence had been diluted and Indian captors of colonial days had become phantom figures of history, their nations long dispersed or decimated. At the same time, with those eastern Indians out of view, the Noble Savage myth could gain sufficient impetus to soften the devil images of captor husbands in books like Lydia Child's *Hobomok* (1824) and Elizabeth Sedgwick's *Hope Leslie* (1827). Temptation did not disappear from printed narratives, guilt did not vanish as a consequence to be faced by the acquiescent captive, yet the reader of the 1820s was allowed to see an Indian through the eyes of a white woman who consented to marry him:

> Sheninjee was a noble man; large in stature; elegant in his appearance; generous in his conduct; courageous in war; a friend in peace, and a great lover of justice. . . . Yet, Sheninjee was an Indian. The idea of spending my days with him, at first seemed completely irreconcilable to my feelings; but his good nature, generosity, tenderness, and friendship towards me, soon gained my affection; and, strange as it may seem, I loved him!

"Strange as it may seem, I loved him!" Those words, representative of what might be called the neocaptivity era, came from octogenerian Mary Jemison, the "White Woman of the Genesee." James

106

Seaver took them down and polished them for a well-circulated quasi-narrative of 1824: *A Narrative of the Life of Mrs. Mary Jemison: Who Was Taken by the Indians . . . When Only About Twelve Years of Age, and Has Continued to Reside Amongst Them to the Present Time. . . .* When Sheninjee (a Delaware) died, Mary Jemison took a second husband, Hogadowah (Hiakatoo), a Seneca, older, fiercer, but sexually potent, apparently, until age 103. She had nice things to say about him too.

Mary Jemison would have been out of place in a movie. Few white women spoke well of Indian husbands on the silver screen. Candice Bergen was reasonably decent about hers in *Soldier Blue* (1970), but in the tradition of her less laudatory predecessors and successors she headed for white civilization as soon as she got the opportunity. Actually, things rarely reached the point of marriage (or the equivalent) where a captured movie heroine was concerned. That is where those coincidences of history and geography come in. The frontier thriller of the motion picture owed its being primarily to encounters with Indians in a setting far west of New England and two centuries later than the Puritan captivities. The Indians of the movies were not the Noble Savages of the neocaptivities or the eighteenth-century Indian plays; they were Indians of the West, as seen through the field glasses of popular culture. When the movies were born, the Indian wars of the West were almost contemporary events (in fact, many actual participants, both Indian and white, were still alive to serve as advisers or performers for several decades of film evolution). Lurid and fanciful interpretations of frontier skirmishes in Wild West plays and pageants, not to mention the dime novels of the Buffalo Bill species, offered photoplays their most immediate sources of inspiration and imitation, while the Old West itself, with its sweeping vistas and galloping horses, was unmatched as a movie milieu. Even the wider-than-high aspect ratio of the theater screen gave an advantage to broad prairies over tall forests (the locale of most printed captivities); and, if those factors were not enough, American movies were shot in the West, those with eastern locales generally included. (*Unconquered,* one of the proverbial exceptions, had Pennsylvania location shots, but was a Western, in form and spirit).

What did geographical setting have to do with the absence of romantic potential in an Indian captor? More, perhaps, than it should have. Here is Richard Slotkin in his respected literary history of 1973, *Regeneration Through Violence* (p. 357):

. . . The expansion of the nation into the Far West brought the Americans into contact with a very different group of Indian cultures, far more nomadic and barbaric, far less sophisticated in their forms of government, far more brutal to captives than the eastern tribes. Rape, for instance, was virtually unknown in the Indian wars of the East, since women captives were wanted for adoption as brides. The western tribes had no taboo against rape and, in fact, made it a part of their celebrations of triumph, along with torturing and sexual mutilation of male captives.

Now that generalization might well be challenged as one perfectly suited to Manifest Destiny, anchored in scant statistical data, and taking no note of rape or mutilation in reprisal for similar actions by white riffraff. But Slotkin merely echoed a prevailing East-West comparison, cemented when the eastern Indian had vanished into mythology. Covered with a blanket marked "nomads" (even if they inhabited quiet villages), western Indians suffered all the allegations customarily heaped upon rootless wanderers. Their press clippings in the burgeoning mass-media dailies were often on a level somewhat lower than that of motorcycle gangs today. On the eve of the movies' birth generals, politicians, and empire builders were calling for their extermination as murdering rapists, and as the screen form developed, screenwriters (with a careful eye to the censor) showed those horseback raiders not in a light of pagan temptation but in all their legendary menace.

Where words did not tell the story, actions could. At the climax of D. W. Griffith's influential Western of 1913, *The Battle at Elderbush Gulch,* the frontier cabin of the Cameron brothers is surrounded by an unstoppable band of aroused Indians. Trembling in the face of the onslaught is a young woman, played by Lillian Gish, who soon will be at the mercy of the frenzied attackers. As the huddled girl sobs in fear, however, a revolver slowly moves into the film frame and and descends toward her head. One of the cabin's defenders will send a bullet into the young woman's brain rather than let her be taken alive. But that bullet is never released. The sound of charging cavalry reaches the unseen protector's ear across the din of battle.

Twenty-six years after *The Battle at Elderbush Gulch,* a memorable feature-length motion picture would employ a similar sequence. As Apaches close in on a racing overland stage, John Carradine, playing a courtly gambler, eases his silver pistol toward the head of another young woman curled in terror. This time the audience can hear the faint bugle call that signals rescue—at the very moment that an Apache bullet strikes down Carradine. The pistol falls before the fallen knight can discharge it to save a well-bred woman from the misfortune his desperate action implies. The film, of course, is *Stagecoach*, and, interestingly enough, the printed screenplay does not contain the pistol sequence. John Ford, the director, likely interpolated it during the filming, remembering the brilliant use of the device by Griffith a quarter-century earlier. Griffith himself may have gleaned the idea, directly or indirectly, from a popular frontier drama of his youth, though that in no way detracts from his creative framing of it. Ford, by the way, would once again have a white man aim a pistol at a white girl during the climactic moment of an Indian film, but with less chivalrous motivation, as we shall see.[1]

The durability of a line of dialogue having been established, what *did* they do to white women on the motion-picture screen when the cavalry was not there to effect a rescue? Very little *before the camera's eye*—that is, until the 1960s, when an anything-goes approach to sex and violence set in, and gang rapes suddenly, and, one hopes, impermanently, became popular with screenplay writers or their directors. For the especially sadistic crowd a postrape skinning of a female victim was included in one film, there being nothing like a good skinning, apparently, to fan the revenge motif. Such aberrations notwithstanding, movies have tended from the beginning to concentrate upon rescue missions or postrescue adjustment and rarely—in contrast to printed fiction—upon the experiences of a white woman during captivity. Thus in photoplays of the pre-1960s the sexual or physical causes of a white captive's grief sprang largely from the audience's imagination—prodded, naturally, by the "you-know-what-they-do"

---

[1]The most likely source of inspiration for the mercy-shooting sequence in *The Battle at Elderbush Gulch* was the David Belasco frontier drama *The Girl I Left Behind Me.* It was performed on Broadway in 1893 and later, and additionally as part of the Columbian Exposition in Chicago. In the play Kate Kennion kneels reciting the service of the dead while her father, the besieged fort's commander, at her request readies his pistol to save her from the warriors of the vengeful Scar Brow. "Listen—Listen!" she cries, as the cavalry bugle is heard from offstage. "Do you hear it . . . the call of the Twelfth!" The memorable garrison finish to the third act of *The Girl I Left Behind Me,* beyond its special pertinence to the Griffith and Ford films, was emulated by Hollywood for decades, sometimes with almost the same dialogue. Radio too used the device, the special variation of one Lone Ranger episode being a last *silver* bullet in the mercy gun.

business. That kind of imagining, nonetheless, was enough for ample damage to the Indian image, admitting that in some real-life situations what was imagined did take place.[2]

During its early years the American film industry made dozens of films about women or girls captured by Indians, the first, probably, being a mini-drama of 1903 bearing the unvarnished title *Rescue of Child from Indians.* Most of these captive-and-rescue ventures were one- and two-reel films made between 1909 and 1915—the peak period for Indian movies in general. Usually the titles told the story: *A Child in the Forest; Iona, the White Squaw; Company D to the Rescue; An Indian Vestal; Only a Squaw; Prisoner of the Mohicans; Broncho Bill and the Settler's Daughter.*

Despite the pre–World War I abundance of captivity films, however, scarcely any of them survive. One that does is "The Goddess of the Far West," the second chapter in *The Perils of Pauline* (1914). Beyond its significance as part of Pearl White's first chapter play, "The Goddess of the Far West" is remembered for what is often called a classic subtitling gaffe. The error follows a sequence in which several nondescript movie Indians discover Pauline emerging goddesslike from a hole in the ground. They take her captive but wonder whether she is a supernatural being impervious to death. Before long Pauline is hustling down a steep hill a few steps ahead of a mammoth boulder her captors have launched as a test not of her immortal but of "her *immoral* strength." Alas, one never really finds out how Miss White's response to a boulder on the back can be fitted into the Freudian scheme of things. At the peak of excitement Crane Wilbur, the hero, swings to the rescue on a lariat built for two.

It now seems likely that the errant subtitle was not in the original print but was a mistranslation back into English from a European edition of the serial (the American original having been lost). Translation difficulties, however, cannot be offered as excuse for the sorry physical appearance of Pauline's captors. These white men hiding

---

[2]In *The Return of the Vanishing American* (pp. 45–6), Leslie Fiedler suggested that, while "the natives of America did not practice rape generally until they learned it from their European invaders," Shakespeare had no trouble transferring to Caliban, Prospero's grumbling servant of *The Tempest,* myths of faraway satyrs who longed to "deflower and violate rather than worship and woo woman." "In mine own cell," charges Prospero, "thou didst seek to violate the Honour of my child." To that Caliban counters: " 'O ho, O ho! would't had been done! / Thou didst prevent me; I had peopled else / The isle with Calibans.' " Thought Fiedler, an unrestrained Caliban offered the self-condemning threat of making the "whole White world Caliban, which is to say, half-breed."

under turkey feathers are Hollywood's Wild West Indians exemplified —though their strutting and cavorting was captured by the camera not in California but somewhere below Cayuga's waters near Ithaca, New York. Even the runaway boulder in the surprisingly well staged action sequence seems less artificial than the celluloid Sioux who send it on its way downhill. Needless to say, Pearl White looks cute in the already standardized Indian-princess costume which she puts on to have her immorality measured.

When the feature film supplanted the two-reeler as the principal theatrical-film format (starting around 1915) and Hollywood greatly reduced the number of films devoted to Indian subjects, the captivity motif almost disappeared except on the juvenile cowboys-and-Indians level. The 1920s, 1930s, and 1940s passed with no memorable motion picture appearing that depicted a prolonged rescue effort to redeem white maidens. Brief periods of captivity and threatened torture were, however, part of several epic films of the early sound era—when audiences could be thrilled by the aural effects of pounding drums, shrieking dancers, and crackling torture fires. In 1936, for instance, the Munro girls were at the mercy of wild-eyed Hurons in *The Last of the Mohicans,* while, farther west, Jean Arthur, as Calamity Jane, was trussed up alongside Gary Cooper's Wild Bill Hickok in *The Plainsman* (the Cheyenne interrogators were after Custer's battle plans). In later years female captives would be rescued in Technicolor (*Northwest Passage,* 1940) and in Technicolor plus 3-D (*The Charge at Feather River* and *Fort Ti,* 1953). Depiction of the captors in these dramas was barbarous, especially that of some seemingly subhuman Abnakis in *Northwest Passage.*

Although cavalryman John Wayne and troop carried out a brilliant and bloodless mass rescue of a mixed bag of covered-wagon children during the latter half of John Ford's renowned *Rio Grande* in 1950, Ford had yet to do the first major film in which the saving of a kidnapped white girl became the single sustaining motivation of a prolonged narrative. That motion picture was *The Searchers* (1956). In it John Wayne portrayed a heroic character much less respectful of his Indian adversaries than his Lieutenant Colonel Kirby Yorke of *Rio Grande* had been.

The colorful *Searchers* screenplay, derived by Frank Nugent, a former *New York Times* movie critic, from an Alan LeMay novel, depicted a search for Wayne's two nieces, a search commenced by a large band of Texans after a Comanche raid in 1868 and concluded by only two rescuers five or more years later. By that time just one niece (played in turn by Lana and Natalie Wood) remained alive. And that niece had become one of the wives of her captor, Chief Scar—enacted by Henry Brandon at his menacing best. To Wayne the wife of a Comanche is not worth saving, even after a prolonged pursuit. In fact, there is every evidence (just as in the novel) that he will put a revolver bullet into the sullied kinswoman should his younger companion, played by Jeffrey Hunter, relax his guard during the rescue.

John Wayne, in *The Searchers,* is the Indian hater personified, his Ethan Edwards being no one but the revenge-mad Nathan Slaughter of *Nick of the Woods.* Even in his acts of vengeance over the deaths of his kin in the raid, the Wayne character evokes the Jibbenainosay of Bird's novel of 1837. Early in the pursuit, and over the protest of Ward Bond, a clergyman and Ranger captain, Wayne shoots out the eyes of a just-buried Indian raider to destroy his afterlife. Only at the last moment—and after scalping Chief Scar—does Wayne put his revolver aside and convey his rescued niece to the comforting arms of the Jorgensen family, who knew her as a child (in the LeMay book that unexpected compassion costs the Wayne character—called Amos, not Ethan—his life).[3]

The venomous hatred of Wayne for the Comanches is not shared by his white neighbors in *The Searchers,* though they are moved to a full-scale rescue effort by the bloody attack on the girl's household that preceded the kidnapping. To Ward Bond and the others the goal is simply to get the girl back safely. To the Ethan Edwards of John Wayne—especially after he finds the other niece's violated body—the goal is something beyond wrathful retribution. Regrettably, because he is John Wayne, because he is so untiringly skillful in the pursuit, his motivation dominates in building audience attitude. Against a bigger-than-life screen figure, the less fanatical approach of the younger partner cannot offer the balance it does in the novel.

[3]Although Nathan Slaughter (the Jibbenainosay) of the Robert Montgomery Bird novel (and Louisa Medina dramatization) was popular literature's preeminent Indian hater, he had some unremembered fictional precursors, the first probably being Hugh Bradley of James McHenry's *Spectre of the Forest* (1823). Another driven slayer appeared in *Tadeuskund,* by N. W. Hentz (1825). James Kirke Paulding converted the real-life Lewis Wetzel into Timothy Weasel for *Dutchman's Fireside* (1831), while James Hall probed the Indian hater's personality in his frontier sketches of the 1830s, one of the stories providing a basis for Herman Melville's *The Confidence Man* (1857). Many compulsive avengers appeared in the wake of Nathan Slaughter, and new models still appear. For more detailed analysis of the Indian-hating motif see Roy Harvey Pearce, *Savagism and Civilization;* and Richard Slotkin, *Regeneration Through Violence.*

Yet not even the Wayne charisma can counteract the revulsion that arises in a viewer as the hulking uncle prepares to shoot down a defenseless girl just because she had lived with Indians. The relief that comes when the girl is spared—observable as it is when *The Searchers* is shown to a theater audience—hardly justifies the jarringly racist tones that have set it up. With its climax the film says only that at the moment of truth John Wayne cannot murder a *white* girl who also is a close relative. Toward the Comanches themselves *The Searchers* displays not a grain of understanding in word or action, except as it grows from audience distaste for writing and directorial bias in an otherwise well-made film. The year, after all, was 1956, too late for such libel.

A century or more earlier, of course, Wayne's act of mercy would have placed *The Searchers* a grade above its genre. As Roy Harvey Pearce pointed out, most of the Indian-haters of early American fiction could not save themselves from their obsessions (the way Wayne's Ethan Edwards finally did). A rare exception was "The Pioneer" of James Hall's collection of 1835, *Tales of the Border*. That frontiersman's family was killed or stolen by Indians when he was a child. After a life of vengeance Hall's Pioneer was transformed spiritually when he recognized one of his intended victims to be his lost sister, now living as an Indian's wife, "contented, perhaps *happy*, in the embraces of a savage at the very time when I was lying in ambush by the warpath." In Pearce's words:

> The moral was pressed upon him. He had almost lost his sense of civilization and its responsibilities; as an avenger he had been a savage. Only as a savage had he right to such vengeance; for only as savages did the Indians have a right thus to protect themselves from the white men and their ways.[4]

In one regard, at least, Ethan Edwards had regained his sense of civilization—not that this recovery meant placing Comanches in any higher esteem.

Pleased, perhaps, by the critical applause for *The Searchers*, Ford and Nugent again attempted the recovered-captive theme five years later—possibly to demonstrate that Natalie Wood would actually have been better off shot down. *Two Rode Together* (1961), while not ranked with John Ford's better Western dramas, does outline the adjustment problems of the white captive raised by Indians and subsequently

[4]Roy Harvey Pearce, *Savagism and Civilization*, p. 229.

returned to colonial or pioneer society. That there were such problems, and that they were sometimes insurmountable, is not to be denied. For example, the daughter of John Williams, a Puritan leader, after decades of Indian life, chose to return to it following too-intense attention to her redeemed soul by the clergy. In a recently discovered eighteenth-century manuscript a Kansas captive named Anna Morgan, married to an Indian chief before she was rescued by Lieutenant Colonel George A. Custer's Seventh Cavalry, put it starkly: "After I came back the road seemed rough, and I often wished they had never found me."

In contrast to *The Searchers,* which placed greater emphasis upon the passion of the pursuit, *Two Rode Together* (derived from Will Cook's novel) portrays a money-minded lawman (James Stewart) and a duty-minded army captain (Richard Widmark) as negotiators for the return of individuals whom they do not know, individuals missing for so long that they have blended into Comanche mores and life. After concluding a deal with a selfish, conniving Hollywood representation of the half-white chief Quanah Parker (played by former-Scar Henry Brandon), Stewart finds that the ransomed whites are disinclined to accept liberation. One young woman refuses to leave camp—with sufficient violence to cause any thinking person to accede to her wishes. Her intended rescuers readily exempt her from redemption. An older female captive, played with sensitivity by Mae Clark, denies repatriation because a second change in social pattern, late in life, would be too difficult, and because her former associates would see her as degraded by years of living with Indians.[5]

Without doubt both *The Searchers* and the film version of *Two Rode Together* had partial inspiration in the actual experience of the white mother of Quanah Parker, the unsympathetic bargainer of the second Ford film (in the Cook novel the icy trader is not Parker but someone called Iron Hand). Captured by Comanches at the age of nine, Cynthia Ann Parker was not returned to white society until twenty-five years later. Although treated charitably by settlers, the thirty-four-year-old

[5]A never-quite-disappearing Puritan viewpoint saw Indian captivity as what Richard Slotkin called an almost certain "spiritual and physical catastrophe." Those who did not meet death or vanish forever—almost one-half of the colonial captives did—"returned half-Indianized or Romanized, or converted to Catholicism and stayed in Canada, or married some 'Canadian half-breed' or 'Indian slut,' or went totally savage. In any of these cases, the captive was a soul utterly lost to the tents of the English Israel." Slotkin, *Regeneration Through Violence,* p. 98.

woman was unable to make the very transition in cultures which the older female captive in *Two Rode Together* feared. Never happy in her new life, separated from her two Comanche sons, Cynthia Ann several times "borrowed" horses to search for Quanah and his brother, Pecos. At last, when the small daughter who lived with her died, the wretched woman denied herself food until death came. Quanah Parker never forgot his mother. He was an audacious battle leader for many years before leading his followers into coexistence with the white man. *Two Rode Together* demeaned him but through the Mae Clark character did identify the position Quanah's mother ultimately would face.

To resume the *Two Rode Together* narrative: The frustrated rescuers eventually bring back just two whites, a frenziedly unwilling junior brave and the Mexican-born wife of Parker's Indian archrival. The woman (played well by Linda Cristal) tries earnestly to resume a role in white civilization, only to be humiliated publicly when James Stewart escorts her to a military ball at Richard Widmark's post. Although Stewart's impassioned denunciation of the hypocrisy and bigotry of regimental society draws the cheers of Andy Devine, an old sergeant —who at that point in the film is clearly the embodiment of all feeling souls in the movie's audience—it cannot erase the disgrace of the redeemed captive. To complicate matters further, the ransomed young male is responding violently to the pattern of white civilization and has to be restrained with ropes. Never does he leave off shrieking that he is Comanche. Sadly, in *Two Rode Together* being Comanche means that he can unfeelingly stab to death a sympathetic frontier woman who, having convinced herself that she is his mother, frees him from his bonds (in the novel the lad kills a demented woman because he fears her madness). A quick lynching puts the white Comanche out of the way. The outcome of the rescue expedition after all the struggle? Two prisoners liberated: one hanged youth and one humiliated woman.

A plea for understanding does emerge from the Frank Nugent screenplay for *Two Rode Together*. Ironically, however, it is for understanding of those whites who have been tainted by Indian life, hardly for the Indians themselves. In view of the abominable behavior patterns assigned to almost every Comanche in the film, anything more would be too much to ask. *Two Rode Together* really preaches: "Be kind to poison victims." The poison itself is beyond consideration. This John Ford film is a sadly curious example of cross-purposes jammed into a framework of good, if narrow, intentions.

Not that it was especially rare for Hollywood to outline a difficult life for rescued white women. Naturally, if the rescue occurred only moments before the closing titles, the entire matter of adjustment was glossed over by an "everything-will-be-all-right-now" embrace. But when the recovery of an Indian's "woman" came in an early reel, discrimination by whites could be anticipated. Thus the middle-aged Barbara Stanwyck is exposed to small-town scorn in *Trooper Hook* (1957). Joel McCrea eventually takes her to a distant range so that she can begin a new life with him. In *The Stalking Moon* (a 1968 film derived from the novel by Theodore V. Olsen) rescuer Gregory Peck leads Eva Marie Saint and her child to a veritable lost valley, far from white civilization. The isolated retreat does not, however, lie beyond the reach of the relentless, seemingly devil-inspired Salvaje, who wants both vengeance and his heir. Miss Saint's adjustment problem is soon displaced by an exercise in lurking terror.

In fairness to a *Two Rode Together* or similar film one should acknowledge that a message for tolerance of even limited scope in a captivity film is preferable to blissful disregard of a captive's perspective. It does not make up for a failure also to consider the Indian point of view, but it is an attempt at substance, one not found in all rescue dramas. *The Day of the Evil Gun* (1968), as an example, has no decent purpose at all and reveals how superior even a mediocre John Ford opus can be to a routine Western. In *The Day of the Evil Gun,* kept too much alive by television, the two riding together are Glenn Ford and Arthur Kennedy. Ford is a reformed gunfighter, who, returning home after years of absence, discovers that his wife and daughters have been carried off by Apaches. What is more, the crafty Kennedy has somehow managed to become engaged to the roaming gunman's wife. Contrived and absurd might be the best terms for describing the remaining plot of *The Day of the Evil Gun.* Its Apaches are simply the background murderers and ravagers of Hollywood tradition, their rapaciousness accentuated to fit the era of "frankness" that commenced in the late 1960s. Never more than plot devices, these Indians do an atrocity here and an atrocity there until Glenn Ford abruptly ends their connection to the narrative by retrieving his family from them with absurd ease, in broad daylight. The Apaches, presumably, will go on to other depredations while Ford resolves his domestic crisis without using his gun. Charles Marquis Warren was responsible for the original story and part of the screenplay for *The Day of the Evil*

Gun. It was not the first time Warren had linked the Apache with mindless evil.

If *The Day of the Evil Gun's* Apaches are the persistent "bad Indians" of plot convenience, the Kiowas of another frequently televised film of 1968 are mercurial (perhaps even transitional) creatures. Like the monsters of those Abbott-and-Costello-Meet-Frankenstein movies, the Indians of *The Scalphunters* (a Burt Lancaster film written by William Norton) are alternately menacing and amusing. Their first captive is not a young woman—or even a human being. Rather, it is the fur-laden packhorse of trapper Joe Bass (Lancaster), who does not exactly consider the runaway slave left in exchange by Two Crows fair payment for a whole season's pelts. While the wily Bass waits for the celebrating Kiowas to get drunk enough for him to recover his goods, white marauders get to the Indians first, slaying them for their scalps (*they* are the scalphunters of the title, though how many moviegoers would have guessed that in advance?). Only Two Crows survives the raid. Bass, who respects the Kiowas, their unwelcome horse trading notwithstanding, is stunned by the massacre. One suspects that the rugged fur trader has enjoyed his robust economic duels with Two Crows over the years, and that it is not just some lost pelts that encourage him to mow down several of the scalp hunters as a way of balancing the scales.

Given a start by Bass, other Kiowas get the rest of the slaughterers —and, once again, Bass's furs. But there is additional plunder. The Kiowas also make off with the white raiders' camp followers, a wagon-load of raucous pleasure ladies under the tutelage of frontier battle-ax Shelley Winters. At last the Indians of movieland have won the picture's white gals. It is a Pyrrhic victory, however, for not even the liberal-minded Joe Bass is wont to redeem this flock of white captives.

"Good hunting, Joe Bass," calls Two Crows airily, as he leads away his captured furs and fancy girls. Lancaster looks oddly philosophical. Perhaps aware of the anomaly that his misadventure represents in the history of captivity drama, he is reckoning that his longtime Indian sparring mate will regret the day he rode off with the flinty Shelley Winters. Alas, poor Two Crows, the henpecked Kiowa.

Sometimes it was hard to believe that this strange bloody-minded red race was human at all. It was as if giant lizards had come here on horses, mouthing and grunting their unearthly language that so few white men had ever understood.

Alan LeMay, *The Unforgiven*, 1957

7

FROM ANOTHER ADAM

MANY readers and B-picturegoers will remember Bomba, the Jungle Boy. He was the fourteen-year-old hero of juvenile fiction created in 1926, as a kind of of junior Tarzan, by the prolific Edward Stratemeyer (the Rover Boys, the Bobbsey Twins, Tom Swift, the Hardy Boys, Nancy Drew). Bomba's initial milieu, however, was the Amazonian rather than the African jungle, which meant that his local antagonists were not black warriors but South American Indians, some of them headhunters. It made no difference to the Jungle Boy, however. In times of danger, as his author, "Roy Rockwood," so often put it: "For Bomba, to think was to act."

Considering the numbers of reptiles, wild animals, and quicksand traps that Bomba encountered per page, instant reaction was usually an absolute necessity. Once in a while—during a jungle equivalent of being stuck in an elevator—Bomba did find a moment or two for reflection. Still, pure cogitation of more than a paragraph's duration was always a strain for the lad, primarily because of an unconcealed preoccupation with skin color. Bomba, the Jungle Boy, may have been the most absolute white racist ever to reach the printed page. For ethnic reassurance he would now and again pull aside his puma-skin top and announce to no one in particular, "See, I am white!"

Not knowing his parentage, and being an easy victim for any pseudogenealogist who passed by, Bomba used the infrequent action-less interludes of the first book in which he appeared to muse over the difference between himself and, say, Chief Nascanora's band of jungle menaces (he had already concluded that he was of a species different from those of his animal friends, Polulu, the panther, and Doto, the monkey). Further, Bomba's whiteness, as opposed to his adversaries' copperness, became apparent to him somewhere along the line. But there had to be some additional distinction. Language? No, Bomba did not give that a moment's consideration. Both he and the Indians spoke Friday-ese, the only difference being that Nascanora's band (North American in style, save for the headhunting) were addicted to "Ugh!" Around and around the sociological dilemma spun in Bomba's mind:

> To be white meant not only to look different, but to act differently, to think differently, to live differently. What inner thing was it that made those who wore white skin for a covering . . . different from the brown or copper-skinned natives?

Then one day, while Bomba wondered why even the nontroublesome Indians in the vicinity took no joy at the beauty of a magnificent waterfall, the answer began to come to him. Did it have anything to do with the possibility that he possessed what the white men called a soul? "Many, many lonely hours Bomba . . . spent wondering about this." Then the full answer started to come:

> Why did the faces of the natives always wear to Bomba the same dull and stupid look, as dull and stupid, Bomba thought, and often more so, than the faces of his jungle friends? Why were the faces of the Indians always the same, except when they darkened and grew fierce and stern? Why did beauty not appeal to them as it did to him?

Was Bomba actually working toward the idea that Indians had no souls?

> He dismissed his thought as improbable. But perhaps their souls were asleep. Ah that must be it! They were asleep!

Bomba's soul, in contrast, was awake, or at least waking, and the thought gave him a thrill:

> Now he was sure he had found the truth. The natives' souls were asleep. The white men's souls were awake. And he was white!

119

Bomba, the Jungle Boy, working on his personal problem of adjustment while sitting on a tree limb in the jungle, was developing as precisely as it was ever put the apologia for the base treatment of the "wild" Indian in popular literature: an Indian might have a soul, but, if he did, it was assuredly a sleeping one. Take that concept, hold it up to most of the printed or dramatized fiction portraying Indians, and instantly one can look into the mind-sets of hundreds, nay thousands, of writers of books and films and sundry stories about "redskins." They wrote not of people but of creatures, children at best, animals at worst. They wrote, sometimes with good intentions, of missionaries who set out to save souls but could not save what they could so seldom find. How did Father Julian, a Jesuit, put it to Lygon, a schoolmaster, in Grace Zaring Stone's *The Cold Journey?*

> I was fresh from Europe. I walked about talking to them, asking questions here and there, but all the eyes I looked into were like wells, very dark and narrow and cold. And so I have found them, with a few exceptions ever since.
>
> "They are a great disappointment to me too," said Mr. Lygon. "I wondered about them a good deal on coming here. . . . But I had come to believe that nature plays a great part in the conception of moral law. That the truly natural man is the man of perfect balance. That if a man were to return to nature he would return to his instinctive feelings of proportion. I had imagined that I would find among these creatures the sort of man or nearly the sort of man whose morality would be a natural taste for what is harmonious. But you know yourself how far this is from being the case."
>
> "I agree that it isn't the case," said Father Julian, "but I am not like you in expecting anything of the natural man. You forget that Adam's sin destroyed the purity of our instincts. It is Divine Grace alone which is capable now of saving us."
>
> Mr. Lygon sighed. He disagreed but nevertheless he liked the Jesuit.

Stone, less insentive than most writers of frontier adventures, was letting her characters talk out the myth of the Noble Savage -in an isolated setting rife with concerns about "popery." Father Julian's soul searching over soul saving saw print in 1934. Almost a century earlier Robert Montgomery Bird, having comfortably resolved the moral dilemma before putting pen to paper, spoke directly to the reader about Indian barbarity in his image-changing novel *Nick of the Woods:*

Such is the red-man of America, whom courage—
    an attribute to all lovers of blood, whether man or animal;
misfortune—
    the destiny, in every quarter of the globe of every barbarous race,
    which contact with a civilized one cannot civilize;
and the dreams of poets and sentimentalists have invested with a character wholly incompatible with his condition.

Animal courage, then, but an unadaptability to civilizing, says Bird.
And the higher values?

Individual virtues may be, and indeed frequently are, found among men
in a natural state; but honor, justice, and generosity, as characteristics
of the mass, are refinements belonging in an advanced state of civilization.

Explain, Mr. Bird, how an Indian can juxtapose laughter and the
infliction of pain:

It is only among children (we mean, of course, *bad* ones) and savages,
who are but grown children, after all, that we find malice and mirth go
hand in hand.

Children, when looked at for their pleasures, *unfortunate savages,*
when looked at for their calamities (to which ignorance of civilization
perforce brought them), *animals,* when looked at for their blood lusts.
Now that was an appraisal a jungle boy could have lived with, had it
ever reached him in his tree. But who would have thought that in his
isolated—but not savage—state (for he *was* white) that Bomba, the
Jungle Boy, would have contemplated those same dark and cold eyes
that would trouble Father Julian in a novel not yet written? Yet even
more perplexing, how did Bomba replicate the theoretical processes
of a sixteenth-century Swiss alchemist-physician? For what was he to
Paracelsus or Paracelsus to him?

Paracelsus, or Bombastus von Hohenheim (1493–1541)—surely
his given name is linked to Bomba's by pure coincidence—plunged
into the early conjecturing about the state of humanity of the New
World's natives with the proposition that they were not among "the
sons of Adam." Adam's descendants, he reasoned, could never have
made it to those faraway American islands. Paracelsus saw the Indians
as beings descended from another Adam, a postDeluge Adam, and
hence of a different flesh and blood. One more tidbit from Paracelsus:
as a race generated after the Flood, *"perhaps they have no souls"* (italics
Bomba's).

Now in 1520 the idea that there were two Adams could only have been considered heretical, so no one in Paracelsus's era seconded the outspoken thinker's polygenesis proposal, in writing at least. But that still left a philosophical and practical argument about whether America's inhabitants were human enough for salvation. The fuss was sufficient to occasion a papal bull (*Sublimus Deus,* 1537) declaring that Indians were not of some subspecies but, rather, were "*true men.*" As such they could receive the Catholic faith and were not to be enslaved. That proclamation effectively limited formal debate on the matter of souls. Still, the pecuniary promise of Indian slavery (begun by Columbus, who had written about rounding up seven *head* of women) brought that section of the bull to various religious or quasi-religious courts of appeal. There Father Bartolomé de Las Casas, who had lived in America, stood out as the Indians' staunchest defender. Once, however, the natives of the Caribbean had been decimated by the tens of thousands and, moreover, had been supplanted by Africans as the New World's slave force, the slavery debate lost its impetus. Now it was for the French and English, with their new colonies, to determine what the indians were, savages noble or savages irredeemable. Michel de Montaigne, in *Des Cannibales* (1580), saw in "Brazil" a picture surpassing that which poets had drawn of the Golden Age. To him even the most negative element of the new civilization, cannibalism, was less barbarous than the calculated brutality of the European torture chambers, where men were "eaten" while still alive.

William Shakespeare took this essay of Montaigne regarding natural civilization, attached it to a shipwreck plot inspired by the celebrated (and generally pleasant) marooning of the *Sea Venture's* passengers in 1609, and produced *The Tempest* (1611). Montaigne (whose essay Shakespeare read in translation) had wished that Plato could have commented on the new world where

> there is no manner of traffic, no knowledge of letters, no science of numbers, no name of magistrate or political authority, no use of services, riches or poverty . . . no metal, no use of corn or wine,

and so on. Shakespeare, in close paraphrase, put Montaigne's description into the mouth of the trusted Gonzalo as a projection not of a land that already existed but of one that the stranded Europeans could set up (act 2, scene 2, 11. 147–54):

> . . . no kind of traffic
> Would I admit; no name of magistrate;
> Letters should not be known; riches, poverty,

And use of service, none . . .
. . . .
No use of metal, corn, or wine, or oil.

But Prospero's magical island had an enslaved aboriginal inhabitant with a personality not at all in keeping with the kind of individual appropriate to Gonzalo's utopia. What is more, Shakespeare (with an unseen bow to the "other Adam" of Paracelsus) brewed a polygenesis in which the aborigine had been born of a witch and fathered by a devil. To produce a name for the creature, he shuffled the letters of the newly coined word "cannibal" and came up with Caliban.

Caliban, the grumbling, misshapen, lascivious servant of Prospero, is not a Noble Savage. He is an animalistic lout, seemingly beyond the reach of the civilizer's hand. His coarse god is Setebos, the Patagonian deity mentioned by an over imaginative survivor of the Magellan voyage who reported giants living in that South American country. Plied with liquor, Caliban eagerly joins two ridiculous servants who were stranded on his island along with their masters in a projected mutiny. It fails miserably. Caliban, after believing he has found a new god in one of the white servants, is driven in defeat through bush and brier by Prospero's spirits in the form of hunting dogs—a once-favored method of keeping West Indians in line. As Prospero and the other Europeans make ready to depart from his island, Caliban is a beaten man, ready for whatever subservient role his white master will have him perform. In a sense he has been tamed, no, *domesticated.*

Shakespeare was portraying the effect of white civilization upon native culture, even if his outlook was colored by negative appraisals of the American native's potential expressed by several Elizabethan colonizers of Virginia. The playwright's childish, soul-asleep, Paracelsian aborigine, however, would in lesser hands be kept alive to poorer purposes during century after century. He would block progress, fall upon caravans, carry off women and children. He would sulk about trading posts in numberless frontier tales, often showing animal cunning, but rarely human feeling. The enormity, variety, and near-universality of the literary crime against the Indian cannot be fully recognized until one has let hundreds of books and films and dramas pass before his eyes in a fixed period of time. One after another, upright characters of frontier fiction are heard talking like Ben, the hero of Alan LeMay's novel of 1957 (and movie of 1960), *The Unforgiven:*

"There weren't any people here, Mama. Those were Indians."

Even schoolbooks would play their part in the libel—furthering the crime by encouraging budding writers to see America's first inhabitants as something less than enlightened beings. One text of 1898 had the subspecies neatly categorized. Collectively the original dwellers of the Americas were "so unlike others" that they were called "red men." Within the circle of red men, the western and northern Indians were "generally called savage Indians" ("repeat that, children: *savage* Indians"). East of the Rocky Mountains, continued H. A. Guerber's *The Story of the Thirteen Colonies,* the Indians "knew a little more than the savage Indians," so they were called "the barbarous Indians" ("again, children: the *barbarous* Indians"). And at the top of the Eclectic reader's aboriginal ladder were the *southern* Indians, the creative Mayas and Incas included. Not that this distinction meant much. The history book gave the southern Indians no more than a D-minus grade—"half-civilized."

With such foolishness being placed into the little hands of future paperback and screenplay writers by their educators, is it surprising that the not-quite-human Indian dominated the dime-novel era, and then was carried over to the Western fiction of the twentieth century, motion pictures included? Notice how Alan LeMay in *The Unforgiven* picked up the old history-book kind of stratification for a bit of dialogue in which a youth reassures Rachel Zachary, his adopted sister and the book's central figure, that she was not—heaven forbid—Kiowa-born:

"And another thing," he said, through the moon-tempered dark, "You're not an Indian—not a red-nigger kind, not a Civilized Nation kind, not any other kind. So quit fooling around with the notion you might be, you hear?"

Earlier in the novel another character, a woman who had been a captive of some "Horse Indians," had showed the reader why Rachel, who already leaned toward the notion that Indians were "half human," had vital reason to be concerned about her ancestry:

"This one thing I know. The red niggers are no human men. Nor are they beasts, nor any kind of earthly varmint, for all natural critters act like God made them to do. Devil-spirits, demons out of red kill, these be, that somehow, on some evil day, found way to clothe themselves in flesh. I say to you, they must be cleansed from the face of this earth!

Wherever one drop of their blood is found, it must be destroyed! For that is man's most sacred trust, before Almighty God."

Biting words those, but in genesis not so much bitter recollection of a fictional captive from the late 1800s as fear-inspired libel by Puritan settlers of two centuries earlier. Into the mouth of a stern plainswoman LeMay had put the arguments, almost the very words, of Cotton Mather and other New Englanders who, in the era of the witch trials, extended the earlier Spanish defamations of Aztec or Inca "devil worshipers" to the extreme by visualizing Indians as demons in human shape. Allegations of ghostly visitations by spectral Indians, Satan-focused explanations of New England's Indian wars, sermons about woodland orgies, ravings by the redeemed captive, Mercy Short, and devil-oriented interpretations of them by Cotton Mather came to a peak in the 1690s. To the "wolves" and "lions" derogations that Mather and other Puritan writers had assigned the Indians were added epithets like "spirits of the invisible world," "hellish conquerors," "horrid sorcerers," and, of course, "divels" and "daemons." In the first chapter of *Savagism and Civilization,* Roy Harvey Pearce explains why Puritans were so ready to see those devil spirits that LeMay's Eumenides indicted:

> The logic was inexorable and unrelieved. Wherever the Indian opposed the Puritan, there Satan opposed God; Satan had possessed the Indian until he had become virtually a beast; Indian worship was devil worship. . . . Satanism, it was abundantly evident, was at the core of savage life. . . . Indian witch doctors clearly were sharing diabolically in the wonders of the invisible world.[1]

And still are, one might add, through the supernatural-based Indian books and films inspired by the success of *The Exorcist* in the 1970s. The Puritans, it should be remembered, were America's champion exorcists, and Indians were their demons.[2]

With soul asleep—or possessed by the devil—or eliminated altogether—the paperback or celluloid savage was, from the first, too often indistinguishable in behavior from an animal. Whether that prevailing condition disturbed the slumber of any action-story writers we do not know, but assuredly it made for easier composition to leave

[1]Roy Harvey Pearce, *Savagism and Civilization,* p. 22.

[2]The Indian connection to the witchcraft phenomenon of New England is too extensive for proper consideration in this book, but Richard Slotkin examines it fully in *Regeneration Through Violence,* especially in his fifth chapter.

the Indian in his habitual low station. No effort-requiring shifts in point of view had to be devised to show how the other side (the Indian side) looked at things (does any writer bother with the pouncing leopard's perspective in a Tarzan picture?). No twinges of conscience had to be allowed for when the number of slain Sioux or Apache attackers reached catastrophic proportions (who considers the number of *animals* trampled in a jungle stampede?). No charging brave ever had to be connected to a grieving mother (why even bother with women, older ones at least, when one can concentrate upon the colorful male of the species?).

For the motion-picture industry, devoted as it was to thinly disguised remakes and interchangeable plots, there was an added (if not fully recognized) convenience in the sleeping-souled Indian. When a screenplay writer was required to let a decent interval pass before redoing a Western plot, he could always take a jungle scenario, move it to the American frontier, and let some Indians assume the roles of any restless natives (the peaceful bearers being replaced by pack animals). If the relocated plot required no restless natives, Indians could replace some jungle beasts. The latter substitution probably was not a conscious action by the film writers; it was a product of the centuries of Bomba-like rationalizations about sleeping or missing souls. Yet, uncomfortable as the Indians-for-animals trades may be to accept, the exchanges are not difficult to locate, even when Indians make only incidental filmic appearances. Recall, for instance, the screen's many pith-helmet-and-machete dramas in which the still-fresh safari members pause in their journey to watch a stock-shot flock of flamingos rise from the water or a startled herd of giraffes race by. Now call to mind one of the wholesome wagon-train epics of movie theater or television in which some natural wonder is hurled at the viewer every five minutes. What happens to the stock shots? The images of flamingos and giraffes (or parrots and monkeys) are replaced by a rumbling batch of bison and a distant line of not-quite-identifiable plains Indians on the trail:

"Look, Pa, Injuns!"

Then back to the story till the next phenomenon arises.

When, however, violent action has been ordered by the film producer and scenic wonders turn into perils of the wild, those nebulous Hollywood-eclectic warriors give up the roles of flamingos and giraffes to become the prairie equivalents of crocodiles or piranhas. Should their lair be intruded upon by the Union Pacific or Western Union or prairie schooners or supply wagons, they pounce instantly and instinctively upon their unsuspecting victims, as if no other course of action were conceivable for them but attacking on sight. Since they seem to have no function in life but to lie in wait for the next traveler who would bring civilization to the frontier, the predator Indians must be moved aside, removed entirely, or confined to the counterpart of an animal reserve—in the interests of progress.[3] And what if, instead of waiting in place, like pit-lurking dragons, for the white man to come to them, the predator Indians deliberately follow at a distance, like coyotes or hawks looking for the right moment to attack? Why, then they clearly show how well they deserve the defeat and subjugation that awaits them when the cavalry finally appears. Whatever the animalized Indian's mode of gaining his prey, however, the picturegoer meets him for the first time to the accompaniment of a sting of menace music that underlines his inherent bloodlust and, were it not for the tom-tom motif, could be used in the studio's upcoming jungle film to signal the first camera appearance of a lion on the prowl. In contrast, the trek of the pioneers or the labors of the advancing railroaders are accompanied by a musical theme of Manifest Destiny worthy of the Great Rotary Club in the Sky.

In keeping with the animallike function of the predator Indian, he does not speak, even to the rest of his kind. When closing in on his prey, he may, if he is the leader of the pack, make a few sweeping gestures to signify attack. Otherwise he howls or yowls or spews out some kind of inhuman sound—even at moments when any lion of average intelligence would recognize the prudence of silent approach. To anticipate the question of a zoologist reading these words, let me say that the Hollywood Indian is a *daytime* predator. He does a lot of skulking around in the dark, periodically issuing various animal calls (which never fool white scouts), but he strikes only by daylight. His dietary habits are unknown, though, if he finds whiskey among the effects of his victims, the merest drop affects him in the same silly way it does a pet animal who is slipped a nip by a prankster at a celebration.

As a matter of fact, our predator Indian, if properly reformed and

[3]Vine Deloria, Jr., used irony when he wrote: "It is fortunate we [Indians] were never slaves. We gave up land instead of life and labor. Because the Negro labored, he was considered a draft animal. Because the Indian occupied large areas of land, he was considered a wild animal." *Custer Died for Your Sins,* pp. 7–8.

civilized by a white mentor, becomes the veritable duplicate of that pet animal. Like the tigers and lions who through the years have played with Dorothy Lamour and other princesses of Technicolor jungles, the domesticated aborigine is ever faithful to and protective of his owner—though he does make other whites uneasy by his presence: ("Are you sure that Shoshoni of yours can be trusted? He looks plenty mean and dangerous to me").

Sometimes it is possible to take advantage of a Hollywood Indian's natural hunting instincts by using him as a bloodhound to smell out pesky varmints of one color or another. He can work well singly —*The Iroquois Trail*—and in groups—the Pawnee scouts of John Ford's *The Iron Horse.* If properly motivated, he can join a good-Indian posse in rooting out miscreants of his own group—*Drum Beat*—or enlist in an elite, white-trained Indian force—Rock Hudson and other "Apaches" in *Taza, Son of Cochise.* The closer he is linked to white civilization, of course, the more his soul awakes, as he changes from wild animal to pet animal to man-child.

For those redeemed Indians whose contacts with white civilization are not too close—say those living on reservations—the transition is difficult. Sometimes, like many creatures of the wild, they get the wanderlust, or a longing for the old haunts, and steal away from their white-made Edens. To the screenplay writer it is the opportunity to dust off yet another jungle-movie chestnut: the "bring-em-back-alive" plot, also used on occasion for wild-horse roundups of the B picture. When large herds are involved, the technique of choice is to lasso the lead stallion, a good wild Indian, and lead him into the corral. His entourage will then follow easily enough. More often than not, however, there is in the shadows a tough customer—he can be called Diablo in jungle, Indian, and wild-horse films—who does little but cause trouble for both sides. It is the death battle with this rogue that provides the movie's climactic action sequence. His opponent may be one of his white pursuers or the leader of his own company (the latter situations being another easy plot twist for a tired writer).

Related to the bring-em-back-alive plot, but only in its pursuit sequences, is the one built upon the running to ground of what in a jungle drama would be called a man-eater. Here the emphasis is upon heinousness of offense and the desperate necessity to destroy the creature before he kills again. This format brings the Indian movie close indeed to the horror film—the inhuman monster must be destroyed—but what is a blood-maddened tiger or lion but a monster?

The ravaging animal must be brought to bay. The hunter must be hunted. The killer must be killed. Each strike by the "angry devil" brings the terror closer to characters and audience and enlarges the case for not simple execution but vengeance. When the creature is at last struck down, the crescendo of viewer reaction reflects the emotional investment generated by the coldly systematic murders of the offender. Salvaje of *The Stalking Moon* (1968) deserves nothing more than the death that comes to him from that last white man who stands between him and his evil purpose. That the evil purpose has something to do with recovery of his offspring born of a captive white woman who found shelter with Gregory Peck is of no consequence in either the film or Theodore V. Olsen's book. In the book we are told that Salvaje was always a wild one, and in both versions so many hideous killings (a dog's included) are piled atop each other that onlookers forget everthing about paternal rights. Salvaje is just too bad to live.

As Hollywood begins to find it tactful to select its purest villains from less ethnically conspicuous forms than Indians or blacks or Italians, one can expect to see more emphasis upon "renegades" (when Indians do really nasty things as a group) and upon the "poor creature gone mad" (when one of them sins individually). Close to the time of *The Stalking Moon* movie was *Tell Them Willie Boy Is Here* (1969), in which, though the business of the hunt occupies more time and characters than it does in *The Stalking Moon,* the object of the chase is shown to have been pressed into his crimes by white tormentors. Since similar filmic sympathy has been increasingly extended to harassed Indians being hunted as groups, the pathological motif will no doubt be more and more necessary if movie (or television) makers wish to haul out those truly bad Indians of yore.

Nonetheless, ostensibly sympathetic screenplay treatments with perfunctory references to renegades or rogues explain away only those Indians who commit violent acts. That still can leave a lot of on-screen Indians with souls half-asleep and tongues slow and eyes empty and throats primed for whiskey. That still will leave a lot of on-screen Indians with not much to show in matters of what Robert Montgomery Bird called cultivation.

Bomba would not sit still long enough to do it, but put Paracelsus to a month of Indian watching through only movie screen, television set, or paperback page, and from what he would see thereon he still might go conjecturing about "another Adam."

KICKAPOO INDIAN HUNTING BUFFALO FOR TALLOW TO MAKE KICKAPOO INDIAN SALVE.

KICKAPOO
INDIAN SALVE!

**Made from Buffalo Tallow, combined with
Healing Herbs and Barks.**

It is a perfect cure-all in Skin Diseases—for the various forms of
Tetter, dry, scaly, moist or itchy, for **Erysipelas,** recent
or chronic; **Pimples or Blotches on the Face,
Scald Head, Barber's Itch,** and all annoying,
unsightly eruptions of the skin; also, painful soft
Corns, and **Burns** and **Itching Piles.**

SOLD BY ALL DRUGGISTS.   **PRICE 25 CENTS.**

TRY IT!   *KEEP IT IN THE HOUSE!*

BONNETS ARE HIGH. A fashion journal says; "Bonnets come high this
season." We do not remember when they did not, as any man who has been
compelled to pay for them can testify.

130

It did not take long for the commercially minded to realize that Indians could sell merchandise. In the medicine shows of America, feathered "chiefs" were there in person to do the selling, but even in effigy braves and maidens were, and are, effective sales aids —on the sidewalks outside cigar stores, on printed page or poster, and on the television screen.

131

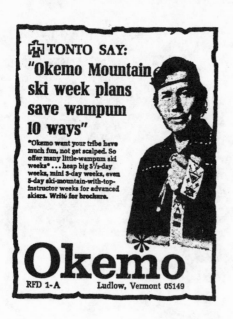

Indian names or credentials can mean good business for every kind of product from giblets to shoes (Sioux brand) to sweaters—for which, the Whitehouse and Hardy advertising tells us, Geronimo "would have traded his loin cloth."

132

AUTHENTIC REPLICA OF
COCHISE

*Sometimes the advertising agents become part of the merchandise, including the wooden
Indians photographed by Clay Frederick.*

133

*It was simply that evolution had played a terrible trick
and pitted against each other two civilizations that
were thousands of years apart and wholly unable to
understand each other.*

Christopher Lehmann-Haupt, *New York Times*,
November 22, 1974

8

THE ENEMY

ON NOVEMBER 14, 1493, with the sun high overhead Christopher Columbus, full of enthusiasm on his return to the Indies, sent out a small boat to examine a landing site at Santa Cruz (Saint Croix), in the Virgin Islands. It was Carib territory his boatmen were pulling for, and trouble was possible, but the first villagers whom the landing party encountered took flight the way the peaceful Tainos of other islands often had during Columbus's first voyage. Satisfied with their reconnaissance, the two-dozen mariners were rowing back to their ships when they spotted and decided to intercept a canoe bearing six surprised Caribs, two of them women. It was a mistake. Infuriated, the Caribs snatched up their bows and arrows, doggedly battling the numerically superior interlopers even after their canoe had been overturned. Then, while the Spaniards were busy playing cat and mouse with a wounded captive, those supposedly terrified Carib villagers angrily took up positions on the shoreline. Soon dozens of arrows were flying toward startled spectators on the waiting ships, changing amusement into alarm. Not at all reluctantly, Columbus and his party said farewell to lovely Santa Cruz.

From that day until 1890 and Wounded Knee there would be few, if any, seasons during which some Indian force, large or small, did not find itself in armed conflict with a force, large or small, of European visitors (or their descendants). To the Indian the white man sooner or later became fixed in mind as the invader. To the white man—not really seeing his "opening" of the New World as invasion—the Indian, by resisting the advance of civilized immigrants, became the enemy. Peaceful interludes, temporary alliances there might be, but the prevailing pattern during four centuries would be one of distrust, hostility, conflict, and, in the end, surrender and internment. On hand to strain the emotions of one side or the other were angry accounts of torture, enslavement, greed, treachery, warfare by disease, ambush, and atrocities to civilians. Popular literature, needless to say, would be selective in its reporting, for that which made money was not necessarily that which was true. And even when profit was not involved, when all that mattered was spinning a good yarn, a dash of ginger never hurt the basic flavor.

OUTLINE BY COLUMBUS

Distortions notwithstanding, it is surprising to see how many elements of the "hostile-Indian" thrillers emerged in 1493 or shortly after. We have already looked at the skirmish in the Virgin Islands, which foreshadowed what might be called the ipso facto clashes of novel and screen: white man suddenly meets Indian, and for no other reason than that they fight. The lesson conveyed, in movies especially, is one of perpetual, and inevitable, warfare, and, alas, it is a lesson that generations of youngsters have been drilled in through their wild-frontier entertainments. Staccato prose, fortissimo musical backgrounds, drammatico camera setups have told them what to expect any time the two cultures accidentally cross paths on forest or prairie trail.

Sad to say, Columbus would offer us trial runs of yet other familiar scenes during his second voyage. Leaving Santa Cruz behind to continue what he expected to be a triumphal return to La Navidad (the Españolan garrison he had built from the wreckage of the *Santa María* at Christmastime, 1492), Admiral Columbus was soon to discover a leveled ruin of his pioneer town. Like the cavalry riding into a burned-out fort or way station, Columbus and his men found no survivors, no logbook to explain the disaster. Only from the few Tainos still willing to try the path of friendship could the admiral piece together a tale of provocations and excesses by the garrison keepers that had precipitated a fatal confrontation with a tough chieftain named Caonabo (who had learned his battle skills from the Caribs, if he was not one himself). After Caonabo annihilated a gang of marauding gold thieves and rapists from La Navidad, he moved on to the outpost itself, which quickly fell to his attack despite the aid given the desperate Spaniards by a Taino detachment led by Columbus's faithful Indian friend Guacanagari. The few Spanish survivors took to the outlands, where they were run down by Caonabo's fighters. Thus one brief piece of American history brought together the staples of the Indian uprising tale: lustful white fools who stir up a conflagration, an enraged native genius of battle, the siege of a fortress, "good Indians" fighting alongside their white friends, a burned settlement, and the relentless pursuit of fleeing pioneers. Screenplay writers would need little more for their flaming-frontier adventures, but Columbus was not finished yet.

Subsequent months in the Indies brought many close calls and fleeing confrontations of the kind that often had to suffice when production budgets or studio space limited the range of action. Columbus, in his perambulations of the islands, methodically broke up volatile demonstrations with a burst of cannon fire. Meanwhile, he kept the trade lines open by holding respected villagers hostage until their comrades were willing to be fleeced. Before long, though, the skirmishes began to escalate, as word of Spanish brutality spread from island to island. At Jamaica the explorers, thwarted in a landing attempt, resorted to their crossbows and then let loose a huge dog to finish the action.

Back on Española bands of impatient colonizers were roaming the island looking for treasure. The Tainos, unable to match the invaders in weaponry, turned to that most familiar of all Indian-movie devices, the ambush, picking off small parties of gold hunters one by one. Unfortunately, these acts of desperation mainly fed the thesis that Indians could be subdued by force alone. Here, moreover, was the excuse Columbus needed to implement a policy that he had been impatient to push: Indian slavery. Spaniards on horseback, hunting dogs running at their sides, rounded up fifteen hundred Tainos and herded them to headquarters for processing.[1]

[1]The best five hundred were dispatched to Spain for sale. After the colonists had taken their pick of the remaining thousand, the leftovers were allowed to go home. The transported slaves (and those sent over subsequently) fared badly on the trip—and in Spain. By order of the royal government, which from the beginning had been lukewarm to Columbus's enslavement schemes, the sordid business was put to an end.

136

Incredibly, Columbus Productions, the company that gave us *Action at Jamaica Harbor* and *Ambush at Taino Pass,* had even more scenarios to offer. First came *The Charge at Puerto de los Hidalgos; or, Guatiguana's Last Battle.* Guatiguana, a major cacique on Española, had been one of the Tainos selected for slave shipment to Spain. He made a spectacular escape, however, by biting through his bonds, and soon he was raising an army. Had outlying caciques joined Guatiguana's cause, his force might have been strong enough to push the Spaniards into the sea. But his potential allies believed themselves too far away for real danger from marauders (or so it has been reported, the idea of Indian cooperation against the invader generally being downplayed by historians more than by fiction makers—who like to pile angry tribe upon angry tribe).

Allies or no, Guatiguana led an impressive legion to the valley of Puerto de los Hidalgos during March, 1495. In an action seldom associated with Christopher Columbus, the admiral (now a general) marched to meet Guatiguana at the head of an army of two-hundred foot soldiers, twenty horsemen, and a large body of cooperating Tainos under the leadership of the faithful Guacanagari. Not familiar with the photoplay clichés, however, Guatiguana pulled his army tightly together in the open, while Columbus set up an ambush by concealing his troops on both sides of the valley. Spanish firearms shook the Indians; a cavalry charge by frightening monsters of war (who seemed part man, part animal, routed them. Those Indians left alive were packed for shipment to the slave market, a denouement totally unacceptable for screenplays—in a movie the end-of-film destination would have had to be a reservation, where the white man would promise to attend to all their needs just like kindly plantation owners.

With Guatiguana eliminated, Columbus had only one Indian problem, a still-alive, and still-dangerous, Caonabo—that "vengeance-mad devil" who had laid waste La Navidad. Operating from a distant stronghold, and impossible to defeat by ordinary means, Caonabo could be taken only through treachery. As Osceola and Mangus Colorados and Crazy Horse would in later centuries, Caonabo learned the bitter price of trusting the invader when there were civilized ends to be served. One of Columbus's officers, with a ten-man patrol, parleyed his way into Caonabo's stronghold with warm promises of, yes, a treaty. Would the great leader go to the Spanish fortress at Isabela to talk of peace with the wise commander from across the sea? If so, the bronze bell atop the white man's church would be his (Caonabo was apparently more vain and selfish than his

137

latter-day counterparts would be). The Indian leader acquiesced, but he took along a larger escort than the Spaniards had expected. At a trailside encampment, as a result, they duped him into thinking that a set of brass chains, loosely fixed, was the proper ceremonial attire for Spanish royalty. Trustingly, but with his escort close at hand, Caonabo allowed himself to be ceremoniously draped with the chains. Then, to rehearse his formal entry into Isabela, he climbed into the saddle with the Spanish officer. Instantly the gulled victim was shackled to his deceiver, who thundered away with the prisoner before the eyes of a stunned escort that was unable to keep up the pursuit on foot. Caonabo, tormented beyond endurance, died on a ship bound for Spain and soon was forgotten. In later years, however, the deceiving of Indians would become so viable a technique in fictional as well as real life that it could be used for humor (the Indians trying on women's hats in Cecil B. DeMille's *Union Pacific*) or for tragedy (the false treaty conference that brought down Osceola in *Seminole*). Caonabo's sad fate seemed to embrace both.

Undoubtedly, Columbus's varied adventures and misadventures with the enemy, while largely overlooked today, established patterns and precedents for dealing with balky Indians and thus influenced popular fiction. Some of Columbus's subalterns and lieutenants, remember, would ride with or advise the famed conquistadores of later expeditions. In fact, a Moorish-wars veteran, Juan Ponce de León, one of Columbus's lieutenants on that trouble-ridden second voyage, would lead expeditions of his own—after first using the lessons he had learned on Española to subdue Puerto Rico's inhabitants in 1509. It would be difficult, of course, to establish how many of the Columbus techniques and reactions were deliberately carried over to confrontations with the Indians of North America. After all, some recurrent situations may simply have been functions of the juxtaposition of an invader with a European heritage and a native American with a heritage of his own. Nonetheless, the possibility of a John Wayne plot going all the way back to Columbus is fascinating.

SHADINGS BY MANY HANDS

Having observed how far back the principal historical elements of the "Indian-enemy" stories can be traced, we can turn with greater pertinence to examining what popular literature has done with those elements through the years. Let us look first at that nearly universal ingredient the surprise attack. Obviously, not many ambushes are laid by white soldiers in novel or film, nor do military records demand that they should abound. But that is not the same as saying that virtually all surprise attacks on peaceful travelers from concealed positions were the work of Indians, which is what the dime novels and movies told us for decades. It is impossible to estimate the number of soft-cover or celluloid thrillers in which silently waiting warriors emerge from hiding to cut down unsuspecting marchers and wayfarers, who, if the plot will allow them to survive, must "Dismount and fight on foot!" or "Take cover behind those rocks!"

Surprise attack by white forces in popular fiction has been limited to special situations, almost all of them directed at the recovery of captives. By convention the victims of the impending raid are seen as miscreants who by their actions have made the sudden strike necessary. Silently, cautiously, the hero and his companion—a gnarled frontiersman or a stiff-backed army officer—slither on their stomachs to a point from which they can overlook the native encampment. Then, one by one, feathered sentinels are soundlessly dispatched, while the reader or viewer prays that neither dog pack nor horse herd will signal alarm.

What the Indians themselves are up to during the approach of the rescuers can be both revealing and demeaning. Not-too-savage communities are shown going about the routine business of living, which at night means sleeping, with guards outside the tents of the captives. Generally shiftless bands, on the other hand, whoop it up on white man's whiskey until they fall in drunken stupors outside their dwellings.[2] Most to be feared by buckskin commandos are the aggressively nasty stereotypes who scream and dance around fires, not in response to applications of firewater but in anticipation of the next day's tortures.

[2]Benjamin Franklin discoursed on the fireside cavortings of Indians, having observed one group around a giant bonfire during a treaty conference of 1750 in Carlisle: . . . "They were all drunk, men and women, quarreling and fighting. Their dark-colour'd bodies, half-naked, seen only in the gloomy light of the bonfire, running after and beating one another with firebrands, accompanied by their horrid yellings." Rum, Franklin concluded, would be the most likely means of extirpating the "savages" to make room for the cultivators of the earth—should extirpation be the design of Providence—for, as he saw it, rum had already annihilated all the tribes who had formerly inhabited the sea coast. Benjamin Franklin, *Autobiography* (Garden City, N.Y.: International Collectors Library 1923), p. 171.

Peril notwithstanding, a single rescuer can be expected to work his way into the Indian village itself, a technique employed to perfection in *Nick of the Woods* (1837) long before dime novels or movies came along. A few deft cuts by the hunting knife on the bounds of captives at the stake, a bold slash down the side of a tipi, and the last phase of recovery is begun. Once the prisoners are safe in hand, the jittery horse herd driven off, a waiting white force can charge the startled captors—resultant carnage seemingly confined to the male householders of the encampment. Until the Vietnam War, with its obvious parallels, the inevitable deaths of women and children in such melees could be disregarded (or, more likely, not even realized) by adventure writers, who ordinarily restricted verbal or pictorial dust biting to howling braves. Rare indeed was a *Northwest Passage* (1940), in which the orchestrated mass extermination of Abnaki villagers by Roger's Rangers was a filmic celebration of virtue over evil. Even in the dark, says an ancient premise of frontier fiction, attackers in coonskin caps or army blue can easily determine the age and sex of any moving target and aim their rifles accordingly. Most writers and audiences long accepted the premise without thought—and may still.[3]

When fictional brave meets fictional soldier on a open plain, of course, civilian casualties among the enemy can be ignored as two male armies clash. Exceptions have been few. In movieland Linda Darnell, playing a white-educated "princess," was shot down while riding with her plains Indian brothers in *Buffalo Bill* (1944), yet her fate stemmed as much from unrequited love for Cody as from tribal loyalty. Linda's death eliminated a forced romantic triangle.

This is not to suggest that the most of the Indian-white wars filmed for theater or television have taken place in classic battlefield

---

[3]Although deaths of Indian noncombatants were relatively late additions in fiction and film, John Underhill's narrative in 1638 on the Pequot War, New England's first significant struggle between settlers and Indians, contains a vivid recollection of an attack that he had led: "Many [Pequots] were burnt in the fort, both men, women, and children. Others forced out . . . our soldiers received and entertained with the sword. Down fell men, women, and children. . . . Great and doleful was the bloudy sight . . . to see so many souls lie gasping on the ground, so thick in some places, that you could hardly pass along." The massacre had been an act of irrational fury, which Underhill had to explain away as heaven authorized: "Sometimes the Scripture declareth women and children must perish with their parents. Sometimes the case alters; but we will not dispute it now. We had sufficient light from the word of God for our proceedings." John Underhill, *Newes from America* (London, 1638 ed.), p. 25, as quoted in Slotkin, *Regeneration Through Violence*, p. 76.

locations. Some have, the many Custer-related epics in particular. But even during Hollywood's golden years the production expense and logistical problems of a massed battle limited the military spectacles to one or two from each major studio a year: *They Died with Their Boots On, Fort Apache, The Charge at Feather River,* and so on. The printed page, needless to say, has no similar restraints—hence the abundance of cavalry paperbacks.

When, on the other hand, the focal point of a fictional military clash is narrowed to a threatened fortress or cabin, the presentational advantage shifts back to the dramatized format. Cooper did make capital with the Indian as a besieger in the Leatherstocking tales, as Robert Montgomery Bird did in *Nick of the Woods,* but somehow a siege seems more vivid in a theatrical framework, where lighting, sound, and special effects can increase the tension. Never, in the decades that preceded the motion picture, did theater and the valiant defense of fortress come together more spectacularly than in a play that brought the Indian thriller back to Broadway in 1893 after a long period of dormancy—the David Belasco–Franklin Fyles melodrama *The Girl I Left Behind Me.*

Offering a marvelous lesson for the Hollywood inheritors of his melodramatic tradition, Belasco, with his collaborator, created one of the great sustained-suspense sequences of all time—without showing a single Indian on the attack. He did it through suggestion, pacing, and an attention to detail that not all economy-minded filmmakers recognized when they attempted to enlarge their fortress settings with stock shots or with awkward posturings of a few extras in feathers. Ironically, it was two film directors not usually associated with production restrictions—D. W. Griffith and John Ford—who best grasped the Belasco inheritance, even if, as in the case of Ford, it was transmitted through Belasco's theatrical heirs.

David Belasco (1859–1931) may not have originated a single device of the now-familiar genre, but working on *The Girl I Left Behind Me* during the decade that saw both the massacre at Wounded Knee and the birth of the motion picture, he assembled successfully virtually all the dramatic elements of the soldier-versus-Indian struggle. Even his villain was memorable. As the *New York Times* put it on January 29, 1893:

Scarbrow, the educated Indian demon, who is briefly but effectively in evidence . . . has caused a good deal of talk this week. [Theodore] Roberts is very real in his looks and manner, if not his speech. . . . He is much more like one of the fiends of the frontier than our dear old Metamora or any of Mr. Cooper's preposterous redmen.

Three days earlier the *Times* reviewer had praised the play itself, despite the elements within it that called to mind pieces of earlier melodramas (not about Indians). In the noble General Kennion's readiness to shoot his daughter to keep her from Indian hands, for instance, the critic heard an echo of John Knowles's play *Virginius.* Belasco, however, connected that sequence, and the inspiration to have the attackers remain unseen, to an actual incident related to him by General Crook's widow, who, in a similar situation of anxious waiting, accepted a revolver so that she could take her own life if necessary. The memorable last-minute relief of the outpost in *The Girl I Left Behind Me* reminded the *Times* critic of Dion Boucicault's *Jessie Brown; or, The Relief of Lucknow* (1858), a play that appeared only five months after the twelve-week siege of the city during the mutiny of 1857 in India (this would not be the last exchange of plot devices between India and America). Also recalled by the *Times* reviewer in the same regard were the rescues in three Belasco-era thrillers: *Rosedale, Under the Gaslight,* and *Blue Jeans.* Point was made, however, that, while some of the situations of *The Girl I Left Behind Me* may not have been new, Belasco's deft use of them made his play exceptional melodrama.

We have already seen how two film directors, D. W. Griffith and John Ford, later duplicated the mercy-killing threat of Belasco's drama to produce suspense in *The Battle at Elderbush Gulch* and *Stagecoach.* These (and other) directors' delight in a last-minute relief of besieged defenders, moreover, needs no elaboration for observers of the motion picture. For example, Griffith (who may well have seen *The Girl I Left Behind Me* in one city or another) built toward nick-of-time rescues from Indian attackers in *The Last Drop of Water* (1911). *Fighting Blood* (1911), and *America* (1924). What might not be realized is the number of additional Indian-trouble devices within *The Girl I Left Behind Me* available for transmission, chain-letter style, first to playwrights, then to scenario writers.

A midmessage severing of the military telegraph line? John Ford used it in *Stagecoach* (1939), adding drama by making the last word "Geronimo. . . ." A desperate race through Indian lines as the hero seeks help for the garrison? Ford's *Drums Along the Mohawk,* of course (the device having been perfected by Griffith before Walter D. Edmonds wrote his book). A military ball on the eve of battle (which Belasco may have gleaned from *Childe Harold's Pilgrimage*)? Ford's *Fort Apache.* A spunky young woman enlivening the post? Shirley Temple in the same Ford film (or Mae Marsh in Griffith's *Elderbush Gulch*). Overstated garrison humor? *She Wore a Yellow Ribbon* (another familiar army-song title) or almost any other John Ford cavalry piece.

The Belasco bequest continues. A serenade by the regimental singers? One graces *Rio Grande.* A stern, intractable, Indian genius? Scar Brow's nominative near-equivalent, Chief Scar, of Ford's *The Searchers*—or his Quanah Parker of *Two Rode Together;* after all, Henry Brandon played them both. A good soldier, falsely accused of another's crime, who saves the day before facing charges? Ford's *Sergeant Rutledge.*

Director Ford and his writers did not have much truck with Indian princesses, but Belasco's Fawn Afraid, daughter of Scar Brow and admirer of Lieutenant Hawkesworth, was picked up by other filmmakers needing a love-struck plot agent to link conflicting forces. Marisa Pavan served that purpose in *Drum Beat,* and Maria Elena Marques in *Across the Wide Missouri.* The forced romantic triangle of *The Girl I Left Behind Me* (good officer–bad officer–confused woman) was likewise passed over by Ford's team, but not by others, who frequently made the good officer an army scout and his uniformed rival more gauche than evil. In *Arrowhead* (1953) director Charles Marquis Warren manipulated not only the frontier triangle and an educated Indian demon (Jack Palance) but also the pervasive ghost-dance agitation of Belasco's play—though the cinematic ghost dancers were changed into Apaches, Warren's favorite fiends.

Does the detailed enumeration of the now-familiar elements of *The Girl I Left Behind Me* tell us that one successful drama, more than any other vehicle, shaped the soldier-versus-Indian screenplay? Considering the time of the play's appearance and the public attention it garnered, the case could be made. Attribution aside, however, the rundown reveals, if nothing else, how much of the filmic cloth about to be unrolled in cavalry movies was ready, in proved dramatic form, just before the narrative film came into being—not to mention how slightly plot conventions would change during the years that followed. While looking at *Stagecoach,* Frank Nugent, the *New York Times* film critic of 1939, would, in the spirit of his drama-page predecessor of 1893, delight in the "thuds" with which "Redskins bit the dust" as part of John Ford's portrayal of what the reviewer called "the scalp-raising

Seventies." In fact, Nugent's delight would take him west to write the screenplays for Ford's famous Indian-wars cycle, screenplays that would contain many of the Belasco devices.

The Girl I Left Behind Me was for three of its four acts a within-the-walls story of a fortress facing attack (the last segment covering the hero's vindication). Thus, handy as it was, Belasco's piece did not consolidate and enhance every element of the Indian-wars framework for imminent transfer to the screen. But in earlier brave-versus-soldier melodramas most if not all of the remaining situations of frontier warfare dating from the Columbus era had been brought before the footlights, their most vivid effects lingering in memory in the early 1900s, perhaps even being kept alive by touring-company interpretations of actions like Custer's Last Stand, which found their way onto opera-house stages in many a small town. Whatever accentuated the "fiends-of-the-frontier" mood in a theater seemed to find its way onto celluloid.[4]

Most of the nineteenth-century battle plays (imitated or not) are now no more than passing references in histories of the theater—*Tecumseh; or, The Battle of the Thames* (1837), *Pontiac; or The Siege of Detroit* (1838), *The Battle of Tippecanoe* (1840). What specifically these sometimes one-performance productions added to the Indian melodrama's bag of tricks other than mass action is uncertain. The better-known *She Would Be a Soldier; or, The Plains of Chippewa* (1819), however, closed with a peace-treaty scene promising a new Indian-white relationship —business that would tidy up so many filmic bouts with the Indian enemy. James N. Barker's history-based *The Armourer's Escape; or, Three Years at Nootka Sound* (1817) showed the value of mood-building dances and ceremonials—even if moviemakers seldom got those things right—while dramatizations of Cooper's Leatherstocking novels and Bird's *Nick of the Woods* demonstrated how to strip a complicated narrative to its melodramatic Indian-eluding basics. As suggested, more than one frontier-wars epic had elaborate battle

---

[4]During the 1870s Buffalo Bill (and imitators) presented crudely written, action-dominated stage melodramas, which, as the numbers of Indians, horses, and panoramas increased, gradually evolved into Cody's outdoor Wild West shows. Enjoyable for what they were, but not taken seriously by the theater crowd, the dime-novel theatricals had counterparts in some of the haphazard Western adventures of early movie days. As dramas, however, they really presaged the skirmish-filled serials and B pictures of Saturday afternoon—which by the 1930 were almost Indianless. Buffalo Bill's tent shows, therefore, pointed to the frontier epics of the screen, while his stage shows were echoed temporarily by low-budget, long-departed thrillers known as "cowboy pictures."

scenes onstage, with dress extras ranging from real Indians to United States Marines.

Yet the only play that could have approached *The Girl I Left Behind Me* in direct influence upon the motion picture was *Metamora,* the Edwin Forrest vehicle, which, unlike the other so-called Indian plays, became part of a major theatrical company's repertoire and was performed occasionally as late as the Grant era. Forrest, who died in 1872, could still pull off a production of the tragedy written in 1829 long after Indian pieces—especially ones about noble chieftains—had departed the Broadway scene. The theater crowd still remembered *Metamora* when Belasco's play appeared. Although waterlogged by stilted dialogue, the John Augustus Stone dramatization had action sequences as complicated as those to come in many small-scale adventure movies. With its many changes of scene and swiftly moving passages, *Metamora* would at times have had a cinematic quality, especially considering its precise musical and sound effects. The stage directions indicated: "Hurried music"; "Clock strikes twelve as scene opens. Thunder distant"; "Slow music, four bars." *Metamora* also anticipated the movie thrillers with a near-burning at the stake, a peace-parley trap from which the Indian leader has to make an escape like that of Jeff Chandler's Cochise in *Broken Arrow,* an Indian raid on a village to the accompaniment of much howling and drumming, and dialogue amply spliced with expressions like "war whoop," "massacre," "paleface," and "happy . . . hunting grounds." And how about this order from a brave chieftain provoked beyond toleration by whites: "He must die! Drag him away to the fire of the sacrifice that my ear may drink the music of his dying groans!"

Edwin Forrest, like John Wayne, could fix his eye upon some impulsive would-be captors and dissolve their nerve by asking, "Which of you has lived too long?" Like Wayne, he could also spare a rash young challenger through a seeming rebuff: "Boy! Thou art a child, there is no mark of war upon thee. Send me thy elder or thy chief. I'll make talk to him."

But when Forrest bade farewell to *Metamora,* it was, for all its once-impressive stage effects, a dated drama, surviving only because the virile actor carried it off so well. Without him it was nigh unperformable.

What is more, Metamora was a good Indian. David Belasco, in *The Girl I Left Behind Me,* gave audiences breathtaking stage effects, contemporary dialogue—and a chillingly bad Indian. That is what was wanted at the end of the nineteenth century. After its New York bow *The Girl I left Behind Me* was chosen for presentation during the World's Columbian Exposition in Chicago in 1893. A staging in New York City in 1894, though disliked by Belasco, pointed to what was soon to happen in movieland. The spell of the unseen battle, carefully woven in the audience's imagination in the original production, was shattered by a troop of mounted cavalry that came roaring onstage at the end of act three. William Winter a critic and historian, did not like that artistic gaffe either, but, as he put it in 1918 in his biography of David Belasco, the "groundlings" loved it.

If the groundlings loved spectacle on stage, they adored it in the motion picture. To the basic theatrical situations film could add the epic action and scenic grandeur that talented craftsmen, led by Belasco, were so earnestly attempting to reproduce artificially at the end of the nineteenth century. Almost overnight the moving picture became the most influential means of presenting the action-oriented fiction about hostile Indians that it had appropriated from the stage. For the American Indian the consequence of that preeminence was devastating.

To those who arranged the tableaus of popular culture, the shock value of a raised hatchet or a flaming arrow was quickly realized, and never forgotten, down to the last years of the twentieth century.

Massacre at
Fort Mims

The painting of Jane McCrea's death was the model for the illustration that students saw in Current Events. *It may also have inspired the raised tomahawk drawing for a children's history book of the 1970s* (left).

The real Geronimo (1884) and his impersonator in a film of 1939, Chief Thundercloud.

Guerrier Iroquois.

Scalping—brutality—torture. The images abound.

Winter or summer, against man or woman, the attacking Indian of the movies is relentless. Jack Holt is the butt of the attack in The Thundering Herd *(1925), Martha Hyer in* Blood on the Arrow *(1964).*

151

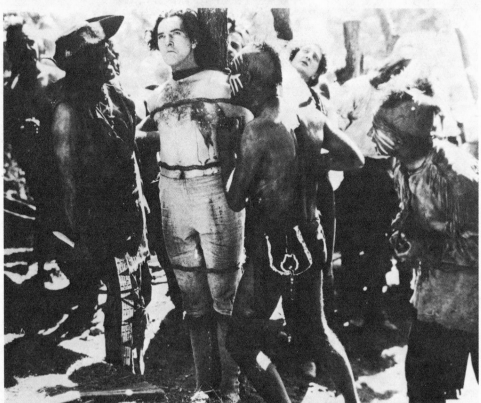

The contrast between "saintly" white and "savage" Indian is never starker than in a burning at the stake (above right). **Below:** *The scene is from D. W. Griffith's* America *(1924).* Above left: *Henry Wilcoxon is prepared for a fiery test in* The Last of the Mohicans *(1936).*

Gary Cooper's temporary indisposition in The Plainsman *(1936) is much like the captive of the Natchez's rather permanent one.*

As Wallace Beery (Magua) points out a course of action in the Maurice Tourneur version of The Last of the Mohicans *(1920), Lionel Barrymore views his Mohawk squadron at mess in* America.

"That's one good Indian!"

Gary Cooper as Chris Holden,
Unconquered, 1947

9

FIXED IN FRAME

WITH the coming of the movies, the Indian was ensnared, then filmically embalmed, by a coincidence of history—actually a double coincidence. First, of course, the motion picture arrived at just the time when the theater was striving for a realism in outdoor melodrama that could be achieved only on film, a circumstance that gave the hungry new medium both ready-made merchandise (Indian thrillers included) and primed audiences. Second, the playwrights who created the theatrical merchandise, the critics who accepted it, the moviemakers who appropriated it, and most of the waiting audience knew the Indian wars of the West not just from the history books but also from their daily newspapers. Geronimo did not give up his struggle until 1886, and the famed Apache leader was still a prisoner of war when he died in 1909. The ghost-dance phenomenon, the death of Sitting Bull, and the misfortune at Wounded Knee marked the winter of 1890–91. While these were the last major clashes between Indians and soldiers in the West, the people of that day had no sure knowledge that hostilities had ended.

David Belasco, for instance, set to work on *The Girl I Left Behind Me* scarcely more than a year after Wounded Knee. As the play's reviewer observed in 1893, the "fierce insurrection" of the Sioux, the "lamentable slaughter of the gallant Custer," and the "rising under Sitting Bull" were "much on the public mind." In writing about an

155

uprising sparked by army restraint of a forbidden ritual, Belasco was dramatizing an actual conflict fresh in mind, one that could conceivably break out again as far as his audiences knew. Disarmed or not, confined or not, displayed in shows or not, the Indian at the turn of the twentieth century was, even in the most liberal conception, a recent enemy. At the other extreme he was still a potential enemy, though allegedly soundly licked. Sitting Bull, remember, brought an over-reacting army down upon him five years after he toured with Buffalo Bill.

Minor but colorful incidents would arise to stir active imaginations (some of them belonging to scenario writers) during the years that the motion picture was becoming established commercially. Most of the central figures in these disorders were what the media called "renegades." Nino, "the Apache Kid," was the stuff of newspaper accounts or frontier legends long after the reward for him was lifted in 1894. The storied manhunt in California for a Paiute erroneously referred to as Willie Boy came in 1909, several years after the first Indian movies. In 1911 a fellow called Shoshone Mike led a small raid in Nevada, and reports of sorties by the remnants of Geronimo's band circulated until World War I.

Purists might claim that in such instances the Indians involved were not collective enemies but isolated gangsters on horseback— though that distinction was seldom made during Geromino's heyday. Yet, even if we disregard any possible impact from the vestigial skirmishes, we are still left with a historical fact worth considering: during the first half-century of the entertainment film those who fashioned its major Indian-fighting dramas had come into the world during the nineteenth century, some of them while the frontier wars were still going on. These moviemakers—and the list includes D. W. Griffith (born in 1875), Cecil B. De Mille (1881), Thomas Ince (1882), John Ford (1894 or 1895), and also Raoul Walsh (1892), King Vidor (1894), William Wellman (1896), and Henry Hathaway (1898)—would have grown up in a land in which most of the adults had lived through, and perhaps experienced, the very desert and plains wars celebrated on the screen. Certainly their history teachers would have.

Correspondingly, every Indian play or story known to these pioneer filmmakers before they stepped onto a studio lot would have been written by an author who had come of age while the western battles were raging. Every Indian-war situation or cliché transferred from the nineteenth-century theater to the twentieth-century motion picture was a situation or cliché transferred from a time of war to a time of peace. It is often observed that D. W. Griffith, for example, was influenced by regional recollections of the Civil War, in which his father had served. Might not he and other moviemakers born before 1900 have been similarly influenced (or prejudiced) by both the memorable historical events that fell in or near their lifetimes and the popular interpretations derived from them?

The era of the Wild West—in dime novel, touring melodrama, and outdoor pageant—paralleled the innocent years of pioneer directors like Griffith, De Mille, and Ince. D. W. Griffith was a toddler when the Buffalo Bill melodramas were filling theaters and was turning eighteen when the more sophisticated *The Girl I Left Behind Me,* with its innovative blending of realistic staging and frontier suspense, first caught the fancy of New Yorkers. Thomas Ince, who would one day hire a Wild West company for his photoplays, was born about the time Buffalo Bill made the transition from theater to arena, and he had been working as a child actor for five years when Belasco showed the stage world how to do the soldier-versus-Indian play. Cecil B. De Mille, one year older than Ince and close to the New York theater (his father had worked with Belasco), may or may not have been one of those awed by the Scar Brow of Theodore Roberts, but we know that he used that actor in his earliest films and that a De Mille epic carried the visual stamp of the Wild West pageant, from showmanship to massed action. It is difficult to believe that these highly observant film pioneers and their contemporaries were untouched by the fictional re-creation of recent history that flourished during their youth. That the work of some directors was not entirely unsympathetic to the first Americans is a product more of their consciences than of their cultural environment.

As a group moviemakers so thoroughly abused the Indians, and so early, that in 1911 representatives of four western tribes journeyed to the national capital to protest their screen treatment to Congress and President William H. Taft. Actually they could have made a case for themselves just by reading the titles of some of those early films: *On the Warpath* (1909), *The Flaming Arrows* and *Poisoned Arrows* (1911), *Incendiary Indians* (1911), *The Indian Raiders* and *The Cheyenne Raiders* (1910), *Attack by Arapahoes* (1910), *The Dumb Half-Breed's Defense* (1910), and *Saved from the Redmen* (1910), not to mention *Love In a Tepee* (1911) and *The Hair Restorer and the Indian* (a comedy of 1911).

157

The motion-picture industry in its infant years did make some Indian-centered minidramas, several of them featuring Native American performers. But once audiences caught sight of flaming arrows, wagons forming circles to repel attack, burning fortresses—the substance of movies mixing Indians and whites—those ethnic one- two- and three-reel films quickly disappeared. A film about life as an Indian, even if done with some authenticity, was to audiences steeped in Wild West tradition more of a fantasy than was a film about an attack on a wagon train. Action sequences, to be sure, were important in arousing audiences, but Sioux versus soldier was demonstrably more attractive to moviegoers than Sioux versus Crow. D. W. Griffith, whose low-keyed *The Redman and the Child* (1908), *The Mended Lute* (1909), *The Mohawk's Way* (1910), and *Song of the Wildwood Flute* (with Mary Pickford, 1910) were among his thirty Indian dramas, brought out the faceless-savage image in 1911 and settled upon that approach for his final Indian dramas. His white actors, dressed as Sioux or Mohawks, bashed skulls, molested women, scalped settlers, and brained babies with the best of them. Cecil B. De Mille, after ridding himself of his *The Squaw Man* fixation—he filmed the play of 1905 three times (in 1914, 1918, and 1931)—administered adrenalin to the almost-dormant Indian-horde genre with *The Plainsman* (1937) and continued the treatment through *Union Pacific* (1939), *North West Mounted Police* (1940), and *Unconquered* (1947).

Like D. W. Griffith and John Ford, De Mille had control of plot and direction of most of his films, a perquisite not accorded most directors. Nevertheless, restriction solely to direction does not excuse an established filmmaker from all responsibility for on-screen distortions of the Indian image. Screenplay writers play their part, of course, as do second-unit supervisors. Yet for accented violence, shrieking savages, inhuman tortures, and absurd costumes or actions, one looks to the contribution, not just the acquiescence, of the director.

How, for example, can one say that the subhuman Abnakis of *Northwest Passage* (1940) derived their principal cinematic sting from sources outside director King Vidor? The screenplay dictated their genocide; the shooting instructions of Vidor intensified a negative image to the point that *Northwest Passage* could fairly be called "one of the most viciously anti-Indian films ever made."[1] Vidor, a director of recognized talent but discouraging blind spots (that he later ac-

---

[1]George Fenin and William K. Everson, *The Western* p. 246.

knowledged), had warmed up for *Northwest Passage* through a large-scale faceless-Indian raid in *The Texas Rangers* and then afterward showed what a "half-breed" seductress could do in the sleazy sex scenes of *Duel in the Sun.*

The dime-novel dust biting of anonymous hordes in *Ten Gentlemen of West Point* and *The Garden of Evil*—exciting as it may have been—should likewise be examined with a director, Henry Hathaway, in mind. Could even a Gary Cooper have mowed down so many hard-riding pursuers had not a director sympathetic to the one-white-can-outfight-twenty-Indians thesis lent a talented hand? The epic *Buffalo Bill* (1944), with its modest bow to the paradoxical hero's adversaries —and its abundance of stereotypes and clichés—was the work of William Wellman (who in a public television series blamed everything on Fox executives). Wellman also guided Robert Taylor and his Indian-harried wagon girls in *Westward the Women* and turned gentle Ricardo Montalban into a meaner-than-mean chieftain in *Across the Wide Missouri.* The spectacular *They Died with Their Boots On* (the Custer myth) was mounted by Raoul Walsh, who learned moviemaking under D. W. Griffith but remembered too well the lessons on accentuating stereo-types when assigned to *Distant Drums, Saskatchewan, The Tall Men,* and *A Distant Trumpet.*

Few directors worked in contrasting tones. Seasoned campaign-ers who guided the "wild Indian" adventures never seemed to turn up at the helm of films sympathetic to Indian resistance. An exception was George B. Seitz. The good and bad Indians of *The Last of the Mohicans* (1936 version), as well as the tireless warriors of *Kit Carson* (in which Geronimo's grandson, Charles Stevens, played a sniveling "half breed"), were overseen by that *Perils of Pauline* veteran, who in 1925 had directed *The Vanishing American* (in which Stevens played a dis-hearted Navajo veteran of World War I). Seitz, however, found his most comfortable movie home with the Hardy Family series of MGM, a different kind of American myth.

All but frozen in their nineteenth-century dramatic mold, the Indians of the motion picture played their collective role of the Enemy year after year, doing many of the same things their action-novel counterparts had been doing even longer, but with the special theatri-cality that delighted an accepting public. Each month millions watched those movie Indians fighting soldiers on the open plain, attacking their forts, falling upon unwary settlers, and, when seemingly sub-dued, rejecting the bounty of the reservation to go on one last bloody

159

tear. Most of all, as the century advanced, the screen Indians inter-
fered with economic progress. They raided railroads (*The Iron Horse,
Union Pacific, Canadian Pacific*); they raided stagecoaches (*Geronimo,
Dakota Incident,* the two *Stagecoach*'s); they raided supply trains (in
innumerable films), trail herds (*Red River*), telegraph lines (*Western
Union*), the mails (the three *Pony Express*'s), and even a fur-trading ship
(*This Woman Is Mine*). Possibly the only transportation-communication
stock-exchange listing not jolted filmically by Indians (airlines excepted, of course) was Postal Telegraph, whose most renowned movie
rider Mickey Rooney of *The Human Comedy,* got through every time—
no doubt because the Indians living around Fresno in the 1940s did
not attack boys on bicycles.

As the Enemy, the Indian of the movies was, by common understanding, treacherous, frenzied, vicious. A master of torture to gain his
ends, he lurked behind every calculatingly photographed rock, tree,
or prominence, always with enough confreres to outnumber his victims. Although destined to lose the overall struggle, he was a terrifying
opponent, the equal of the Japanese or Germans in Hollywood's
World War II movies. In fact, only when those European and Asian
foes confronted the nation was the ongoing character assassination of
the original American diminished—though just in frequency, not in
degree.[2]

When global war ended and Japanese or Germans were softened
into rather decent chaps for the periodic battle dramas of the postwar
decades, the still-unsoftened Indian was returned to his unsought

---

[2]When it comes to classification, do the soldier-versus-Indian Westerns belong more
properly to the war-film genre? Scholar Stanley J. Solomon has proposed that the core of that
genre is not the physical disaster of battle but the attitude of those confronted by the struggle,
real or impending. That attitude emerges as a resistance to the "spiritual" force that is the
enemy. The heroes defend their side against a totalitarian adversary, "usually depicted only
from the heroes' point of view . . . as a source of evil." Stanley J. Solomon, *Beyond Formula:
American Film Genres,* p. 244.

Without realizing the possible source of his dilemma, another student of film, Will
Wright, struggled with the soldier-versus-Indian melodrama in *Sixguns and Society: A Structural
Study of the Western*. After preparing sixty-four profitable Westerns for analysis, Wright elimi-
nated three because he could not recall their plots well enough (one was *Cheyenne Autumn*).
Then he deleted four more Westerns because they did not fit his analysis scheme. The four?
Little Big Man, The Charge at Feather River, Fort Apache, and *She Wore a Yellow Ribbon*—in all of
which military actions are of major importance. Freed of these complications, and those
represented by virtually every other cavalry drama (he also avoided *They Died with Their Boots
On* and *Rio Grande*), Wright had little trouble arranging his remaining Western money-makers
according to plot. The vexing war-film equivalents were out of the way.

position as barbarous theater-screen enemy number one, a niche he would occupy without serious rival until various economic and social factors caused him to share the honor. These factors include the poor economics of filming battlefield epics in the United States instead of Spain or Yugoslavia; the plethora of European-made spectacles featuring pagan hordes (some of them Indians, naturally); and the retrospective celebration of World War II through blockbuster movies like *The Longest Day* or *Patton.* They also included the special-mission vogue represented by *The Dirty Dozen* and *The Eagle Has Landed;* the rise of the invader from alien worlds—or the fantasy battles of outer space given acceleration by *Star Wars;* and, during the Vietnam era, a set of motion pictures by message-minded moviemakers that denigrated the soldier—the oldtime hero—and sometimes used Indian-wars frameworks to parallel contemporary civilian massacres by the military. A developing moral consciousness regarding Indians also played its role, of course, but would have meant little had Sioux or Apaches been the most profitable wide-screen agents for biting the dust on a grand scale in the later twentieth century. It assuredly has not yet led to the elimination of the Indian enemy from the frontier films made for television—the medium which, needless to say, also keeps all the talking film's Indian thrillers on rotating display so that youngsters of any year know them as well as their elders did, a fact to be borne in mind throughout this chapter.

Examiners of the cinema should always remember that, during intervals of peace, battle dramas have never declined appreciably in number. They have simply changed locales and enemies. When it has not been a proper time to hate the beasts of Berlin, some other adversary—some other recent, if more confined, threat to white civilization—has always been found; the native tribesmen of the Khyber Pass or the Sudan (Britain's favorites), the desert warriors of the Sahara, the massed Zulu infantry, and, to be sure, the American Indians. With an eye more to the box office than to historical truth, producers have selected the enemy of convenience, in terrestrial or galactic milieu. True, Darth Vaders and Khyber khans may show more signs of education than do taciturn chieftains of desert or plain—just as German commanders showed more polish than those of the Japanese in World War II movies—but the distinction is minor. The various subspecies of war films have been almost identical in substance and format. Only the costumes, locales, and pseudodialects need to be changed to identify the guilty.

161

Thus after the success of *Stagecoach,* Paramount's *The Lives of a Bengal Lancer* (1935), with a change of continent, a selection of stock footage from various Paramount Westerns, and an Apache demon-in-chief, lived again as *Geronimo* (1939), a sun-scorched garrison of men in blue, not white, braving the terrors of a frontier too large to defend. Although Geronimo's warriors seemed more thuggees than Apaches, Chief Thundercloud, in the title role, delivered a chilling performance vastly removed from his likeable Tonto of the Lone Ranger movie serials. Meanwhile, rugged captain (Preston Foster) and jolly scout (Andy Devine) helped end the alienation between stiff general (Ralph Morgan) and gentle lieutenant (Bill Henry). To get an actress's name onto the marquee, Paramount inserted Ellen Drew into the cast, but the writers kept her out of the way of the old Bengal plot line by rendering her unconscious before she could utter a line of dialogue and keeping her that way till the end of the picture.

A more obvious Indian-to-American transfer was *Sergeants Three* (1962), a Frank Sinatra harlequinade easily recognized as a misconstruction of a *Gunga Din* (1939). Not as readily recognized was the derivation of Columbia's *The Last of the Comanches* (1952) from that studio's Humphrey Bogart movie of World War II, *Sahara* (1943). Film scholars, by the way, differ about whether Sahara itself came from a Russian movie *The Thirteen* or from a story of soldiers isolated during World War I that John Ford filmed as *The Lost Patrol.*

Recognizing transplanted screenplays is always fun, but in war films exchanges of basic situations have been more common than exchanges of entire plots. With a John Wayne, Spencer Tracy, Gary Cooper, or Randolph Scott in the lead, Indian films have duplicated every combat format—the special mission into enemy territory, the defense of the outpost, the dangerous escort, the harried retreat. For example, although the preliminaries are different, it is not difficult to see the parallels between Warner Brothers' Errol Flynn movie of World War II, *Objective Burma* (1945), and that studio's Gary Cooper adventure of the Seminole wars, *Distant Drums* (1951). Both films were built upon carefully planned but improbable sorties (launched by parachute in the Flynn movie, by superboat in the Cooper film). Both films had dramatic commando raids, followed by torturous retreats from near-maniacal adversaries. And, perhaps not incidentally, both films had the same director: Raoul Walsh. British journalists objected that Flynn and the Americans appeared to have won the Burma war on their own. American historians, in turn, could wince at both the foolishness and the technical inaccuracies of *Distant Drums.* In neither effort, of course, was the enemy up to handling a much smaller group of American soldiers, the same weakness holding true in other special-forces missions into Indian territory, such as *Major Dundee, Fort Ti,* and *Northwest Passage,* as well as in the thrillers in which the focus was upon a beleaguered garrison or a line of attack (Custer's blunder excepted). For those interested in comparing an uncharacteristic softness of the Khyber Pass enemy with that of the Canadian Indian—when a little child is pulling the strings—consider one last pairing: Shirley Temple as a peacemaker, first in John Ford's *Wee Willie Winkie* (1937), then in William Seiter's *Susannah of the Mounties* (1939).

Bonded to interchangeable military situations are the many aural and visual clichés associated with the Enemy. Did those Japanese jungle fighters of World War II movies use psychological weapons or deceit to lure American soldiers from their positions? Did they taunt their GI adversaries with challenges—pretending to be buddies in trouble, torturing a captive within hearing distance of the American lines? Movie Indians had done the same things years earlier, though favoring drums or false bugle calls over speech mimicry. Geronimo, in his feature of 1939, even got inside the army's entrenchments by donning a soldier's uniform, much as the Germans would do in *Battleground* later on. Oddly enough, the dressing-up trick has usually been employed by *heroes* in action movies, but when Geronimo used it, careful camera work and music scoring brought out the nastiness of it all.

A particularly insidious stratagem of the Enemy is the bullet or arrow that reaches its target after the battle seems won, striking down the hero or someone close to him. In the South Pacific, Sergeants John Wayne and Richard Widmark died that way in *The Sands of Iwo Jima* and *Take the High Ground,* and, back in nineteenth-century America, Sergeant Arthur O'Connell was a similar postbattle victim in *A Thunder of Drums.* Treachery of that kind comes from two basic sources, the cruel-eyed sniper or the wounded-but-not-quite-dead warrior. In either case the assassin's action usually is signaled by a camera shot showing him readying his weapon. The cue gives the audience the opportunity to say, "Oh, no!" while simultaneously emphasizing the infamy of the action.

Burlesques by stand-up comedians notwithstanding, no villain exceeds movieland's advancing Enemy in viciousness of facial expression or abrasiveness of sound. Shouts of "Banzai!" can be readily

163

equated with Hollywood's indispensable war whoops, the gradually discovered drone of approaching bombers with the swelling din of hoofbeats across canyon or plain. The piercing buzz of a diving Zero also contrasts with the reassuring hum of an Air Force fighter plane in the same manner that the whine of a deadly arrow contrasts with the steady boom of the scout's Old Betsy. Fully as disquieting visually as he is aurally, the Enemy, when photographed from below in starkly lighted close-up, takes on a demoniacal countenance that has by now been securely locked in the memories of veteran moviegoers—and may never be fully erasable.

Any adversary who looks and sounds so devil-possessed is not above torture and atrocity, of that a spectator can be certain. To discover a prisoner's secret, the Enemy will apply rack or fire or blade or water in precise and painstaking manner until the captive talks— or can never talk again. To draw out a dying victim's soul power or to deface a slain foe's corpse or just to gather a souvenir or talisman, the Enemy uses knife or lance or bayonet, a rare smile crossing his face. When the business at hand is public execution, the Enemy finishes his captives by putting them to the flames or the machine gun, staking them under a hot sun, or burying them up to their heads and then letting charging lancers take the pleasures of human target practice. Who is the creature who conceives such horrors? Agent of the Gestapo? Soldier of the emperor? Warrior of the Mahdi? Horseman of Cochise? In the movies the answer is simple: the Enemy.

But who portrays the Enemy? In wartime, obviously, he is rarely an actual representative of the global foe. For the American Indian, however, there has always been an agonizing dilemma because he is close at hand for acting duty. That availability for mock-battle service has made him party to his own undoing. Since the infancy of the movies the Indian has been given the opportunity with some regularity to enact or even to reenact the battle against the invader. Although D. W. Griffith usually preferred to offer his Indian assignments to white impostors in feathers and fright wigs (just as he used whites to portray his black characters), Thomas Ince, in 1912, signed up the Miller Brothers' 101 Ranch Wild West Show, which spent the winter in Los Angeles. With a ready-made cast of real cowboys and real Indians, Ince turned out *War on the Plains*, then *Battle of the Red Men*, then *Blazing the Trail*, *Indian Massacre*, and *The Lieutenant's Last Fight*, finally working up to a three-reel spectacle called *Custer's Last Fight*.

The principal Indian of these adventures was William Eagleshirt, a Sioux.[3]

Not long after Ince's flurry of Indian films, an older showman grasped the possibilities of real Indians in on-screen battles. With a boost from the government and a guest appearance by General Nelson Miles and cavalry troop, Buffalo Bill Cody produced and starred in a panoramic movie called *The Indian Wars.* Reportedly the Indians (who were re-creating the very battles in which some of them had fought) contemplated employing real ammunition in the grand finale —filmed at the Pine Ridge Reservation. Buffalo Bill, it is said, had to talk them out of it. True or not, the anecdote is more flattering than the many stories of Indian petulance and menace that dot press accounts and recollections concerning Indian performers. Still turning up, especially in film histories, are stories about the drunkenness and petty thievery of those called upon for film duty. Cited often in such narratives is Colonel Tim McCoy, a youthful adjutant-general of Wyoming, who, in 1924, drew attention to himself for his marvelous handling of the government's wards during the filming of John Ford's *The Iron Horse.* Even so, there was gossip about whiskey and pilfering, as there would be in almost every account of the Indian extra well into the sound era. The clichés about the Indian backstage apparently are as locked-in as those that unfold on screen—"brightly colored props" being particularly attractive both to allegedly light-fingered performers and unthinking film historians (steeped, no doubt, in the shiny-baubles notions of Columbus and successors).

It is on television that the photoplay Indian fights most of his battles now—in thrillers made for the home receiver or the innumerable reruns of Hollywood's feature-length libels that will keep the Enemy image fixed in frame for the rest of this century. If cameras are to roll for a new production, an old masquerade probably still awaits the Indian performer. For a modest amount of money and a box lunch he puts on a forest or frontier attire that may be incorrect not only for his ancestors but for the ancestors of the group that he and his fellows

---

[3]In a radio interview Indian actor-teacher Dennis Wilkerson isolated two problems in satisfactorily employing Indians in motion-picture or television parts. First, to go beyond the roles of extras they must have training as actors. Second, Indians of one tribe may not know much about the heritage of another tribe. The latter aspect has troubled producers little over the years, but the former in part explains the frequent use of trained white performers to portray Indians. Interview on WOR, New York City, September 16, 1979.

temporarily represent. On cue he will race shrieking toward the good characters of the drama with bloodlust painted on his visage. No matter how much his fictional behavior of the moment defies both history and mores, the on-camera Indian must either follow directions or stand aside and let an unconcerned non-Indian actor or extra replace him. The audience will never know the difference, he is told. So, once again, he prepares for the charade, ever hoping that the next time he works a technical adviser will strike down at least one piece of foolishness. In the meantime he waits in his Hollywood war-paint and, as the camera rolls, takes another turn as the Enemy.[4]

[4]The challenge facing the motion-picture technical adviser is sharply outlined by Karen Stabiner in "Experts for Hire: Authenticity Hollywood Style," *New York Times,* December 31, 1978. The article focuses particularly on the work and views of George American Horse, a film adviser for more than two decades, who recognized (despite winning many screenplay battles), that, as Stabiner phrased it, "advice is good only as long as it is also good business" and that, in the matter of Indian actors, "it's hardly box-office wisdom to cast authenticity over talent." American Horse, who himself had missed out on a humorous role that had gone to a white actor shortly before the article appeared, conceded that "comedy is not our strong suit."

On fictional battlefields the Indian could be a formidable adversary—when the numbers were in his favor. This attack is from The Vanishing American *(1925).*

Above: *Zorro and Champlain are unfazed by numerical odds.* Below: *Both Night-Hawk George and James Stewart (in* Broken Arrow*) are outnumbered but stalwart.*

The Indian bit the dust...but t

says MAUREEN O'HARA, starred in
"COMANCHE TERRITORY"

SHOOTING INDIANS IN "COMANCHE TERRITORY" WAS ROUGHER ON MY HANDS THAN ON THE R

Although making Indians bite the dust was just a picnic for Wild West show performers, an actress of 1950 could discover that it was rough on hands. The Maureen O'Hara advertisement was for a skin lotion.

BVFFALO BILL'S WILD WEST
AND CONGRESS OF **ROUGH RIDERS OF THE WORLD**

A PRAIRIE PIC·NIC.

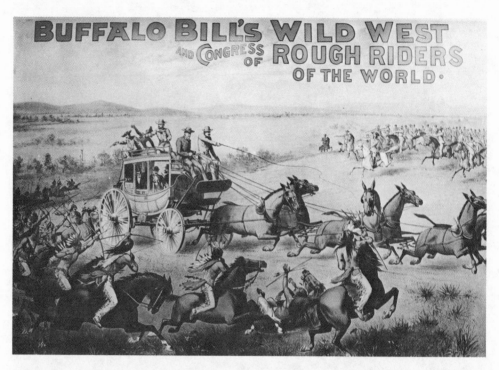

Buffalo Bill's Wild West shows laid out the action sequences for Hollywood's Westerns, in this instance Stagecoach *(1939).*

A frame from John Ford's Stagecoach *catches the moment when the pistol (held by John Carradine) nears the temple of Louise Platt, as he prepares to save her from an expected fate at the hands of attacking Apaches. Similar scenes had occurred in Belasco's play* The Girl I Left Behind Me *and Griffith's film* The Battle at Elderbush Gulch.

Custer's Last Fight (above), *a Thomas Ince film of 1912, and* They Died With Their Boots On *(1941) are among the few motion pictures in which the Indians are the victors.*

10

VANISHING AMERICANS

IN act 1, scene 2, of *The Tempest,* Caliban, William Shakespeare's
tortured aborigine, reminded his white master:

> This island's mine, by Sycorax my mother,
> Which thou takest from me. When thou camest first,
> Thou strokedst me and madest much of me,
>   wouldst give me
> Waters with berries in't, and teach me how
> To name the bigger light, and how the less,
> That burn by day and night; and then I loved thee
> And show'd thee all the qualities o' the isle,
> The fresh springs, brine-pits, barren place and fertile.
> Cursed be I that did so! All the charms
> Of Sycorax, toads, beetles, bats, light on you!
> For I am all the subjects that you have,
> Which first was mine own king; and here you
>   sty me
> In this hard rock, whiles you do keep from me
> The rest o' the island.

Flattery, gifts, liquor, lessons, then subjugation. Would anyone
among the audience of first-nighters in 1611 have realized how accu-

173

rately Shakespeare, in a comedy fantasy, was outlining the destiny of the Indians of the Americas for the next three centuries and more?

Caliban's exacting master chose, of course, to return to Europe, leaving the subdued wretch to his island. But the Europeans of real life who came to the New World would, for the most part, stay on, matching well the précis set forth by Caliban. And two centuries after Shakespeare, in the early days of the American theater, another Indian character would take center stage and echo the sentiments of the Bard's tormented aborigine. He was that nameless chieftain of M. M. Noah's *She Would Be a Soldier* (1819), who, remembering when only the woodland bears were the enemy, rebuffed an American general offering amity:

> You came with the silver smile of peace, and we received you into our cabins; we hunted for you, toiled for you; our wives and daughters cherished and protected you; but when your numbers increased, you rose like wolves upon us, fired our dwellings, drove off our cattle, sent us in tribes to the wilderness, to seek for shelter; and now you ask me, while naked and a prisoner, to be your friend.

Actor Edwin Forrest, who spoke those lines in Noah's play, conveyed similar emotions a decade afterward in the long-lived *Metamora*. What is more, playwright J. A. Stone's noble Indian could offer only bittersweet solace to his comrades as they looked to a future that inevitably would be dominated by the white man:

> ... when our fires are no longer red ... when the bones of our kindred make fruitful the fields of the stranger, which he has planted amidst the ashes of our wigwams; when we are hunted back like the wounded elk far toward the going down of the sun, our hatchets broken, our bows unstrung and war whoop hushed; then will the stranger spare, for we will be too small for his eye to see.

And so it was. Metamora's words, written before the reservation era, foretold the neglect that would mark the decades following the end of the Indian wars. While those wars were being reenacted again and again in the popular media, the Indians who had fought them faced problems of existence that were not dime-novel stuff. Their problems were those of any people vanquished in war who must then live among or beside their far more numerous former adversaries. However they privately regarded their lot, those who had fought an irresistible tide had become a burgeoning nation's conquered people.

174

Their hunting or farming land was now occupied territory. Scattered survivors of lost wars had become displaced persons, forced to seek shelter with not-yet-defeated Indian groups or to eke out a living on bits of land not coveted by the victors. For larger groups there were government-designated refugee or internment, centers called reservations. There they were to remain (for their own protection) eternally —or at least until they could be educated to white men's ways. Reconstruction funding, however, was minimal in the pre-Marshall Plan era and did not match that extended to the defeated Germany or Japan. Nor has it yet.

As might be surmised, popular literature frequently would reflect the halfway-house status of the Indian attempting to live in another culture in the days following the wars (or in the days in which some of the wars had ended but battles still raged on other fronts). Thus plays and novels would focus, sometimes briefly, sometimes at length, upon war brides (white men's "squaws"), orphaned children caught between two cultures, racially mixed young people in a white-dominated civilization, and also the exploiters: frontier black marketeers and postwar profiteers. Psychological cripples and disillusioned alcoholics would be revealed as embittered products of defeat. Even when subdued, the Indian of popular culture would remain a problem and in some eyes the white man's burden.

Believers in *Robinson Crusoe* had long known, of course, how matters would have to be. The Indian had entered Defoe's novel and, hence, popular fiction as only a footprint in the sand. Temporarily, though, that footprint brought anxiety to the mind of the white man, who perceived a sinister alteration of his well-ordered domain. Robinson Crusoe, alone, yet clearly the master of a new world, found in the footprint of a never-identified Indian a sobering reminder that he was not the unrivaled possessor of the rough land that lay around him. He recognized that he would survive or not depending upon how he could take the measure of his unseen rival. Still, never did Crusoe entertain real doubt that he, as a white Christian, was the superior of the barefoot savage, or that as such he could prevail. His dispersal of the cannibals, his domination of the rescued Friday, merely reinforced Crusoe's parochial assumption, which subsequent fiction generally accepted without challenge. After all, was not contemporary history adhering to the long-range plot line?

Yet, when sharing the land with the native no longer was a matter of white survival but, rather, of Indian removal, that assumed superiority repeatedly blurred the focus of popular literature. How many times, for example, would an Indian princess step aside, or die conveniently, so that the white man she loved could live a better life with the often insipid white woman who had done markedly less than the brave Indian maiden to earn her romantic trophy? The Indian male could be equally unselfish when a white hero was to be served. In the film *Apache Rifles* (1964), Red Hawk, betrayed and captured, readily rides out of the way so that Captain Stanton (Audie Murphy) can marry the pretty teacher at the Indian school, whom Stanton has earlier backed away from because she is half-Comanche. Red Hawk gives the couple his blessing and heads for a reservation *in Texas*—where "the water is good."

One can only hope that Red Hawk knew more about water tables than he knew about reservations. Texas, which uniquely did not lose its public domain when it attained statehood in 1845, was singularly short of land set aside for Indians, and what little had been set aside was far from utopian in either setting or freedom from disturbance. Could it be, on the other hand, that Red Hawk had perceived what usually happened in popular fiction to mixed marriages, especially when children appeared? Where would he and the half-Comanche schoolmarm have taken up wedded life? Would the educated woman have traded blackboard for wickiup? As a matter of fact, what kind of existence did she face with Captain Stanton?

Whatever a person's degree of Indian-ness, actual or attributed, getting along in a white man's world was often a tough proposition. Everett Stonequist described the difficulties facing what he called a marginal man (of any race or culture):

> For the individual, the contrast . . . is not merely a conflict between two culture systems, each having its subordinate groups. . . . The individual may have to readjust his life along several points: the language in which he communicates, the religion he believes in, the moral code he follows, the manner in which he earns his living, the government to which he owes his allegiance, as well as the subtler aspects of personality. The duality of cultures produces a duality of personality—a divided self.[1]

At times, as Joseph W. Whitecotton points out in his foreword to John Rogers's *Red World and White: Memories of a Chippewa Boyhood,* marginal

---

[1]Everitt V. Stonequist, *The Marginal Man: A Study of Personality and Cultural conflict,* pp. 216–17.

men "may completely reject the old world, the world of their ancestors, or they may experience a blind, passionate nostalgia for it."[2]

In its own way popular culture reflected the struggle. William C. De Mille (Cecil's brother), in his play *Strongheart* (1905), described the plight of Soangataha (who shares one of the names given to young Hiawatha when he killed the deer). After becoming a football hero at Columbia, Soangataha-Strongheart falls in love with Dorothy Nelson, a white woman whose brother he has earlier saved from death. Thinking that his coveted college education will surely soften any apprehension about union between races, he and the young woman consider marriage. But Dorothy's brother and another male classmate challenge the Indian's right to make love to her or to any other white woman. Stunned, Soangathaha wonders what use it was to be transplanted from his western home so that he might enter modern life if he is not to be treated as the brother they have pretended him to be. It is Soangataha's own people, however, who stand in the way of the marriage, for he is called to be chief, and the expectation is that the Indians will not accept a white bride. "Oh, great spirit of my fathers," cries the departing Soangataha, "I call upon you for help, for I am in the midst of a great desert alone."

Zane Grey wove a similar theme into *The Vanishing American,* which first appeared as a printed serial in 1922. An orphaned Navajo is raised by prosperous foster parents from the age of seven. Like Soangataha, he is educated well at an eastern university, where he too becomes a notable athlete (Jim Thorpe, who attained sports fame after De Mille's play, must have been in Grey's mind as he wrote *The Vanishing American,* if *Strongheart*—filmed in 1916—was not). Despite the adulation heaped upon him for his achievements, the Navajo is seen by Grey as the representative victim of white encroachment upon an existing civilization.

When filmed in 1925, with Richard Dix as Nophaie, Lois Wilson as the white teacher he loves, and Noah Beery as their antagonist, *The Vanishing American* was given an elaborate historical prologue showing one group after another displacing their predecessors from a single panoramic setting. That extended prologue sometimes is attacked as racist for its thesis that any civilization is inevitably supplanted by a more advanced one, though, as some writers have pointed out, not all

---

[2]John Rogers (Chief Snow Cloud), *Red World and White: Memories of a Chippewa Boyhood,* p. xiv.

177

the supplanters are white.[3] Strikingly photographed, with tinted film stock used to advantage, *The Vanishing American* was directed for Paramount By George B. Seitz, whose career, as mentioned, spanned both Pearl White and Andy Hardy productions. Seitz and a good cast made the most of a screenplay that tried to be sympathetic to the Indian without offending the Federal government, and romantically sentimental without letting its interracial lovers walk into the sunset together—as they were allowed to do in the *Ladies' Home Journal* serial (but not in the subsequent Harper book version, in which Nophaie dies from influenza).

The main portion of the film spans the years before, during, and after World War I and has as its dark force an Indian agent (to whom was transferred the mantle of villainy worn by a missionary in the novel). In another change, perhaps more meaningful, Nophaie has no college background or athletic stardom, having to learn to read at the white teacher's feet. He does, however, become a battlefield hero, only to return to a land being exploited by Indian-agent Beery, against whom Nophaie had repeatedly stood firm before the war. Self-restraint having prevented the noble Navajo from revealing his love for the white woman (who at the end of the film confesses her love for him), Nophaie dies while trying to put out the flames of a confrontation between infuriated Navajos and agency scoundrels.

After the success of *The Vanishing American,* Hollywood turned out several features presenting as the principal figure an Indian who was either a war hero or an outstanding college athlete enamored of a white woman. In fact, in *Red Clay* (1927) William Desmond was qualified by both battlefield valor *and* college education. William C. De Mille's *Strongheart* reached the screen again in 1926 as *Braveheart,* with Rod LaRocque in the lead. And Richard Dix was recycled as an Indian for *Redskin* (1929), a silent film with music and sound effects added. Shaky execution, perhaps, kept this two-color Technicolor movie from matching *The Vanishing American,* and *Redskin* more or less closed out

---

[3]Mordaunt Hall, the reviewer for the *New York Times,* considered the prologue, with its successive waves of Indian, then white conquerors, to be the strongest part of the film, the battle scenes ranking next. The modern tale of the West he found "somewhat ordinary." "Food for thought," wrote Hall, was the title used at beginning and end in reference to the striking outdoor location used throughout the film: "Race may come and go, but the mighty stage still stands." *New York Times,* October 25, 1925. The British name for the film, incidentally, was *The Vanishing Race.*

178

the cycle of photoplays about enlightened Indians just as the talking picture was appearing on the scene.[4]

Precisely when the motion picture industry could have let audiences hear articulate Indians, the market was left open for practitioners of the Friday-Tonto school of speech (Tonto himself being introduced to radio listeners in January, 1933). Two exceptions to the talking-film pattern before the television era were Richard Barthelmess as a sophisticated show-business idol turned activist in *Massacre* (1934) and Robert Taylor as an honored Civil War veteran turned fatalist in *Devil's Doorway* (1950). For both of these educated Indians going home again means leading their peoples against white oppressors, the difficulties of side-by-side existence, in Barthelmess's case particularly, having been exacerbated by the Indian's taste of worldliness. A Warner Brothers' message film of the New Deal era (as MGM's *Devil's Doorway* would be in the era of *Gentlemen's Agreement* or *Pinky*, which also had a racial themes), *Massacre* shows Joe Thunderhorse (Barthelmess) as a darling of society. He is applauded for his Wild West-show feats at Chicago's Century of Progress exposition and lionized by white socialites, Claire Dodd especially, for attractions of a different nature. But when Thunderhorse, in white double-breasted suit, races his fancy roadster into the old reservation to visit a dying father, there is nothing but trouble for an Indian who does not know his place. Convicted of murdering a white undertaker, who has raped his little sister, a fugitive Barthelmess saves his people in a contrived ending that suggests that all will be well on reservations now that Washington officials know of the Indians' plight through Thunderhorse's daring journey to the Potomac. The producers may have seen some justification for an optimistic finish in the Indian New Deal of President Franklin D. Roosevelt (which is described so concisely in

[4]Although a *Films in Review* history of Technicolor (June-July, 1964) does not mention *Redskin*, Kevin Brownlow called the film's color scenes "breathtaking"(*The War, the West, and the Wilderness*, p. 344). In contrast, Jack Spears, who first had analyzed "The Indian on the Screen" for *Films in Review* (January, 1959), considered the color used in *Redskin* "glaring" (*Hollywood: the Golden Era*, p. 372). Brownlow called *Redskin* a film "long overdue for rediscovery," while Spears considered it a "glossy conception of the redman's problems." Brownlow called *Redskin* a better film than *The Vanishing American*, while Spears considered it "infinitely poorer." Most film histories say nothing at all about *Redskin*, perhaps because of its weaknesses, perhaps because it was one of those films caught between silent and sound worlds, just as its hero, Wing Foot, the first Indian at Thorpe College, was caught between white and Navajo life—till he discovered oil.

relation to the public image of the Indian by Robert Berkhover, Jr., in *The White Man's Indian*). Roosevelt made John Collier his Commissioner of Indian Affairs in 1933, but Collier's far-reaching plans were soon undercut by Congress, just as the serious message of *Massacre* was undercut by a happy ending.[5]

Burt Lancaster, as *Jim Thorpe—All American* (1951), fought no wars against the white man but profited little on screen from the education he received at Carlisle. His movie biography, though, is as much an exploration of the problems of an athlete unprepared for the situations of ordinary life as it is a portrayal of an Indian in a white world. Thorpe's battle with drink nonetheless reinforces the firewater refrain of popular literature associated with Indian-white contacts. A sadder portrait of a hero turned alcoholic was *The Outsider,* a film of 1961 (and earlier a television drama) about Ira Hayes, a Pima who was one of the Marine flag raisers at Iwo Jima. Uncomfortable as a hero, unsuccessful as a representative of his people, Hayes (Tony Curtis) dies in a drunken stupor.

Designed for television was another troubled-Indian movie with a contemporary setting, *Run, Simon, Run* (1970). In it released-prisoner Burt Reynolds is loved by a rich white woman, who enjoys dressing him up and showing him off to her cronies. Reynolds takes her foolishness with good nature, but cannot set aside his long-planned vengeance against the white man for whose crime he was imprisoned. The film ends in mindless violence, the kind expected of wronged Indians.

In 1955, incidentally, *The Vanishing American* was filmed again, this time by Republic Pictures, which was not far from closing its doors. The director was Joseph Kane, whose name had appeared on the credits of the studio's final serials almost two decades earlier. It is not difficult to see, then, why this variation on a title by Zane Grey moves in agitato fashion from action sequence to action sequence right down to the last-minute resolution, in which the Indian hero (called Blandy)

[5]Although the Saturday-afternoon B westerns seldom had Indian-related plots, when they did, the Indian was often treated proportionately more sympathetically than he was in higher-budget features. Among the more ambitious early-sound-era attempts to show the Indian's side of frontier problems was *White Eagle* (Columbia, 1932), in which Buck Jones, as a Bannock riding for the Pony Express, fights criminal-inspired abuses of his tribe and forms a suppressed attachment to a white girl. The ending of convenience reveals him as a white man and allows an end-of-the-film clinch with heroine Barbara Weeks—whom he had saved from a mountain lion, Metamora style. A more serious study of Indian problems within

makes a startling recovery from a rifle wound as the marshal announces the capture of leftover baddies. In the best Republic cliff-hanging style recurring menace comes from a sinister double quartet of Apaches—all wearing black hats and vests—who skulk about the agency, waiting to ride off to some skulduggery at the villain's bidding. Those Apaches not felled by Blandy die from arrows unleashed by Navajos, who are shaking off their agency oppressors.

Although the Indian-rights theme is submerged by all the heroics, tough-guy Scott Brady brings a surprising amount of dignity to the role of Blandy—except when he is consciously posing with head upturned, perhaps in imitation of Richard Dix. And Audrey Totter is impressive as the perceptive white woman who loves, and physically embraces, Blandy. Still the vanishing Republic's *Vanishing American* stands as only a minor item in the history of the Western film and as not much more in the movement toward decent portrayal of a minority on the screen. But for action lovers who watch old movies on television, it does provide a rare opportunity to cheer for the Indians during the rousing charge at the climax.

Indeed, before the *Broken Arrow* round of noble-warrior Westerns movie audiences could pull for Indians in battle (or see Indians and whites laboring side by side) only in films depicting doughboys or GIs overseas. Struggling heavy-handedly to introduce notes of brotherhood into wartime message films, producers created squads or platoons in which every conceivable ethnic minority (save, usually, blacks) had at least one representative. Here, at least, the Hollywood stereotypes, whatever their backgrounds, could get along with each other—though possibly after a few reels of misunderstanding. The token Indian in such melodramas said little but, when action sequences came along, did a lot. It goes without saying that if the Indian was a Navajo not only his marksmanship but his linguistic skills were called upon to confound the dull-witted enemy through secret messages received by a second Navajo on another phone. GI Indians also excelled at tracking and such.[6]

a B-Western budget was Tim McCoy's *End of the Trail* (Columbia, 1933). McCoy portrayed an army captain cashiered for allegedly supplying arms to Indians to whom he is known to be sympathetic. Having lived with them for a year, McCoy is able to persuade the Indians to break off a much-provoked attack, but seemingly is martyred in the process. A revised ending brings him back to life, though the original "death scene" remains. At the close of the B-Western period another Columbia film, Gene Autry's *The Cowboy and the Indians* (1949), depicted the Indians in the title from a sympathetic viewpoint.

But the overseas war films came and went, and after they were gone, the camaraderie of the battle front gave way to frontier strife, with Indians and whites seemingly incapable of coexistence. Although ever more frequently a white criminal or corrupt Indian agent was seen as the provocateur, traditional misunderstandings arose whenever the two civilizations crossed paths on the screen. Novelists, despite their predilection for "half-breeds," followed much the same motif as scenarists, attracted, no doubt, by the possibilities for an exciting climax that lay in bloody confrontation or grisly retribution.

One set of novelists perhaps should be excepted from the preceding generalization. With much greater frequency than those writing books for adults, the creators of literature for children showed a willingness to undertake quiet studies of Indian or Indian-White existence. During the long period in which ethnic authorship was not the fashion, the work, flawed or not, had to come from white authors, including Laura Armer (*Waterless Mountain,* 1931); Ann Nolan Clark (*In My Mother's House,* 1941; *Circle of Seasons,* 1970; and many other works); Evelyn Sibley Lampman (*Treasure Mountain,* 1949; *The Year of Small Shadow,* 1971); and Weyman Jones (*The Talking Leaf,* 1965; *The Edge of Two Worlds,* 1968). Although about a white girl, *Caddie Woodlawn* (Carol Ryrie Brink, 1935) suggested that frontier hostilities were not inevitable where fair-mindedness existed. *The Island of the Blue Dolphins* (Scott O'Dell, 1960) showed the inner strength of a marooned Indian girl. Despite limitations of viewpoint many pre-1970s juvenile novels opened paths to understanding.

Not that they did not face continued competition for library space or bookclub listing from the wild and woolly school of children's novels, as exemplified by the one-sided award-winner of 1941, Walter D. Edmonds's *The Matchlock Gun.* There were painted savages aplenty to harass white settlers in *Tomahawk Shadow* (Nancy Faulkner, 1959), *One Week of Danger* (Cateau de Leeuw, 1959), *Fear in the Forest* (de Leeuw, 1960), *Captured by the Mohawks* (Sterling North, 1960), and *Mary Jemison, Seneca* (later *Indian*) *Captive* (Jeanne Lemonnier Gardner,

---

[6]The use of Navajos as "code talkers" is, of course, well documented, 350 of them having served in that capacity during World War II. The Navajo language, with its many variations, would have been difficult for code breakers even if they had possessed a textbook (none existed at the time). As Carl Gorman, one of the original code talkers, explained in "Navajo War Code was Unbroken," *New York Times,* January 7, 1979, a message in Navajo "was done fast. It took just a few minutes, and it never did fail."

1966). Representing a welcome change of approach for the juvenile thriller—in that some time was spent in developing the Indian's reasons for the inevitable uprising—was Theodore V. Olsen's story of the Black Hawk War, *Summer of the Drums* (1972).

Influenced, perhaps, by Oliver La Farge's Indian-centered (but condescending) Pulitzer Prize novel, *Laughing Boy* (1929), adult-market authors examining adjustments to a white world produced *Fig Tree John* (Edwin Corle, 1935), *The Man Who Killed the Deer* (Frank Waters, part-Cheyenne, 1941), and *Old Fish Hawk* (Mitchell F. Jayne, 1970). Pocket Books, Inc., put all three into paperback in 1971–72, with cover paintings similar in style. Just before those reprints and four decades after *Laughing Boy,* a Kiowa-Cherokee author, N. Scott Momaday, had won the Pulitzer Prize of 1969 for his depiction of the reservation-to-World-War-II-and-back-dilemma, *House Made of Dawn.* White interpreters of things Indian would now have to share the market place with Indian authors like Leslie Marmon Silko (*Ceremony,* 1977) and James Welch, a Blackfoot-Gros Ventre, who attracted much critical favor with his *Winter in the Blood* (1974), perhaps because his Blackfoot narrator was not bogged down by conventional storybook Indianness.

The two most celebrated non-Indian authors to take on the problem of frontier coexistence during the era of social consciousness begun in the middle of 1960s were Elliott Arnold, of *Blood Brother* (*Broken Arrow*) renown, and Jessamyn West, remembered for *The Friendly Persuasion.* Was it coincidence that at a time of grasping for historical redress both writers were drawn to actual group murders of Indians planned by white civilians? The titles of both mid-1970s historical novels were anchored by a significant word: "massacre."

Jessamyn West's *The Massacre at Fall Creek* (1975) was built upon the scanty records of a trial of 1824 in Indiana wherein four white men were found guilty of the premeditated murder of nine Indians—men, women, and children. Three of the convicted murderers were hanged, very likely the first time such an action was taken in the United States. West's purpose was to reveal the dilemma faced by both sides in the unprecedented court action. Would the men actually be found guilty by a white jury and, if so, executed? Or would the Indians of the territory be forced into lightning raids of vengeance, the sentiments of their religious leaders against capital punishment notwithstanding?

For the most part, the author of *The Massacre at Fall Creek* succeeded in giving perspective to the viewpoints of both settlers and

Indians. The primary weakness of the novel comes from the interruptive love affairs of the book's principal figure, one of the defense attorneys. In "naughty" sequences jammed into the narrative either to please an editor or to titillate a cloistered reader, Charles Fort has sexual relations (one assumes) with Woman A (mature), only to have Woman B (blooming) discover the couple lying naked and asleep. Later Charlie takes a turn with Woman B (again discretely offpage), this time with Woman A stumbling upon recumbent nudes. The sexual silliness demeans an otherwise thought-provoking novel.

Eschewing the romantic encounters supposedly necessary for a modern novel, Elliott Arnold focuses upon the day-by-day approach of *The Camp Grant Massacre* (1976). Like Jessamyn West, however, he develops both sides of the climactic clash, describing, as she did, atrocities that molded the vengeful personalities of the perpetrators of the massacre of 1871. Both authors, though obviously sympathetic to Indians, successfully avoided becoming mired in the kind of breast-beating or mea culpa that, as we shall see, distorted other Indian-related works of their era. In *The Camp Grant Massacre,* Arnold treats in parallel narratives (1) the achievement of Lieutenant Royal Whitman in persuading Eskiminzin and his Arivaipa (Aravaipa) Apaches to surrender their rifles and take up quarters (and farm duties) near the small outpost outside Tucson and (2) the smoldering wrath of a group of ranchers and townspeople that erupts in a devastating surprise attack by a white-led force of Papagos upon the virtually defenseless Apaches.

One of the more interesting aspects of Arnold's book is the subtle evolution of the Apache image in Royal Whitman's mind. As the officer gradually moves from curiosity about "wild Apache women" to the first perception of the Arivaipas' humanity and finally to an appreciative recognition of their culture and family life, the textual descriptions of Eskiminzin's people advance correspondingly. The overall effect is almost subliminal, and the final tragedy is all the more affecting because the reader has made friends with characters by degrees, instead of being confronted by wooden paragons on page one.

Whenever peaceful coexistence is explored in frontier stories, there inevitably arises that nagging question: Could it have worked? Was there a path that did not involve confinement, self-internment, or relocation? The experience of the Cherokees in the South suggests that no accomplishment on the part of the Indians could have turned the tide of Manifest Destiny in the nineteenth century.

Late in the 1700s the Cherokees set out to prove to the white men that Indians could be just as "civilized" as whites. They learned to use looms, spinning wheels, and factory-made farm implements. They used Sequoyah's Cherokee alphabet in a well-set-up newspaper. By 1827 they had a written constitution for a government similar to that of the United States. They had schools, churches, roads, mills, and a rich economy. They even had a verdict from the Supreme Court protecting their right of self-government against attempts at sovereignty by the state of Georgia.

And what came of this demonstration that an Indian people could meet every conceivable white-conceived criterion of civilization—and within only one generation? President Andrew Jackson, disregarding the Supreme Court Decision and having pushed Congress into adopting the Indian Removal Act of 1830, began moving the southern Indian nations to what he would call "highly favorable" land beyond the Mississippi. As he expressed it to the Congress in his message of 1835: "All preceding experiments for the improvement of the Indians have failed. It now seems to be an established fact that they can not live in contact with a civilized community and prosper." With Jackson's encouragement regional officials harassed the Cherokees, giving away their homes, their developed land, and their public buildings in illegal state lotteries. In 1838 a force of seven thousand soldiers moved most of the "unremoved" Cherokees into stockades and then, by detachments, to the western lands. As many as four thousand Cherokees may have died in the stockades or in the harsh journeys to Oklahoma in the late 1830s.

With the embarrassingly successful Cherokees out of the way, with the eastern agricultural Indians (who had kept many early colonists alive) long since decimated, the myth of the savage nomad who did nothing to develop the land over which he aimlessly roamed could be nourished—especially if attention was directed only to the open plains. Both history books and popular fiction readily accepted that explanation of convenience, justifying the eventual subjugation of all Indian groups in face of Manifest Destiny. Here is George Armstrong Custer reassuring his wife about reservations in a youth-level biography still in print during the 1970s:

"I know how you feel about it, honey," he said gravely. "I pity the poor redskin with all my heart. He is the unfortunate victim of circumstances. I don't blame the present-day Indians for not wanting to go onto the reservations to take up the white man's mode of life. Their existence has been free and to them very pleasant. But it is a way that cannot go on. Savagery cannot be allowed to block civilization."[7]

Custer explains to his dutiful wife that reservation life will be hard on "this generation of Indians" but that education and care will turn them into "good American citizens." The sooner the Indian "bows his neck to civilization," the better it will be for him. Custer, in this biography, sees himself as hastening the process. After all, "the progress of civilization is more important than the native's wild way of life."

"Of course, it is," Libby said, her eyes sparkling with pride in the husband she adored. "Do your fine job for civilization, my brave, good man."

While less conspicuous, perhaps, than the attacker of fort or village, the Indian left to his own way of life in the fertile valley—or untapped gold field—was an obstacle to white advance. Side-by-side relationships, in that light, were perforce obviated through the only rationalization possible: the Indians were useless savages. All else— relocation, internment, extermination—followed logically. As Shannon Garst summarized it in the Custer biography: " . . . it was written in the pages of destiny that savagery must eventually give way to progress."

Longfellow's Hiawatha put things more euphemistically when he gave way to the Black-Robe chief—the Pale-face:

"I am going, O my people,
On a long and distant journey;
Many moons and many winters
Will have come, and will have vanished,
Ere I come again to see you.
But my guests I leave behind me;
Listen to their words of wisdom,
Listen to the truth they tell you,
For the Master of Life has sent them
From the land of light and morning."

Indians and white men living side by side as equals? The Trail of Tears told the story. Popular fiction kept alive the myth.

[7]Shannon Garst, *Custer, Fighter of the Plains*, p. 120. The book had its seventeenth paperback printing by Pocket Books, Inc., in 1965.

186

When popular culture chooses to have a good Indian, nothing on the face of the
earth can match that character in stolid nobility (or pristine femininity). Wooden
Indians have long been with us.

The noblest pose of them all: arms folded, head erect. Executors of this position (used to signal "delay-of-game" in football) are A. S. Lipman in a play of 1897 (left) *and Rod La Rocque in* Braveheart, *a film of 1926.*

These chiefs are not demonstrating phases of the signal for a touchdown. Solemnity is their message. Above: Naked in the Sun *(1957)*. Center: The Great Sioux Uprising *(1953)*. Below: The Way West *(1967)*.

"If the white man speaks the truth he is our friend; if he lies he shall meet death by club and fire."

189

Above: *Vision improvement. Linda Darnell in* Buffalo Bill. *Below: Vision of an ethereal nature. Trevor Howard in* Windwalker.

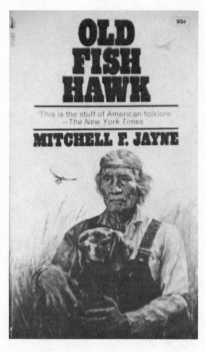

The "noble elder" face, in three paperbacks published at about the same time.

191

The real Sitting Bull, with two feathers, is haunted by a paperback illustrator's "swipe" of his countenance with nine.

*"Yes, . . . said Injun Joe. . . . Five years ago you drove
me away from your father's kitchen one night, when I
come to ask for something to eat, and you said I
warn't there for any good; and when I swore I'd get
even with you if it took a hundred years, your father
had me jailed for a vagrant. Did you think I'd forget?
The Injun blood ain't in me for nothing."*

Mark Twain, *Tom Sawyer*, 1876

11

BLOODLINE

I
N what was known as the wilderness, the purely social problems of
an Indian-white family were minor. No mountain man or north-
woods trapper would have raised an eyebrow over the eminently
practical decision of some colleague to take upon himself an Indian
wife. Correspondingly, in an Indian village a white captive was likely
to be fully integrated, perhaps becoming an adopted daughter, son,
or brother. It was primarily in the developing white community that
real or imagined aboriginal roots became a liability, with Indian-ness
being the heart of the matter.

Thus in a film portrayal of the problem, *Flaming Star* (1960), Elvis
Presley would grow up with a white father and an Indian mother
(Dolores Del Rio) but never gain acceptance in a white town. His
attempt to be peacemaker between warring sides would only bring
tragedy. On the other hand, in *The Unforgiven* (novel, 1957; film, 1960)
Audrey Hepburn could live a respected life with the white family that
had adopted her until a Kiowa raid threatened the ranchland and an
accusation was made that she had red skin. Then, suddenly, angry
settlers were ready to "strip her down" to find the truth.[1] Even pure-

---

[1] In the novel (also called *The Siege at Dancing Bird*) the racial question was left open; no

193

white parentage could mean little if one had been raised an Indian and had come to "think savage," a vivid case in point being the turmoil surrounding True Son, the central figure in Conrad Richter's *The Light in the Forest* (1953), filmed superficially by Walt Disney in 1958 (*Hombre*, a Paul Newman movie of 1967, treated the subject more challengingly).

While there is a certain cachet about having a bit of Indian ancestry—Will Rogers, President Calvin Coolidge, and Vice-President Charles Curtis would claim it proudly—for the first generation of Indian-white offspring and their parents fiction writers seldom would offer anything but torment (movies simply took over the precedents already established in novels and short stories). To several generations of Americans the most familiar literary product of a mixed union no doubt was Ramona, an actual figure who was brought to national attention through the Helen Hunt Jackson novel of 1884 that bore her name. Later her story was kept alive through play and film.

Ramona's real-life Indian husband, Juan Diego, distraught over the civil and criminal injustices inflicted upon the Mission Indians of California, unaccountably appropriated a horse owned by Sam Temple and used it to ride to his home. Temple caught up with him the next day and immediately shot him dead. Temple then calmly rode off with the recovered horse, not at all worried about being prosecuted for murder. Nor had Temple's sangfroid ended. After his vicious action had become the climactic point of the Jackson novel—Juan Diego having been renamed Alessandro Assis and Sam Temple having become the brutish Jim Farrar—the calculating Temple tried to wangle bids for personal appearances at both the Chicago and the Saint Louis world fairs. In a recording of 1900, moreover, he boasted of having put twenty-two buckshots into "Alessandro's" chest before breaking his rifle over the Indian's head and finally putting three revolver bullets into the dying man. Despite this seeming overkill, claimed Temple, the suspect still "laid on the ground on his back and cut the ground four or five times most viciously" with his knife.[2]

Ramona herself disagreed with the Temple account because it gave the impression that the slayer had merely acted in self-defense.

one knew whose baby William Zachary had found abandoned. In the film adaptation of Alan LeMay's book, however, the girl's foster-mother ultimately admits that Rachel is an orphaned Kiowa. This revelation is enough to cause Cash, a previously protective foster-brother, to move out of the house, blinded by his hatred of "Injuns."

[2]Don Battle, "The Man Who Killed Alessandro," *Westways*, February, 1962.

She also asserted that Temple had fired even more times than he had admitted. For both approach and accuracy Jackson's description (with changes of name and era) was the version Ramona endorsed, and that is the one that has endured.

In Jackson's book the daughter of Angus Phail and his Indian wife is raised from infancy on a California rancho as part of a proud Mexican family. Ramona Ortegna, unaware that her mother was an Indian, falls in love with Alessandro Assis. Only when she announces that she plans to marry him does she learn of her parentage—from a matriarch who does not wish to think of Ramona as part-Indian and would not have her step beneath her caste by marrying one.

Nonetheless, Ramona and Alessandro elope. Their marriage is idyllic until the dissolution of land titles caused by the change from Mexican to American governance costs them their property. As a result they are pushed from one shelter to another by encroaching American roughnecks. Following the murder of the mentally tortured Alessandro and Ramona's subsequent acts of courage and fortitude, Felipe, her foster brother, finds and marries Ramona, taking his bride to Mexico when the old rancho too is lost to American interests. Ramona, while remembering Alessandro, finds happiness in a return to her former style of life.

In the last event, as Albert Keiser pointed out in *The Indian in American Literature* (1930), lay one reason that *Ramona* fell short of Jackson's hopes for it as a social document uplifting the lot of the Indian. Ramona is Mexican in breeding and bearing. So, for that matter, is Alessandro, though his rancho status was below that of his wife-to-be. During their married days in Indian society they are more sophisticated than their fellow villagers, though without pretentiousness. Their romance, furthermore, dominates the other aspects of *Ramona* so dramatically that the Indian cause espoused by Jackson is easily overlooked by readers. As a novel and in its motion picture and outdoor-pageant manifestations, *Ramona* is remembered as a bittersweet love story.

Although Hollywood filmed *Ramona* more than once—with Mary Pickford, Dolores Del Rio, and Loretta Young among those in the title role—about all that echoes from those efforts is the popular song associated with the Del Rio version of 1928. In the photoplay of 1936, directed by Henry King, rich-voiced Don Ameche, newly arrived in Hollywood after radio stardom, looked uncomfortable as Alessandro, while the beatific Ramona of Loretta Young appeared only a halo away from canonization. Times were changing. The nice, if sometimes hoydenish, "half-breed girls" of Hollywood's earlier days—Jees Uck of *The Mohican's Daughter* (1922), Mescal (Bebe Daniels) of *Heritage of the Desert* (1924)—were giving way to the earthier Indian-white women Hollywood seemed more at ease with after the Roaring Twenties— Clara Bow in *Call Her Savage* (1932), Paulette Goddard (the scheming "klootch") in *North West Mounted Police* (1940). A Ramona, it would seem, no longer exuded the sensuality that the depiction of a half-Indian woman dictated. More commercially desirable were glimpses of, say, Joan Taylor skinny-dipping in Roger Corman's *Apache Woman* (1955) while Lloyd Bridges ogles in genial fashion (as is a white hero's cinematic privilege when discovering an Indian maiden in the nude).

Taylor's Annie Le Beau, however, was as honorable as she was sexy. Hollywood's monumental insult to the part-Indian female would remain the Pearl Chavez essayed by Jennifer Jones in *Duel in the Sun* (1946). Disregarding the good (or, if one prefers, the *white*) side of Pearl's character—which Niven Busch sporadically acknowledged in his novel of 1944—the film team of *Duel in the Sun* emphasized what Busch chose to call the "trashy" nature of the "half-breed" young woman (well, after all, before many pages had passed Pearl had swum naked with two men and had stopped mopping a floor to fornicate with another). Faced with that kind of challenge, the film's makeup men and bodice enhancers strove earnestly, and with embarrssing results, to give Jennifer Jones (best known for her Saint Bernadette) the smoldering appearance of the book Pearl:

> The Indian blood showed in Pearl's long legs and ropy bluish-black hair and in her lips which had a slight bulge even when they were closed. She had rather light brown or brown-greenish eyes, lighter than her olive skin. . . . Witnesses to her arrival will declare and swear that they spotted Indian the first time they laid eyes on her.

It may have been the wide apart, slightly slanting, Indian-looking eyes, but whatever racial feature gave Pearl's heritage away brought trouble for her from the ranch folk. Even her benefactress and guardian, Mrs. McCanles, knew how to handle out-of-line Indian stragglers, as Busch offhandedly advised the reader:

> Once when Laura Belle put a mustang-grape pie to cool in her kitchen window a Keowa buck reached for it and then for her. Laura Belle McCanles took the carbine which was standard equipment over her stove and blew one side of the Keowa's head off.

Good prairie fun, getting back at pushy bucks. What could Pearl expect, then, but to be misunderstood, by both westerners and film makers. "Desperately Pearl wanted proof that she came from some-where . . . that she was a real person." But Hollywood knew what she was: a female "half-breed," who couldn't keep her seductive juices under control when the character whom wags called "lewd Lewt, the brute" (Gregory Peck) was around. She wound up abetting his law-breaking. The studio gave Pearl a marvelous death scene (in keeping with movie mores of 1946) as she crawled through the desert to the lover she had shot, finally bringing a seemingly interminable cowboy-drama-cum-heavy-breathing drama to a panting conclusion. In the novel, by the way, Busch had let the misdirected girl marry and settle down with a good white man once Lewt was out of the way. The movies, though, were not yet ready for such startling considerations. As Preston Foster, a Mountie, warned a marriage-minded Robert Preston in *North West Mounted Police:*

"Never trust a blue-eyed squaw!"

When it comes to *males* of mixed backgrounds, it is hard to tell whether they received greater mercy on paper or on celluloid. Cer-tainly Mark Twain did not do much for the sons of Indian-white unions with his depiction of a twisted creature who was written off as just plain bad:

"Say, Huck [whispers Tom Sawyer], I know another o' them voices; it's Injun Joe."
　　"That's so . . . that murderin' half-breed! I'd druther they was devils a dern sight."

In *Tom Sawyer* (1876), Twain set out for apprehensive readers and imitative writers a definitive literary archetype. Here Joe is at his demoniacal best during the moonlight struggle in the graveyard:

Injun Joe sprang to his feet, his eyes flaming with passion, snatched up Potter's knife, and went creeping, catlike and stooping, round and round about the combatants, seeking an opportunity. All at once the doctor flung himself free, seized the heavy headboard of Williams grave and felled Potter to earth with it—and in the same instant the half-breed saw his chance and drove the knife to the hilt in the young man's breast. He reeled and fell partly on Potter, flooding him with his blood. . . . The half-breed muttered:
　　"That score is settled—damn you."
　　Then he robbed the body.

Minutes later, he convinced the awakening Potter that it was he (Pot-ter), not Injun Joe, who had plunged the knife. Deceit as an encore to

197

robbery and murder was, after all, nothing out of the ordinary for a character called by his author, as well as his fellow characters, a "half-breed."

That Mark Twain did the historical model of Injun Joe a disservice is revealed, more's the pity, in Jerry Allen's *National Geographic* tour of "Tom Sawyer's Town." Allen called the real-life Indian resident of Hannibal, Missouri (Sawyer's Saint Petersburg), a "kindly old ragpicker toward whom children were cautious." The townspeople took care of him for many years until "he died in the town of his fame . . . an aged and wrinkled half-breed Indian." The legends attached to Injun Joe after his fictional infamies, reported Allen, made twentieth-century tourists uncomfortable when visiting his haunts, the cave in particular. Said one schoolgirl visitor to Cardiff Hill (her details garbled), "This is the place where Indian Bill murdered the widow." Her mother "looked warily around for 'Indian Bill' and uneasily herded her family from the treacherous ground of fiction."[3]

Curiously enough, fiction writers generally saw more difficulties in being part Indian than in being all Indian, primarily because of the consequences of living in two worlds, a situation that writers liked to give full play.[4] Paperback publishers were most receptive to novels built around the mixed-blood with problems. From the 1950s on, store racks were not complete without at least one book with blurbs like those that follow:

> Had Pawnee Perez been a white man, you would know his name as you do Custer's or Kit Carson's. But history has no use for half-breeds.
> Clay Fisher, *Red Blizzard,* 1951

> The lawman was part-Indian, so he couldn't look for help when he caught a ruthless white killer.
> Peter Dawson, *The Half Breed,* 1962

> Brent was a half-breed and anybody could see it in the sharp jut of his

---

[3]Jerry Allen, "Tom Sawyer's Town." *National Geographic,* July, 1956, pp. 131–32.

[4]In a novel of 1936 based on the Lone Ranger radio series (begun in 1933), Tonto is inexplicably called a "breed." Subsequent novels, however, gave him the full-Indian status associated with his career on the airwaves. It would be interesting to discover the source of the confusion, since Fran Striker, writer of the radio drama, was ostensibly the author of the novel. Was Tonto, whose tribal relationship and language ("Kemo Sabe") have always been a bit shaky, originally conceived as a person of two backgrounds? Or did a hack novelist substituting for Striker make the slip? Whatever the answer, the Lone Ranger's creators would not long have brooked a troubled creature of two worlds as a riding companion, for in Tonto they had called up the ghost of Chingachgook.

nose, the high cheekbones and the angry slit of his mouth. And Brent had spent most of his life mad at the world for what he was.

Wade Everett, *The Whiskey Traders,* 1968

For the first time in his life, Benito thirsted after another man's blood. He no longer felt himself a half-breed; he was an Apache. . . . He savored the fate he would inflict on the murderer. First he would stake him out and slowly flay him; then he would methodically cut out his eyes and shred his tongue to ribbons.

Glen A. Blackburn, *Apache Half-Breed,* 1971

They called him the white Indian . . . with the flaming red hair of his mother and the dark, fierce eyes of his Pequot father . . . and a heart that burned with with a cold fury.

Maria Sandra Sterling, *War Drum,* 1973

The blurb writers (who seldom quoted the authors themselves) also had fun describing those who procreated two-worlds offspring:

Pete Handy knew the spot he was in, a white man with a Cheyenne wife and a half-Indian son. He stood alone in a savage crossfire of hate and violence.

Lewis B. Patten, *A Death at Indian Wells,* 1970

Lee Tobin was his name. He was tough and sure and he wore the Army uniform. But he was a Squawman and he stood alone.

Gil Martin, *Squawman,* 1972

And even if an Indian youth had a good white upbringing, paperback society offered no favors:

He was a Navajo who had been raised as the foster son of a respected rancher. . . . But he was an Indian.

William R. Cox, *Navajo Blood,* 1963

Raised white, but born Cheyenne—and they'd never let him forget it if the desperate mission failed.

Lewis B. Patten, *Redskin,* 1973

In contrast to the publishing industry, the Hollywood establishment, with its concern for nationwide acceptance of its product, used part-Indian males as central figures of frontier dramas infrequently—and always carefully. Tom Laughlin's *Billy Jack* (1971), with its quietly confident (but much too lethal) hero and peculiar social themes, was atypical and late arriving. Preferring to hold "breeds and such" to minor and generally unredeeming roles, filmmakers apparently felt more comfortable with casual denigration of partial Indian-ness than they did with the glorification seemingly required for sympathetic central characters. Nonetheless, the industry must be saluted for the preciseness of social distinction evidence by a quickie of 1916 called *The Quarter Breed* and by a Peter B. Kyne–based melodrama of 1922, *One Eighth Apache* (the discovery of that 12.5 percent is enough to prostrate the hero's wife).

For *The Only Good Indian,* Ralph and Natasha Friar compiled a list of silent melodramas that, from 1909 to 1913 alone, included *The Half Breed's: Treachery, Atonement, Plans, Daughter, Sacrifice,* and *Way;* not to mention *The Dumb Half-Breed Parson,* and *The Half-Breed Sheriff.*[5] Obviously, there was appeal in the designation.

It was not until 1916, according to film-historian Kevin Brownlow, that a character of Indian-white parentage was treated in a sympathetic light in a motion picture. Some might argue that this was not the first such representation, but with Douglas Fairbanks in the title role, *The Half-Breed* (Fine Arts–Triangle) surely was the most prominent film of its kind. The director was Allan Dwan, who recalled the difficulties in mounting the photoplay because Fairbanks's wife

> ... didn't want him appearing as an unwashed half-breed. To fix that, I had him standing on a rock, nude except for a loincloth. He dives into the river, and rubs himself with sand to get himself oh, so very clean. So I asked Beth "How's that?' She said, 'That's fine.' He was a washed Indian, not a dirty Indian. I only put the scene in to satisfy her."[6]

Although many motion pictures of early days centered upon the problems of Indian-white offspring, the vogue ended before World War I. Of later productions both *Half Breed* (First National, 1922) and *The Half-Breed* (RKO, 1952) bear forgetting, as does *White Comanche* (1967), with its twin brothers of mixed blood, one raised white (good), one raised Indian (bad). *Broken Lance* (1954) was a curious, though not unsuccessful, transplanting of *House of Strangers* (an Edward G. Robinson movie of 1949 which had nothing to do with Indians but lent itself to subsequent variations of different milieus). In *Broken Lance,* Katy Jurado portrays an Indian wife of Spencer Tracy, and Robert Wagner is their son. Both are rejected by Tracy's other sons.

[5]Ralph and Natasha Friar, *The Only Good Indian: The Hollywood Gospel,* p. 301.
[6]Director Allan Dwan to Kevin Brownlow, *The War, the West, and the Wilderness,* p. 335.

In general, the men that the movies called "half-breeds" were unhappy, weak, or vicious. If not tortured by their lives in two worlds, they made evil use of their status by excelling at betrayal and frontier espionage or by leading the Indians they had cleverly aroused against some settlers or soldiers. Charles Stevens, Geronimo's grandson was adept at playing both Indians and part Indians of the weaseling kind whose treachery inevitably resulted in death or torture at the hands of one side or another. When it came to figures of history, for every sympathetic treatment of an Indian leader of mixed blood there would be five of the vengeance-mad kind. The effort of Louis Riel and the French-Indian Métis to establish an independent state in Canada became in *North West Mounted Police* a bloody exercise of a gang of murderers. The many contributions to society of Quanah Parker after his days as a Comanche battle leader went undiscovered by scenario writers. For some reason only Osceola, who may or may not have had white forebears, came off consistently well in movies. Perhaps that was because he was not a western Indian.

The sprinking of Indian ancestry in essentially cowboy heroes like John Wayne's *Hondo* (1953) was scarcely noted by scenarist or viewer. More in the celluloid tradition was the Zach Provo of *The Last Hard Men* (1976), based on the book *Gun Down* by Brian Garfield (author of *Death Wish*). In the film Charlton Heston describes Provo as the "meanest Indian I ever saw" and later as "half-Injun, all killer" (CBS Television brought those words to a nationwide audience on December 13, 1979). When reviewing the film as a theatrical feature for the *New York Times,* Richard Eder found actor James Coburn "hopeless as the maddened half-breed." In the reviewer's words, Coburn "grimaces, shows his teeth, rolls his eyes and gargles his consonants." Standard operating procedure, really, for an heir of Injun Joe.[7]

[7]For a deeper than usual insight into the part-white, part-Indian individual in twentieth-century society, a reader can turn to *Ceremony.* This novel, by Leslie Marmon Silko, herself a person of mixed background, met almost universal approval of critics. Silko—Laguna Pueblo, Mexican, and southwestern white in ancestry—confronted positively the despair that, she wrote, "accounts for the suicide, the alcoholism, and the violence which occur in so many Indian communities today." Tayo, the central character, has dimension not found in the stereotyped mixed-bloods far more common in literature. Although pleased by the success he and his buddies enjoyed with "white girls" while in uniform, he nonetheless recognizes the passing nature of his wartime role and, moreover, finds it difficult to erase the paralyzing memories of the Pacific battlefield. The Indians in *Ceremony* have a fuller range of character than that normally given them in novels, whatever the background of their authors. It is unfortunate that Silko's book has not received the public or commercial attention afforded lesser, and sometimes plainly pretentious, Indian-glorification fiction of recent years.

Being Indian in a white world, or the reverse, created difficulties for both real and fictional individuals. Artists, writers, and filmmakers regularly turned to the marginal man or woman for source material. The "Indian Dandy" was sketched for a travel book of 1882.

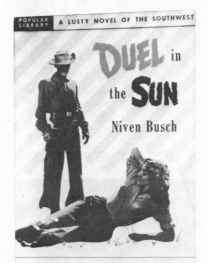

Above: *The genteel Ramona of Loretta Young (with Don Ameche in 1936) was in strong contrast to the lusty women of mixed background who followed her, such as Paulette Goddard in* North West Mounted Police *(1940) and Jennifer Jones in* Duel in the Sun *(1946).*

Three times Cecil B. De Mille filmed The Squaw Man. *From Left: Dustin Farnum and Red Wing (1913); Elliott Dexter in a triangle (1918); and Warner Baxter and Lupe Velez (1931).*

Richard Harris experiences some sort of Sioux tribal initiation in A Man Called Horse
(1970). A portion of the George Catlin painting of a Mandan *ceremony (not initiation)
copied in the movie appears beside him. Above it is Catlin's painting of a* Crow *chief
appropriated for Harris's vision of a Sioux leader.*

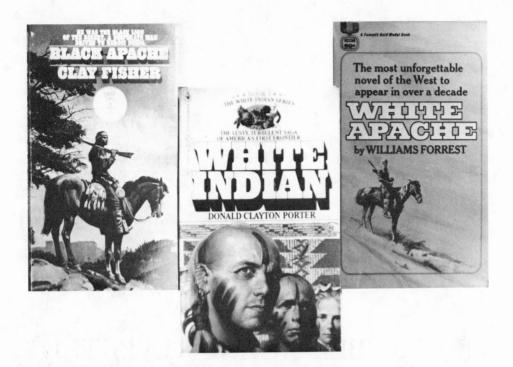

Above: *Traditionally, the best Indian of all in a frontier tale is a white one. The black Apache is an interesting variation.* **Below:** *Indians, and pseudo-Indians, in comic-book land.*

In a way . . . the refusal to see an Indian or a Black or an Oriental in anything less than a favorable light is as much a put-down as the old implicit suggestion that they are all basically volatile children. Total goodness is also less than human.

Richard Schickel,
New York Times, February 9, 1975

12
THE NOBLE SAVAGE REVISITED

I N the late summer of 1950 motion-picture audiences, long accustomed to conventional Indian thrillers, fortified themselves with popcorn and candy at their neighborhood theaters in anticipation of yet another vicarious bout with rampaging Apaches. They may have heard that the new James Stewart Western was a little different, but once its tranquil opening narration had passed, a quick attack on white trappers by a band of Chiricahuas promised the full-color savagery and mayhem moviegoers had come to expect from Apache raiders. It was not even too surprising when the hero, after aiding a young Chiricahua wounded in the attack, vowed to seek a peaceful solution to the endless bloody confrontations that plagued the Arizona Territory. That noble promise, after all, had been heard before. It usually resulted in nothing more than a pageantlike treaty signing tacked onto the end of a melodrama that had been filled with more than enough ambushes and scalpings to satisfy the most aggressive popcorn muncher.

But things *were* different in *Broken Arrow,* and although the film had errors of its own, it disturbed the savage-horde status quo. Unlike conventional Indian films—and that includes potboilers like *Comanche*

Territory (1950), in which a frontier hero saves Indians from exploitation by *criminals*—*Broken Arrow* placed the Apaches at the center of the decision making and solution seeking. It also avoided the heavy hand of pathos that had marked earlier sympathetic treatments of the first American. Elliott Arnold's historical novel *Blood Brother* (1947), which portrayed Tom Jeffords's efforts to arrange a peace with the Chiricahuas through the almost-legendary Cochise, was the physical source of the Michael Blankfort screenplay. That noble nineteenth-century stage Indian Metamora, however, was the drama's spiritual inspiration. Encouraged by Arnold's laudatory characterization of Cochise, 20th Century–Fox brought forth an Indian figure who—according to New York Times reviewer Bosley Crowther, carried himself "with the magnificence of a decathlon champion" and spoke with the "round and studied phrasing of the salutatorian of a graduating class." Edwin Forrest's Metamora to the very gesture and vowel.

It can be perilous for film historians to look with much favor upon *Broken Arrow* today. The movie is regarded as an example of both patronization (a valid judgment) and glorification (also valid). Its Hollywood touches are decried (at times rightfully), and its special award from the white-organized Association of American Indian Affairs discounted (not so rightfully if one considers popular fiction of its era and the favorable mention of the film in *Akwasasne Notes,* an Indian publication). A resurrection of the Noble Savage may not have been the highest course of action for the motion-picture industry in the early 1950s, but that action was, if nothing else, a break in the unrelieved display of the mindless, faceless, attackers that Hollywood had again fallen into with World War II out of the way.

Broken Arrow may have been as lacking in subtlety as the whacks on a donkey's head in a venerable anecdote about motivation. Yet as the wily driver of that donkey explained to a reproachful onlooker: "Shucks, I'll be glad to reason with the critter after a bit. But first I have to get his attention." *Broken Arrow* did get attention, from a general audience bemused by decades of on-screen slaughter. Though Hollywood would in many ways bumble the opportunity to do something constructive after that attention had been won, youngsters in the *Broken Arrow* audience (and they included some future filmmakers) would look at screen Indians less narrowly after cheering for Cochise.

One of the liabilities, historically, of a motion picture that cuts new (or long-neglected) ground is that it is sometimes remembered for its imitations and not for itself. Because it was successful, *Broken Arrow* sparked a wave of action movies, some of them viable, most of them bad, in which saintly or misunderstood Indians were brought down by the treachery, malevolence, or iron-headed stubbornness of whites. Not often did the producers of these wonder-Indian dramas pause long enough in their rush to exploit a new toy to recognize that *Broken Arrow* was successful not because it had nice Indians but because it was fundamentally an entertaining and carefully made film derived from a novel most critics liked.[1]

In *The Western* George N. Fenin and William K. Everson called *Broken Arrow* "a moving and sensitive film with some breathtakingly beautiful camera work."[2] To Jack Spears, Tom Jeffords's "long ride into the Indian country" contained "some of the most sustained suspense yet seen on the screen"[3] These writers, although aware of the film's excesses in glorification, were appraising *Broken Arrow*'s cinematic values, which, of course, was exactly what satisfied audiences had done at the time of its release. Moviegoers applauded the motion picture for what it really was: good romantic adventure. True, director Delmer Daves was sensitive to the peace-oriented story, yet when the screenplay called for violence by some of the Apaches, he brought out the menace in the situations as fully as he later would the sympathetic actions of Cochise's people.

Scholars sometimes forget, by the way, that the Chiricahuas of *Broken Arrow* attack and kill white civilians and soldiers without being labeled "renegades." There is none of the good-Indians-don't-slay-whites, bad-Indians-do dichotomy portrayed, for example, in *Little Big Man* (1970). The early ferocity of Cochise's warriors, in fact, enhances the significance and fragility of the Jeffords-arranged truce, which both sides work to preserve in the second part of the movie. Although

---

[1]Although reviewers such as Oliver La Farge and Stanley Vestal wrote generally favorable reviews of Arnold's book, Hoffman Birney came down hard on the novel in the *New York Times.* He would have preferred to see Chief Joseph or Wovoka (the ghost-dance messiah) as the honored Indian rather than Cochise. His reason bears noting: "The Apaches were the scourge of the southwest for centuries before the white man came." Even if one accepts this selective racism, the obvious reply is: Doesn't the use of a noted "scourge" instead of a "good Indian" make the turnabout that produced the truce with Cochise that much more dramatic? Birney predicted that *Blood Brother* would "delight those who believe that all Indians were as noble as Hiawatha," then closed his argument by stating: "As biography it is inaccurate; as history it is often distorted; as ethnology it is balderdash."

[2]George Fenin and William Everson, *The Western,* p. 281.

[3]Jack Spears, *Hollywood: the Golden Era,* p. 376.

some of the Chiricahuas, notably Geronimo, do not buy the peace idea at all and, as the screenplay puts it, "walk away," they do so in parliamentary fashion. When a few of them attack a party of white men later on, Cochise's warriors perform the necessary police action without undue heroics or self-approval. *Broken Arrow's* only old-fashioned good Indian–bad Indian business involves a jealous Chiricahua who steals into Jeffords's wickiup and tries to kill his romantic rival. Cochise himself executes the fellow summarily for violating the Chiricahua code of hospitality—a chilling action to many viewers, but a reminder that Cochise is not a Presbyterian elder. If there are any stereotyped renegades in *Broken Arrow,* they are the white rabble-rousers determined to wreck the truce through an ambush, not the dissident Apaches who had never subscribed to it in the first place. "Oh, no, don't let them get Cochise," moviegoers implored when it seemed he would fall to the bushwackers—reversing the customary pattern of audience anxiety in an Indian movie.

When Hollywood producers set out to imitate *Broken Arrow,* they took its white rascals and expanded their evilness, an action that in turn made the sympathetic Indians appear that much more noble or put-upon. The difficulty with that approach was that the Cochise depicted in *Broken Arrow* was already at the outer reaches of believability. To stretch the Noble Savage fantasy further was to invite disbelief, which is one reason that the flurry of Indian goodness on the screen from 1950–55 was self-extinguishing. Special circumstances—for example, the novelty of an Indian hero who did not go down to defeat —made it easier for Daves, working with a good story, to pull off the trick ... once. But a postwar receptivity to seeing some traditional movie enemies execute a turnabout and do some nice things for a change would mean less with each successive exercise in exaggerated nobleness.

Then, too, there was something especially fortuitous, and not easily duplicated, in the casting of Jeff Chander as Cochise—a role from which he was never disassociated. Chandler had both the physical and the vocal characteristics of a larger-than-life character, and, just as important, he was unknown to the *Broken Arrow* audience, having played only a few minor parts in unimportant films. Like Michael Rennie, a British actor Fox used a year later for a similar nonpareil role—that of the awe-inspiring yet sympathetic envoy from another planet in *The Day the Earth Stood Still*—Chandler brought no familiar persona with him. He was fully the mysterious (and then not particularly well known) chieftain of a forbidding stronghold. He was Cochise. His carefully orchestrated initial appearance in the film—first by voice from an off-camera position—was developed with as much gradually rising suspense as that of the giant ape in *King Kong,* and with less audience knowledge of what to expect. The appearance of a familiar actor at that point would have destroyed the dynamics, as Daves and others must have known. Later, when imitators tried to capitalize on the noble-Indian motif, they used familiar non-Indian Indians like Victor Mature *(Chief Crazy Horse),* Burt Lancaster *(Apache),* and J. Carrol Naish *(Sitting Bull)* as historical chieftains with less dramatic result. The masterpiece of unwise casting may have occurred, however, in 1962, when tall, blond, blue-eyed Chuck Connors was passed off as a victimized Geronimo.

As counterpart to Jeff Chandler the *Broken Arrow* producers cast a likable, steadfast, and not easily overshadowed James Stewart as Tom Jeffords. The veteran performer added verity to the romance with the lovely Sonseeahray (Debra Paget), a subplot of *Broken Arrow* that bordered on the maudlin, yet still came off better than the romatic interludes of any *Broken Arrow* pastiche. To some moviegoers the film no doubt was seen as an outdoor love story with a nice wedding in white, an idyllic honeymoon, and, alas, a tearful ending—it was not yet time for an unshattered Indian-white marriage on the screen. Needless to say, the Indian-princess market picked up, for Debra Paget and for any actress who looked like her.

In addition to the wedding ceremony various not-quite-right rituals dotted *Broken Arrow,* but they were nonetheless accepted as real because of the care and, sometimes, taste in staging them. A last recital of the names of Chiricahuas fallen in battle was especially affecting. Not readily recognized as an asset of *Broken Arrow,* certainly by imitators, was the use of humor by Cochise. Once, when Jeffords warily tells Cochise that there are a few Indians he wouldn't trust, the chieftain reflects briefly, then says with a slight smile, "Me too." Later Cochise advises Jeffords that his supposedly secret romance with Sonseeahray is "as quiet as the thunder." And after making an anxious Jeffords think that the girl's family will not allow a marriage, Cochise smilingly confesses, "I make a joke."

Slightly forced or not, that humor, coming from a formidable warrior, was a rare note in an Indian adventure. While drunken or comic Indians often were the butts of weak jokes in Western movies, they rarely made the jokes themselves except to terrify victims. Chieftains, in particular, tended to be uniformly stern, almost dyspeptic. In so-called serious, or sociological, Indian dramas the tone was invariably somber, with impending tragedy hanging heavily overhead from the opening titles. Since Indians as a group enjoy wit and laughter—particularly when the outsider is not around—the jokes of *Broken Arrow* were legitimate and amplifying elements of characterization.[4]

Broken Arrow ends almost immediately after Sonseeahray dies trying to protect her husband from white ambushers. Cochise can offer Jeffords only quiet sympathy, and the film closes with Stewart narrating off camera that Sonseeahray's death sealed the peace. That, sad to say, was hyperbole. The Jeffords-Sonseeahray romance was, as Elliott Arnold called it, "pure fiction," constructed from Jeffords's informal comment that he had been intimately involved with a lovely Indian girl. The sealed peace of 1872 did not last long after Cochise —who was actually much older than Chandler's portrayal suggested —died in 1874. Just two years later the government ordered the Chiricahuas to the San Carlos Reservation, despite official promises that they would not have to move and despite the presence at San Carlos of former Chiricahua adversaries. One of Cochise's sons, Taza (or Tahzay), took almost half of his father's people there. A younger son, Naiche (Nachise), went with the others to Mexico and subsequently joined Geronimo. As might be expected, it was Taza, not Naiche, whom Universal Pictures selected for a hero role in its own string of noble-Indians movies in the early 1950s. *Taza, Son of Cochise* (1954) came after *The Battle of Apache Pass* (1952, Cochise in earlier days), *Seminole* (1953, Osceola), and *The Great Sioux Uprising* (1953) but before *Sitting Bull* (1954) and *Chief Crazy Horse* (1955). Jeff Chandler (under contract to Universal) and Rock Hudson were seen as Cochise and son, but also got into a couple of the other films as army officers. By the time Universal had unveiled Victor Mature as Crazy Horse, the Indian extras on the lot no doubt were placing bets on which magnified chieftain would be the first to meet the studio's Abbott and Costello in a comedy feature.

Meanwhile, other studios, though not pursuing the *Broken Arrow* motif as strongly as Fox and Universal, were exploring the concept

[4]Vine Deloria, Jr., presents a colorful analysis of Indian humor in chapter 7 of *Custer Died for Your Sins*.

here and there. Sometimes the effort amounted to no more than allowing a gang of murderous outlaws to abuse some peaceful Indians, as in the dismal *Slaughter Trail* (RKO, 1951).[5] Sometimes the adjustment lay in letting the white hero use an Indian maiden to further his schemes (as Clark Gable did in MGM's *Across the Wide Missouri*) only to realize too late the prize he had lost. Close to the pattern was RKO's *The Big Sky* (1952), based, but not too skillfully, on A. B. Guthrie's novel, in which the effect of white civilization upon Indian society is portrayed through individual victims as opposed to faceless tribes. Howard Hawks produced and directed the film.

Devil's Doorway (MGM) examined the post–Civil War difficulties of an educated Shoshoni who had served in the Union Army with sufficient distinction to win the Congressional Medal of Honor but could not win fair treatment for himself or the Shoshonis on his return. The otherwise straightforward narrative suggested, then backed off from, a love affair between Broken Lance Poole, the Shoshoni (Robert Taylor), and Orrie Masters, a white attorney (Paula Raymond). That equivocation was a mistake, unstated taboo or not. Although the ending of *Devil's Doorway* was less Pollyanna-like than that of *Broken Arrow* —Taylor and his followers dying in a hopeless defense of land to which they have been denied title—a romantically sterile film with a tragic ending was not what audiences were looking for. What is more, when a bitter Broken Lance Poole told Orrie Masters just before his death that in a hundred years a romance between them might have worked, he was really saying that, while *Devil's Doorway* was all for decent treatment of Shoshonis and their cousins, it was not about to portray the unthinkable: physical love between a white woman and an Indian man (even if played by Robert Taylor).

Equivocation notwithstanding, MGM executives reportedly anguished over *Devil's Doorway* after seeing the completed film with its downbeat theme and its reversal of sympathies in the well-staged showdown between Indians and their oppressors—soldiers and posse. The studio did not put the motion picture into general release until after the appearance of Fox's *Broken Arrow,* and then with the scantiest of publicity budgets. *Broken Arrow*'s producers, in contrast, knowing how to play the Indian love theme of the time—Indian

---

[5] *Slaughter Trail* was one of those Westerns of the 1950s in which a male quartet was used Greek-chorus style to accent the plot—a device usually more ludicrous than imaginative.

woman, white man, love, death, victory—won both the critical and the monetary laurels in 1950.[6]

Through the years, incidentally, other than death for the Indian male the safest way out of the interracial dilemma lay in a last-reel discovery that the chap really was white. Buck Jones and *White Eagle* come to mind here. So does the musical *Whoopee* (1930). In *The Savage* (1952), Paramount let the audience know right away that Charlton Heston was a Sioux-adopted brave who, as Warbonnet, had eventually to choose sides. That, however, was about as far down the road toward understanding Indians as Paramount seemed willing to go during the *Broken Arrow* era. *Warpath* (1951), which bore a curious resemblance to that year's *Bugles in the Afternoon,* coupled a cashiered officer's vindication with Custer's Last Stand. *Pony Express* (1953) saw Wild Bill and Buffalo Bill (Heston again) getting the mail through. *Arrowhead* (also 1953), based on W. R. Burnett's *Adobe Walls,* was just what would have been expected from a film written and directed by Charles Marquis Warren: every Apache the whites put their trust in was downright bad —exactly as the Indian-hating army scout (yes, Heston) said they were. Toriano (Jack Palance), the white-educated ghost-dance reincarnation of David Belasco's Scar Brow, was bad. Heston's part-Apache girl friend (Katy Jurado) was bad. "Spanish," her brother, was bad. Scout Jim Eagle was bad. All of them had pretended to be friends of the white man before revealing their true colors so that Heston could smirk, "I told you so." And to think that old Charlton had been a pseudo-Sioux just one year earlier.

At least Tyrone Power did some nice things for Indians in late 1952, but he was working for 20th Century–Fox. As a Canadian Mountie in *Pony Soldier,* Power helped a group of starving Crees who had been roughly handled in the United States. Then with the aid of a pretty princess he snuffed out a near-uprising. Actor Guy Madison, in contrast, spent most of his time fighting or escaping from Indians, undoubtedly because his studio, Warner Brothers, was experimenting

[6]In *The Hollywood Indian,* the finely turned out catalog to a symposium, film series, and exhibit of the New Jersey State Museum in 1980, John E. O'Connor stated that (Broken) Lance Poole, the central character of *Devil's Doorway,* was, in the original draft, a white drifter. According to O'Connor, Poole was changed by stages into an Indian war hero to add the feature to the cluster of postwar message films on tolerance that included *Gentleman's Agreement, Crossfire* (both 1947), and *Pinky* (1949). The corporate cold feet about the finished product could seem to be a contradictory response if the use of an Indian was a ploy to cash in on a postwar marketing trend, but Hollywood action or reaction cannot be presumed to have consistency from day to day—or hour to hour.

with wide-screen and three-dimensional effects in *The Charge at Feather River* (1953) and *The Command* (1954). Naturally, battle scenes allowed for more spectacular visual sequences than did truce talks. *Hondo,* with John Wayne, was another Warner Brothers 3-D exercise, though it had more depth than most other such movies. Oddly enough, *Hondo* was developed from a Louis L'Amour short story called "The Gift of Cochise." Since that Chiricahua, as represented by Jeff Chandler, had become the virtual joint property of Fox and Universal, Cochise was instantly transformed into another chieftain, Vittoro, for the movie of 1953 and its subsequent "novelization." With each change of medium the image of the *Hondo* Apaches worsened. Warner Brothers' only real nod to *Broken Arrow* was *Drum Beat* (1954), an Alan Ladd movie with a derivative story line (but no Cochise). The resemblances are not surprising since *Drum Beat* was written as well as directed by *Broken Arrow*'s Delmer Daves.

Revived in the early 1950s was the idea that the best Indian was one who tried to be just like a white man. In *Apache* (United Artists, 1954) Burt Lancaster, as Massai, had loads of trouble after his escape from a Florida-bound prisoner train until he discontinued a personal vendetta and took to the hoe and plow. His reward was the quiet life on a nice little farm with an Indian wife (Jean Peters). The Indians of *White Feather* (princess Debra Paget included) also went through the tortures of adjustment to white men's ways in that Fox film of 1955, but the white protagonist's closing narration of the Delmer Daves–Leo Townsend screenplay was upbeat in the *Broken Arrow* style: "I said at the beginning: this was a true story. Appearing Day and I were married at the Methodist Church in Council Bluffs. Broken Hand lived to see his grandson enter West Point." How's that for Middle West America —even if the mixed marriage was merely announced?

By 1956, Delmer Daves must have been exhausted by his efforts to chip the last piece of flint from *Broken Arrow*. For Fox's *The Last Wagon,* as director and cowriter, he brought back "Bible-Reading" Howard (the general who had made the peace with Cochise). He also presented Richard Widmark as a frontiersman whose Comanche wife (like Jeffords's Apache bride in *Broken Arrow*) had been killed, along with his two sons, by white yahoos. But *The Last Wagon* was really a doomed-caravan film, caught in the wake of the noble-Indian flurry. The film's faceless Apaches were carefully excused for attacking the wagon train, their provocation being the recent Camp Grant massacre, in which the Arivaipas had been the victims. The narrative, moreover, was contorted in such a way that the destruction of the caravan could occur off camera—while a few pioneers who escaped it were down at the river for an illicit swim. All this left *The Last Wagon* a war film without a battle and a brotherhood film without a single Apache whose character had been even lightly outlined.

The *Broken Arrow* motif had run its course. Universal's last serious contribution (also 1956) was *Walk the Proud Land,* the story of John P. Clum (Audie Murphy), the young Indian agent who gained attention through one of his least charitable actions, the capture of Geronimo by deceit. Critics were divided on *Walk the Proud Land,* some finding it a gentle gem, others a dreary preachment. Audiences apparently regarded it as a somewhat tame Western with an uncharacteristically subdued Geronimo (Jay Silverheels). And moviemakers at all studios noticed essentially the box office reaction after a half-dozen years of films about good Indians—meanwhile keeping in mind the developing impact of the television Western. *Run of the Arrow* (1957), though ostensibly pro-Indian, came off the RKO lot loaded with violence and abnormal psychology.

*It was the white people who had nothing; it was the
white people who were suffering as thieves do, never able
to forget that their pride was wrapped in something
stolen, something that never had been, and could never
be, theirs.*

Leslie Marmon Silko,
Ceremony, 1977

13

MEA CULPA

D URING the last half of the 1950s and most of the 1960 the
noble-Indian movie was in temporary decline. Exceptions
would come along—the already mentioned blue-eyed
Geronimo of Chuck Connors, for instance—but no recognizable Indian-glorification strain can be seen in theatrical films of the era. Some
producers, never really having been distracted by the idea that Indians
might be sentient human beings, went on in their old ways. Undoubtedly aware that the Indian-oriented movies, which they considered
dull and actionless, seemed even more so alongside the rip-roarers of
the 1940s and 1950s newly released to television, the old-style
filmmakers brought back the howling hordes, with no more than token
screenplay comments about provocation.

Sometimes they even remade former successes. *Stagecoach* was
one. It reappeared under the Fox banner in 1966, with Alex Cord in
the John Wayne–Ringo Kid role and a jejune Ann Margret as the
exiled woman of the town made memorable by Claire Trevor in the
John Ford film of 1939. In more fortunate casting, Bing Crosby took
over the drunken-doctor part played earlier by Thomas Mitchell. To
complete the alterations, Geronimo and his Apaches were replaced by

Crazy Horse and his Sioux. The tense pacing of the original *Stagecoach* was totally lacking in the remake, but the Indians, in keeping with the violent 1960s, demonstrated considerably more hostility. In the opening massacre (portrayed largely through suggestion in John Ford's film) the Sioux marauders are shown in close view, striking brutally with their axes or dragging victims through fires. One scarcely imagine the frenzy if the logarithmic progression stretches to *Stagecoach III*.

Yet if the Indians were barbarous in the *Stagecoach* of 1966, they were arcane in United Artist's *The Way West* (1967). A. B. Guthrie's well-received novel, in the hands of Hollywood, became the film that taught the lesson: wagon trains and frigid wives do not mix. Let me outline the screenplay reasoning. A cold wife will sooner or later drive her husband into the bushes with an eager young filly (destined to become television's Flying Nun). Once the philanderer-despite-himself begins to feel guilty about his pleasures, he will nervously empty his shotgun at the first Sioux stripling who inexplicably crawls upon the wayside scene of passion disguised as a wolf. That kind of hostility will upset the young brave's elders (carousing nearby) and lead to days of impending danger from the Sioux, who will follow the wagon train into territory they have never entered before so that they can see the face of the murderer and put the boy's soul to rest. A band of Sioux, hovering around with a face fetish, can unnerve any wagonmaster, especially the frequently deranged one portrayed by Kirk Douglas and jaw. To settle his nerves, the wagonmaster will have to string up the accidental killer, requesting, of course, a brief bugle salute to cap the event. But matters will not end there, for the frigid wife is still part of the caravan. Although the Sioux, their conventions satisfied, will withdraw without even a tom-tom reprise to the bugle call, the woman who started all the trouble is free to ruin a wedding by announcing that the bride is pregnant. What is more, she can spoil the wagonmaster's entry into the promised land by taking a knife to the hoist by which he is being lowered down a four-hundred-foot cliff. Now bereft of its testy Moses, the wagon party will have to turn to a half-blind trail scout (Robert Mitchum) and a stolid fellow traveler (Richard Widmark of *The Last Wagon*) to get them successfully to the Willamette Valley— by raft.

Thus ends the lesson of *The Way West*, as Hollywood saw it. And thus was the saga of the Oregon Trail reduced to inanity. The Indians of the motion picture are depicted as a gang of jolly, if bowstring-happy, roisterers until the boy is killed and the "chief of the whole

Sioux nation" (in Mohawk hairstyle and woman's shawl) makes a stately appearance, surrounded by a crazy quilt of accouterments from non-Sioux cultures and bearing the miraculously undecayed corpse of what turns out to be his youngest son. This one noble Indian, however, can do little to offset the impression left by the befeathered revelers who have emoted earlier in the film, nor the impression that will be made in the last reel by a Northwest felt-hat-with-plume archetype whose grunts reveal how dull a fellow he is meant to be.

Out of the absurdity, or crudity, that marked so many Indian dramas of the middle-and late 1960s, and the protesting, demonstrating antiwar temper of that time came a well-intentioned, guilt-quenching, but generally misguided redirection of the Indian film. The theme would be mea culpa, and the revisionist history one-dimensional. Icon breaking and pretentious patronizing would scramble the traditional narratives, adding more heat than light. Feeble comedy and weak parody, moreover, would do little to relieve the obfuscation. *The Hallelujah Trail* (1965), for instance, was at the "drunken-Indians-are-hilarious" level. So was *Flap* (1970)—original title, *Nobody Loves a Drunken Indian.* Said the Mohawk publication *Akwesasne Notes* in May, 1971; "This picture made a joke of Indian rights. We don't mind a laugh at ourselves but this picture made us look like idiots."

Resistant to normal evaluation was a parody of the cavalry-and-Indians epic called *Texas Across the River* (1966). Overdone, but difficult to dislike totally, this Dean Martin movie featured Joey Bishop as an Indian companion with the unlikely name Kronk—that was the name of his tribe too. Possessing nary a trace of the Indianship one would expect of a proper Tonto, Kronk is given to nightclub one-liners and snappy rejoinders usually poking holes in Hollywood fancies about Indians. The running gag of *Texas Across the River,* though, involves a catchall oral command that sounds something like "Ho-oroar, har!" but is never fully deciphered by the bumbling troopers whose fatuous officer bellows it whenever there is needed to charge, retreat, or change direction. Even the Indians under Michael Ansara (television's Cochise) wind up following the cloudy command.

For moviegoers familiar with the cavalry genre there was delight in spotting the photoplay clichés that *Texas Across the River* (a bit laboriously) runs off one by one—smoke signals, fiery arrows, pow-wows, speakers with forked tongues, braves arranged in ordered echelons for the camera, and so on—till every chestnut has been pulled out. Did this deliberate parody put the clichés to rest? Not at all. Each of them turned up in a dozen or more Wild West movies before the passing of thirty moons.

Not every laugh-provoking Indian film of the awareness era was designed as comedy or parody. Some frontier features were maudlin when they were supposed to be funny and hilarious when they were attempting to impart a message. In 1964 director John Ford presented the film which, according to some critics, was designed to make amends for all the Westerns in which he and John Wayne had laid it on the Indian. The picture was *Cheyenne Autumn,* suggested, as the titles announced , by a book by Mari Sandoz. Virtually any source, however, the Omaha telephone book included, would have served as well for this unfortunate and interminable strip of celluloid. It was almost as if John Ford, who had built so many entertaining films around the men in blue, could not put his heart into something in which the motivating figures wore blankets—and did the "Cheyennes" in this pursuit tale ever wear blankets. They wrapped them around themselves dramatically to strike brave poses, droopingly to suggest rejection, and at one point a huddled band of captives produced enough arms and ammunition from within their wraparounds to stock a modest arsenal.

In *Cheyenne Autumn* John Wayne was impersonated by Richard Widmark, a casting decision that automatically reduced the role of the upright army captain from frontier god to ordinary human, thus making the two Indian principals less likely to be overshadowed by their multireel pursuer. Since these principals were arrayed in pompadoured fright wigs that gave them the appearance of the Toni-Home-Permanent Twins, the use of Widmark rather than Wayne was almost providential. The two unfortunate wig wearers—Gilbert Roland and Richardo Montalban—were mere victims of Hollywood circumstance. They did their best under difficult conditions. Sal Mineo, on the other hand, as a wild young brave given to ripping off his shirt, inhaling deeply, and then prancing about in this unnatural attitude, earned a permanent station in the hall of horrible Hollywood Indians. Regrettably, he was left alive until the final reel—when his own chief plugged him, one assumes for overacting.

The prolonged action of *Cheyenne Autumn* involves a long trek by a band of Cheyennes (inflated to the "whole Cheyenne nation") from a reservation to a distant homeland, with a stumbling cavalry under Widmark in pursuit. Along the way the participants pause long enough for a full reel of absolutely extraneous nonsense in a Kansas

219

saloon, with James Stewart making a cameo appearance as Wyatt Earp. Then the Cheyennes plunge on, jabbering and fussing like a troop of exiles from a daytime serial until a sympathetic Edward G. Robinson, as Carl Schurz, helps them on the last leg of their journey.

Tributes of the likes of *Cheyenne Autumn* the magnificent plains tribe does not need. A skeptic could ask why none of the Indian principals was portrayed by an Indian. Only one nonwhite adult was given what might be called a line of dialogue. That was the aged warrior who was permitted some howls of command in a tongue that may be Navajo (the winter songs performed in the film are actually the chants of Navajos, Ford's favorite Indians).

Featured prominently in *Cheyenne Autumn* was a post commander (played by Karl Malden) who would have done well at a Nazi concentration camp. His mistreatment of the Indians within his fort revealed a strong strain of insanity, a characteristic that would become a prominent aspect of the revisionist movies of the next decade or so. All too frequently sympathy would be directed toward Indians not because they were depicted as individuals with whom audiences could identify but because they were portrayed as victims of white madmen. In addition, the Sioux or Cheyennes or Apaches were often being presented as no more than endangered species in photoplays akin to those decrying cruelty to animals. Indeed, in a low-budget movie of 1964 called *Navajo Run,* the much-copied premise of *The Most Dangerous Game* was reworked with the result that a sadistic white rancher first sheltered, then stalked, a "half-breed" played by director Johnny Seven. Was it because human prey made for a worthy adversary in a hunt? No, it was because, to the rancher, all Indians were animals, put on earth to be hunted. Johnny Seven was envisioned as trophy number seventeen.

Still, that number was small compared with the amount of wide-screen carnage open to a white madman in an army uniform. Look at what happened in a movie of 1970 derived from a novel originally called *Arrow in the Sun.* The book, by T. V. Olsen, followed the flight of a young woman escaping from the Cheyennes, with a quiet soldier as accidental escort. The Cheyennes of the book were neither saints nor devils, and the cavalry troop was not under the command of lunatics. When Hollywood purchased the work, however, renaming it *Soldier Blue,* the narrative became a strained historical allusion to the My Lai massacre. The slightly disguised frontier event appropriated for the purpose was the Sand Creek massacre of 1864—a tragic mass murder of Cheyennes and Arapahos that had nothing to do with Olsen's novel.[1]

Colonel John M. Chivington, the coldly ambitious Colorado militia commander who led the attack on Black Kettle's village during the Civil War, became for movie purposes Colonel Siverson, a fanatical leader who rode to the battle site sprawled in an army wagon and boisterously singing "Rally Round the Flag." The number of Cheyennes slain and mutilated in the raid on the village, though depressing enough in real life, was augmented for the motion picture, while minor alterations here and there obscured the source of white brutality. The atrocities of the *Soldier Blue* photoplay seemingly originated in the entire military establishment, America's whipping boys at the time the film was made. Not even hinted was that the Sand Creek massacre itself was essentially a bloody lark that a trophy-hunting temporary militia—Chivington included—set up and carried out just before the expiration of their one-hundred-day enlistments. Shades of gray did not fit the message. The poorly trained raiders who perpetrated the actual slaughter at Sand Creek were scarcely more than vigilantes in uniform, enlisted (and thus escaping Civil War draft service) because President Abraham Lincoln in 1864 had not regulars to spare for protection of frontier civilians against possibly exaggerated dangers. Riding on the apprehensions and racial hatreds of the mining communities they were to "protect" but unable to prod the nearby Cheyennes and Arapahos into the kind of action that would justify reprisal, Chivington and his aides beat the enlistment deadline by attacking an encampment of nonhostile Indians—the very ones whose leaders had enjoyed a warm meeting with Lincoln the year before and for that reason willingly remained at a location cleverly selected by the militia for a last-minute massacre if no better opportunity presented itself. After the barbarous surprise attack Chivington's rowdies displayed their trophies—more than a hundred scalps, plus sundry objects such as tobacco pouches made from genitals. To the Denver citizenry, roughnecks as well as good people frightened by stories of Indian atrocities on a lightly defended Civil War frontier, the Colorado Volunteers were at first heroes to be applauded. Then the true story came out, as officers and men of the First Colorado Cavalry,

[1]For the paperback edition of Olsen's book (given the movie's title and a nude Indian princess for the cover) the Sand Creek massacre was squeezed in through a frontispiece quoting the five-sentence narration with which the film ended.

temporarily attached to Chivington's Volunteers, testified before authorities. There was national outrage and later a federal confession of war guilt, with indemnity to Indian widows and orphans. But Chivington could not be court-martialed. His enlistment had expired.

Soldier Blue could have been a more honest film if it had reflected the climate of fear and intolerance on the Colorado frontier at that point of the Civil War, when not all Indians were pacifists and not all soldiers madmen. Or it could have stayed with its simple adventure story of a woman fleeing from the Cheyennes, with whom she had been forced to live (as a chief's wife) yet who nonetheless gained her respect. But that was not the film's path. The editors of *Akwesasne Notes* thought that the massacre itself was depicted properly enough but that the rest of *Soldier Blue* was "junk."

Those editors had worse to say about a supposedly authentic depiction of the American Indian entitled *A Man Called Horse* (1970). It was rated a "four tomahawk" picture, that is, a "massacre." Expanded from a short story by Dorothy Johnson, this tale of an Englishman captured and later adopted by Crows was loaded with rituals that either did not exist or were earnestly copied from George Catlin paintings of *Mandan* ceremonies. The speaking roles of the fictional Indians went to non-Indian actors of various nations, Judith Anderson included. Crows somehow were turned into Sioux (their ancient enemies), perhaps to take advantage of the Dakota extras available on the Rosebud Reservation. All this would not have mattered so much had the publicity for the motion picture not stressed accuracy of detail and significance of message. Neither was found in *A Man Called Horse*. Since audiences liked the film, however, there was a sequel in 1976, complete with the flesh-piercing ritual that apparently was the highlight of the movie for gore hunters. Vincent Canby of the *New York Times* rightly caught both the patronizing and the white savioring of the sequel—which did indeed bear the title *The Return of a Man Called Horse*.

The adopted Indian's chieftain, incidentally, was played in the first *Horse* film by Manu Tupou, a Pacific Islander. Tupou had earned his feathers by portraying Sitting Bull in Arthur Kopit's play of 1969, *Indians* (and would continue in Indian assignments like that of a Kentucky chieftain in television's short-lived *Young Daniel Boone*). Kopit's *Indians,* a protest drama of unusual narrative framework and staging, connected Buffalo Bill and the destruction of the Indian nations to the slaughters and motivations of the Vietnam War. When the drama reached the screen in 1976 (as *Buffalo Bill and the Indians; or, Sitting Bull's History Lesson*), Tupuo had been replaced by Frank Kaquitts, and the Vietnam War had ended. Producer-director Robert Altman contented himself with poking holes into the remembered image of poor old Buffalo Bill, portrayed by Paul Newman.

The frontier hero who really started taking it on the chin during the revisionist film era, though, was George Armstrong Custer. Ever since his most famous film biography, the Errol Flynn adventure *They Died with Their Boots On* (1941), the Custer screen image had been declining (with minor exceptions such as the feature spliced together from a controversial ABC-TV series). In *Warpath* (1951), for instance, the erstwhile boy general was dashing still but disgruntled over the comedown that fighting mere Indians represented to a commander who had once gone against J. E. B. Stuart. And it is certainly not difficult to recognize in the Colonel Thursday (Henry Fonda) of John Ford's *Fort Apache* (1948) the Custer who led his troops into defeat against all advice and caution, and then in death became a legendary hero. In a dozen other post-flynn films Custer is at best a flamboyant daredevil and at worst a careless popinjay. Cinerama used him for *Custer of the West*—in which the "general" frankly tells an Indian emissary that the Indians are going to be pushed aside by onrushing newcomers and that neither he nor they can do anything about it. Although television unveiled a deranged, impotent "hero" in *The Custer Court Martial* (1977), the dramatic nadir probably had already been reached in *Little Big Man* (1970). The protrayal of the Seventh Cavalry commander is so distorted and defamatory in that film as to invite a turnabout rehabilitation of the historical character in some film yet unmade.

Again, as with *Soldier Blue*, there may have been a notion to offer a little cinematic boost to the Indian people in *Little Big Man,* the story of a white man who moves back and forth betweeen white and Indian civilizations. But by the time director Arthur Penn and Writer Calder Willingham had put on film their adaptation of Thomas Berger's satirical book, even the glorified Indians had been upstaged by yet another insane army officer. The George Armstrong Custer of *Little Big Man* (played by Richard Mulligan, later of television's *Soap*) is, in fact, too ludicrous to be believable before the Little Bighorn engagement. And during that famous battle of the Greasy Grass he is no more than a raving maniac. What adversary can gain stature by defeating such a commander?

The otherwise entertaining and generally well-received motion picture, in which Dustin Hoffman gives a virtuoso performance, does present rare vignettes of Indian life. Chief Dan George is particularly endearing as the venerable (and Hollywood-sanctified) chief who becomes Hoffman's foster-grandfather. The film, like the book, also suggests that a typical Indian village can contain some rather colorful eccentrics, including one chap (a "contrary") who does everything backwards and another who is saucily homosexual. But three surprise attacks by the cavalry on such villages seem more than necessary to make a point, even if the final one does backfire on Custer. Then, too, the film thoughtlessly revives the old good tribe–bad tribe device of Cooper at the expense of the Pawnees, who, after losing a skirmish to Little Big Man and pals, are derided as "always sucking up to whites." It is hard to tell who came off worse in *Little Big Man,* Custer or the Pawnees. Custer, of course, did not have to face society after the release of the movie. Twentieth-century Pawnees do.

With the passing of the war-heightened turbulence that had marked the Vietnam era, the mad colonels and generals were given a bit of rest—though the theatrical film release of 1971 became the televised movie of 1976 or 1977, stirring the cauldron again. For its own purposes television tended to lean toward patronization or historical adjustment in its occasional efforts to uplift the first American. Take the epic of 1975 called *I Will Fight No More Forever.* A story of the incredible retreat toward Canada by Chief Joseph and the Nez Percés, this ABC-Television drama received much advance publicity in press and classroom, the sponsor, Xerox Corporation, distributing instructional guides to schools. When the show reached the air, the critical evaluations were largely favorable, though Jay Sharbutt of Associated Press called the drama "somewhat stolid," and *Variety's* critic called actor Ned Romero's Chief Joseph a "mixture of nobility and facial immobility," a liability found in more than one effort to depict a worthy Indian. More significant was *Variety's* observation that the narrative halted too often for "hindsight philosophy" about American Indians that would have been unlikely discourse in 1877. "Making brownie points with contemporary viewers" is the way the publication aptly summarized the business.[2] At several points James Whitmore (as the ubiquitous "Bible-Reading" Howard) and a junior officer (Sam Elliott) did become so orally entangled in moral aspects

[2] *Variety,* April 23, 1975.

224

of relentlessly dogging a valiant foe that the courageous Nez Percé families were almost lost sight of by the writers.

After the telecast historians entered the scene, not just because of inaccuracies in *I Will Fight No More Forever* but because television was toying with something called the "docudrama." A docudrama purportedly told a true story, such as that of a famous kidnapping or a lost aviator, yet more often than not twisted the truth to serve the immediate message. A viewer who accepted *I Will Fight No More Forever* at face value would have concluded that the peaceful and industrious Nez Percés were unjustly ordered off their land and onto a small reservation as the result of a minor incident in which one of the many despicable white settlers of the Northwest was killed by an Indian— an Indian who was merely punishing the man who had a day or so before gunned down his father. Instantly recognizing the impossibility of reprieve from the eviction notice sparked by the shooting, Chief Joseph's Wallowa band and other Nez Percé groups head for the Crow country and then toward Canadian refuge, pursued, reluctantly, by an agonizing General Howard.

What was wrong with that overview? It was obtained through too many adjustments of history, said the experts, an action not so serious in a typical entertainment piece but improper when twelve-page study guides are distributed to school children to enhance the teachings of the docudrama.

By 1877, the year following the amalgamated Indian effort that culminated in Custer's defeat, General O. O. Howard was fearful that the nations of the Northwest might similarly unite under Chief Joseph. Although not an Indian hater, Howard was in a hurry to get the Nez Percés onto the reservation at Lapwai, even if it meant moving the Wallowas from productive territory onto land obviously too small for their livestock. Howard went so far as to order the complicated removal in a season inopportune for moving animals and with a deadline unrealistically close. That piece of history notwithstanding, the producers needed a sympathetic general for the drama's two-bit moralizing and soul-searching, and in that guise did O. O. Howard appear in *I Will Fight No More Forever.*

To make sure that no one lost sight of the message, the many legitimate but not visually exciting legal grievances of the Nez Percés were shunted aside in favor of a potent but deceptively altered opening incident. Arbitrarily, the shooting of a middle-aged Nez Piercé for alleged horse stealing was moved closer in time to the long flight. As

225

a result, when the accused thief's son, striking swiftly, shoots his father's murderer and then, his righteous fury not spent, turns his weapon upon a store's shelf of liquor, it seems to be no more than simple frontier justice. Certainly it is small cause for displacing every Indian in the area—which is exactly the implication sought for. What docudrama viewer, some program planner must have reasoned, would ever discover that the slain Indian's son (Shore Crossing was his name) would not be moved to take retaliatory action until two years after the death of his father—and then mainly as the result of goading by another Indian? And who would be aware that Shore Crossing really took his vengeance not directly upon his father's slayer (who was long gone) but, instead, upon several white settlers who had nothing to do with the horse-stealing incident? Drunk and aggravated, the young Nez Percé rounded up two companions and in a shooting spree killed two white men and wounded a third. Other Nez Percés, their tempers long frayed from the callous actions of various white scoundrels, also took to the saddle. A dozen more white settlers were killed, several women and children were abused, and some property was damaged before the twenty raiders calmed down.

To a nervous General Howard the raids were the beginning of the war he feared. To Chief Joseph, none of whose Wallowas had participated in the action, the raids were the sign that he must lead his people away, for, innocent or not, he and his lieutenants would draw the suspicion of Howard. The Wallowas started off alone, but a random military attack on a band of Nez Percés under Looking Glass drew that group also into the long dash for freedom.

During that painful, peril-filled, thirteen-hundred-mile struggle not a single act of cruelty or barbarism would be committed by the harried Nez Percés. They fought cleanly and fairly. Still, disguising the attacks that triggered the flight as an act of just revenge by a lone Indian was not the way to truth or television, nor, for that matter, was the omission of the long pursuit's only atrocity—the exhumation and mutilation of Nez Percé casualties by the army's Bannock Indian scouts. However inconvenient to the Noble Savage message, that outrage happened, some Indians perpetrated it, and the moralizing General Howard approved it. It was no worse than many other barbarous actions by whites against Indians through the years. And no reasonable person will condemn an entire race for some dramatized outburst of violence by a single group, when the presentation is balanced. But to conceal or disguise any action that stands in the face of the philosophical message and then to boast of the honesty of your presentation, as the packagers of *I Will Fight No More Forever* did, is either dishonesty or misguided charity. The Nez Percés, like all other Indians, have had enough of both.

Perhaps someday their remarkable saga will be filmed, the inspiring story of Chief Joseph told without conspicuous hand wringing by a few "enlightened" white characters who stand above the universally shallow and money-grubbing white settlers—and without the tragically noble posturing of wooden gods in feathers. Now that would be a real exercise in understanding.

THE HUMOR MAGAZINE

NATIONAL

JUNE 1978

PRICE: $1 25

LAMPOON

IND
34496

THE WILD WEST

EVEN BLUEGIRLS GET THE COWS. COWBOYS OF MANY LANDS.
GAHAN WILSON PLAYING COWBOY.
AND HEATHEN RED INDIAN SAVAGES

Like all minorities, the American Indian peoples have been the butts of ethnic humor since their first encounters with laugh makers. Yet while the offensiveness of demeaning jokes was realized long ago in regard to most minorities, with the Indian it has gone largely unrecognized—even by those who think of themselves as sensitive in such matters.

INDIANS MAKE IT FOUR SOX SCALPS

Uhle and Larry Gardner Keep Sox Subdued, 5-1

CLEVELAND April 21—Cleveland made it four straight from Chicago today, winning 5 to 1. Uhle was effective with men on bases, while Cleveland hit Robertson hard enough in the first inning to win the game. The veteran Larry Gardner went to third base in place of Lutzke, who injured his hand in Friday's game, and made two hits, driving in three runs.

CLEVELAND	ab.bb.po.a.e.		CHICAGO	ab.bb.po.a.e.
Jam'on.lf	2 1 3 0 0		Hooper,r.	3 1 2 0 0
Wambg.2	3 1 2 6 0		Johnson,s	4 0 2 1 0
Sp'ker,cf	3 1 1 0 0		Collins,2.	4 1 2 8 0
Guisto,1.	4 2 12 1 0		Mostil,cf.	4 1 2 0 0
Summa,r.	4 1 1 0 0		Sheely,1..	4 1 6 0 0
Sewell,s.	4 1 1 2 0		Kamm,3..	4 1 2 0 0
Gardner,3	4 2 0 0 0		Elsh,lf...	4 1 6 0 0
O'Neill,c	3 0 7 0 0		Schalk,c.	4 1 2 2 1
Uhle,p...	3 2 0 6 0		Rob'son,n.	3 1 0 2 0
Totals..31	11 27 16 9		To'als..34	8 24 8 1

Innings.... 1 2 3 4 5 6 7 8 9
Cleveland.... 3 0 1 1 0 0 0 0 .—5
Chicago.... 0 0 1 1 0 0 0 0 0—1

Runs—Wambsganss, Speaker, Guisto, Summa, Uhle, Mostil. Two-base hits—Gardner, Sheely, Kamm. Three-base hit—Schalk. Stolen base—Guisto. Sacrifice hits—Jamieson, Wambsganss. Double play—Uhle, Wambsganss and Guisto. Left on bases—Chicago 7, Cleveland 6. First on balls—Uhle 1, Robertson 2. Struck out—By Uhle 5, Robertson 1. Umpires—Hildebrand, Moriarity and Rowland. Time—1h. 45m.

Indians scalp Pirates, 3-2

Braves scalp Davis, Phillies, 12-2

An uprising of Redmen

Until Christmas, St. John's season looked like a downer. Then they won a holiday tournament and have been rolling through the East ever since

The baseball story (above left) was published in the Boston Herald *in 1923, the scalping headlines in 1981 (in another newspaper).* Sports Illustrated *described the "uprising of Redmen" in 1973.*

A GREAT DAY FOR THE INDIANS

Above: *The cartoon is also from the Boston Herald (April 22, 1923).* Left: *Mobil ran advertisements like this one in the Bicentennial Year to publicize a series on public television.*

Presidential death streak may be result of old Indian curse

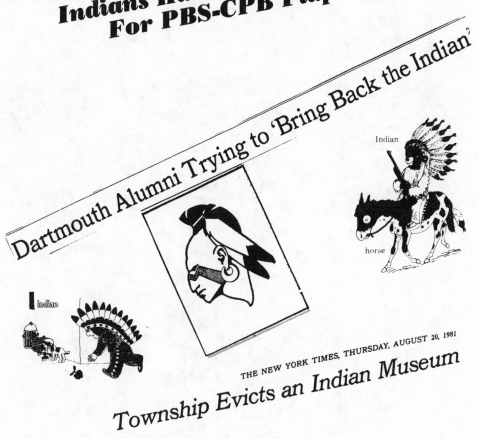

Indians Have A Word For PBS-CPB Flap: Ugh

Dartmouth Alumni Trying to 'Bring Back the Indian'

Indian

horse

Indian

THE NEW YORK TIMES, THURSDAY, AUGUST 20, 1981

Township Evicts an Indian Museum

One way or another Indians continue to attract headline writers—and illustrators of alphabet books.

The "Chief Wahoo" image, in sports logo (center) or comic art, just won't go away.

If we could teach the
Indians to USE **SAPOLIO**
it would quickly civilize them

Metamora: The palefaces are all around us, and
they tread in blood. The blaze of our burning
wigwams flashes awfully in the darkness of their
path. We are destroyed—not vanquished; we are
no more, yet we are forever.

John Augustus Stone, *Metamora*, 1829

14

LINGERING SHADOWS

IN THE WINTER of 1975, *Time's* film critic, Richard Schickel, posted
a challenging thesis in the Sunday *New York Times*. He submitted
that *Ulzana's Raid,* a theatrical film of 1972 (which had just made
its television bow), probably would be "the last movie of its kind that
will ever be made."[1] Ulzana, as delineated by producer-director Robert Aldrich, is a sadistic Apache leader, who, after a prolonged hiatus
on a reservation, has escaped with a gang of roughneck followers and
is making his way across the territory, leaving a string of burning
homes, raped women, and slaughtered homesteaders to mark his trail.
Burt Lancaster portrays the veteran scout assigned to guide a young
lieutenant in the pursuit of warriors who, to the inexperienced officer,
seem evil and merciless beyond belief or explanation. His troopers,
though, are past being surprised. They take the Apaches' cruelty for
granted and respond in kind. As Ulzana's depredations mount, the
confused lieutenant (Bruce Davison) looks ever harder for an explanation, but the best answer he can get comes from an Indian scout, who
says that Ulzana and his followers were weak after the long stay on the

[1]Richard Schickel, "Why Indians Can't Be Villains Any More," *New York Times,* February
9, 1975.

234

reservation and that by torturing a man for hours they believe they can transfer his "power" to themselves.[2]

There is never much doubt about what both soldiers and Apaches will have to do when the two forces finally meet. A peace parley is out of the question; one side must destroy the other. As Schickel saw it, *Ulzana's Raid* represented the last time Hollywood would develop the "them-or-us" situation so strongly and with so patent a moral obligation falling upon the federal policing force in face of unrelieved savagery. Aldrich's production would remain, he believed, "the last movie in which the soldiers and the savages had at one another, with no liberal-minded questions asked."

Schickel understandably expected a new prevailing pattern to be set by movies like *Soldier Blue* and *Little Big Man*—films he derided as distorted attempts to prove that whites "have been since the beginning of time genocidal" in their racism. The critic, therefore, envisioned no more movies in which whites would do "if not just, then justifiable, battle with persons of non-Caucasian persuasion." He expected, rather, the other face of Indian portrayal, glorification. And that trend Schickel regretted, because to refuse to see an Indian "in anything less than a favorable light is as much a put-down as the old implicit suggestion that they are all basically volatile children."

About glorification Schickel was right, of course, though some observers of the 1970s might have found in the neo-*Broken Arrow* atmosphere of a few Indian films if not a favorable wind then at least a break in the weather. But was Richard Schickel right in announcing the demise of the cavalry-and-Indian genre—just at the time when filmmakers like Aldrich "were beginning to perceive, however crudely, that there were possibilities within this material not just for superficial excitements of melodrama, but for a somewhat more interesting, ambiguous, and resonant drama"?

The answer could be yes—but. Undoubtedly Hollywood had recognized, at least on the major-studio level, that new (if neglible) restraints existed, though Schickel himself spotted a throwback to *Ulzana's Raid* when reviewing *The Mountain Men* for *Time* (October 6, 1980). But even with the major studios muted that still left the inde-

---

[2]Richard Slotkin saw prolonged torture as a reassertion of masculine powers and an exorcism of fears, which the Indian accomplished by "inflicting on his defeated enemy the very torments he had feared for himself." *Regeneration Through Violence,* pp. 143–44.

pendent American producers, as well as the foreign producers of English-language Westerns to keep alive the ancient derogations. And, certainly, unpleasant examples of that kind of handiwork did come forth in the years following *Ulzana's Raid.* Moreover, there was already-mentioned false cover involving "renegades," which many producers were finding convenient. Renegades (whom some youngsters might come to think of as a separate nation like Apaches or Sioux) can be assigned any sort of raid or torture because they have "gone bad."

Yet in fully evaluating Schickel's prophecy about Indian movies, a strong rival medium must be brought into view: television. There are two reasons. First, television has given motion pictures a dimension earlier reserved primarily for books. That dimension is longevity (as combined with easy availability). Movies no longer bloom and die in one season, not even pedestrian efforts. They play again and again, year after year, alongside, opposite, or close to movies made decades earlier, much as both freshly printed and well-thumbed books share home or library shelves. And as home-video playback units become commonplace, that parallel will prevail all the more strongly. Just as new books must withstand quick comparison with familiar standards, new movies will have to survive family-room confrontations with those of earlier years. Photoplays intelligently sympathetic toward the Indian (assuming those films win the struggle) may not appear in sufficient numerical or narrative strength to ease traditional "blood-and-thunders" (or embarrassing "glorifiers") to the back shelves for quite a few years. Until then, regardless of what the studios are making, most of the Indian movies that an average person will see during a single year will have been produced in a presumably less sensitive era. Collectively, what has just been released will not be as pervasive as what has long been in circulation. In the way that books denigrating the Indian vastly outnumber those putting him or her in perspective, the accumulated Indian photoplays will paint the scene for a number of years, sins of the past being displayed alongside apologies of the present.

The second reason for looking at television in relation to Richard Schickel's observation of the death of the old-time Indian movie is that television commissions its own film dramas and with the press of scheduling and the desire for ratings is not always painstaking in avoiding the profitable clichés of melodrama. Although makers of television movies (series or single features) may have more time than

236

variety-show producers or comic-book writers to sharpen their efforts and dodge ethnic pitfalls, in practice the margin is not that great. Frequently the cushion of time for those preparing a telefilm is closer to the frantic weeks once afforded those who turned out pulp magazines than it is to the generous buffer of the slick-magazine field. And not very often does it match the unhurried months of a first-line photoplay or a hardcover novel.

Thus we can expect to see television adventure, whizbang style, till the arrival of the next century. The Classics Illustrated version of *The Last of the Mohicans,* first seen as an NBC Thanksgiving feature in 1977, serves as a garish example. Starting with a Lone Rangeresque rescue of a frontier family from marauding Indians, the telemovie emphasizes frenzied action to the very end. Although Hawkeye (Steve Forrest) delivers brief homilies about Indian virtues and white vices during occasional pauses for breath, the dramatization (which was clarioned in schools) could otherwise be mistaken for one of the haphazard B-picture productions of the 1940s and 1950s. Magua (Robert W. Tressler), a throwback to the Goliath of *The Panther Captivity* (1787), is the traditional red devil in a superman's body, a terrifying giant from the perspective of younger viewers. To augment his evilness he is given the familiar Mohawk haircut, while the Huron and Delaware extras are decked out in movieland Plains Indian wigs and rigs, items readily available in Hollywood costume companies and much more suitable for covering miscellaneous bodies than most "Indian suits." About two-thirds of the way into the film the eastern-forest Indians miraculously acquire scores of horses—just in time for the good guys (Hawkeye and the Delawares) to enact a grand chase after the bad guys (Magua and the Hurons). Much of the Cooper plot, and almost all its subtleties, are absent.

At the film's conclusion actor Ned Romero (the erstwhile Chief Joseph) is given center stage to convey Chingachgook's lamentations for his slain son. But Uncas, Le Cerf Agile, has been so much a two-dimensional character throughout the thriller that there is little underpinning for the pathos. As these words are written, Indian movies of the old style may discomfit a greater number of Americans than they did in former days, but through reruns or quickie productions, they are not dead.

Nor have the stereotypes and slanders by any means been erased from films produced for television series (as opposed to special features). *Gunsmoke* opened its penultimate season in 1973 with an episode that *Variety* decried as loaded with "mean, drunken, Indian rapists." A few years later no startling transformation had occurred. A series called *The Oregon Trail* (1977) provided an old scout with a line about how the white man "gave [the Indians] our diseases and took their land." That was only window dressing. Earlier the same fellow had said, "Well, sometimes to an Indian bein' friendly means just stealin' your stock instead of cuttin' your throat." A passing mention of "Indians" leads a child in the caravan to assume that someone is about to be scalped. And in response to an unintended desecration of a burial ground by the hero's son, a band of Indians steals the wagon train's extra horses, kills the guard, and murders the moralizing scout, who had ridden out to parley with them.

The western trek of *The Chisolms* carried the endangered caravan business into the 1980s, with customary menace music at the mere appearance of a few Indian riders outside Fort Laramie and lines that foretold inevitable danger: "Smells like trouble's comin'!" The Sioux spoke in superimposed subtitles: "Let no whites leave the fort!" Recurrent scenes of sneak raids by various parties of warriors produced so vicious a tone that the occasional good deeds of Santee Sioux—returning prisoners taken by bad Indians or curing a white man's tomahawked "squaw"—hardly balanced matters, nor did incessant attribution of Indian misdeeds to "them renegades." Until he bowed out of the series, Robert Preston, whose Indian troubles went back four full decades to De Mille's *Union Pacific,* attempted to offer philosophical leavening in a patriarchal role as outré as *The Chisolms'* Indian activity was clichéd.

Not even the all-out "us-or-them" battles that Richard Schickel believed banished from movies were overlooked by series producers. The pilot for NBC-MGM's *The Buffalo Soldiers* (1979–80) used the *Ulzana's Raid* premise to set up two successful sorties by black cavalry against a force of Comanche raiders twice its size. While *The Buffalo Soldiers* made no apology for its hand-to-hand combat other than the punishing of marauders, a convenient television excuse for hauling out a good old-fashioned battle scene is likely to be some affront or indiscretion committed by a shallow white character before a commerical break. To this lapse the neighborhood Indians respond in staggering number—often with no more logic than would be found in using a cannon to avenge a beesting. In *How the West Was Won* (February 12, 1978) that ubiquitous "whole Sioux nation" was ready for war because a boorish Russian nobleman had celebrated his ransoming from brief captivity by whacking proud-chief Ricardo Montalban on the cheek with a riding crop. As ever, the critical provocation—in this instance the decimation of the buffalo herds—is smothered by histrionics and by the enticing fantasy of an armed confrontation of Romanovs and Dakotas in the Black Hills.

In 1978, *How the West Was Won,* earlier called "The Macahans," fooled some critics with a revival of the noble-Indian motif (some direct or indirect borrowings from *Metamora* recognizable). Other observers may have suspected forked typewriters, especially if they recalled how ridiculously easy it had been in one episode for Jeb Macahan (played by *Gunsmoke's* James Arness) to escape from a gang of stupid and short-tempered Indians, who obviously had not studied dignity under Edwin Forrest or Ricardo Montalban. In another episode of *How the West Was Won* a "renegade Sioux" sneers and snarls in the true spirit of David Belasco's Scar Brow, though dressed, unaccountably, in Apache costume. So much for the film and television decline of the (Wild) West.

With adventure film or fiction still holding on to the ripsnorting patterns, with "earnest" literary and dramatic works tripping over their messages while irritating the very people they are trying to ennoble, and with variety and sports entertainments ridiculing the American Indian in blissful unawareness, is there any curative action that goes beyond letting time take its course—and falls short of censorship? Is there prescription, sans proscription, that can at least reduce the misconstructions that mar the presentation of the American Indian in popular culture? Who can say? The plague has raged for a long time, and many of the symptoms have gone unrecognized. On a particularly rough day of muggings, rapes, and murders a New York police sergeant answers the precinct phone, "Fort Apache!" The name catches on, and in 1980 a film company is shooting a Paul Newman movie called *Fort Apache, the Bronx.* Does someone notice the nominative implication? Oh, yes. A member of the United States House of Representatives expresses regret on WABC Radio not that Apaches are once again associated with violence but that the good people living in the Bronx are stuck with a bad nickname. A parochial focus for the 1980s, beyond question, but is it logical to expect the people of any era, even our own, to recognize their errors or conveniences of cultural perception regarding the Indian any more clearly than their predecessors did? As Robert Berkhofer pointed out in *The White Man's Indian:*

> For most Whites throughout the past five centuries, the Indian of imagination and ideology has been as real, perhaps more real, than the Native American of actual existence and contact. . . . Although modern artists and writers assume their own imagery to be more in line with "reality" than that of their predecessors, they employ the imagery for much the same reasons and often with the same result as those persons of the past they so often scorn as uninformed, fanciful, or hypocritical. As a consequence . . . the basic images of good and bad Indian persist from the era of Columbus up the present without substantial modification or variation.[3]

Sometimes, of course, what brings discomfort to one Indian (the idea of a Washington *Redskin,* for example) brings only a smile or a yawn from another. Still, on the assumption that at least some contemporary distortions and misapprehensions can be seen for what they are when a light is played on them, I respectfully offer a few candles that one might reach for whenever an "Indian" is called into the circle of popular culture:

1. IS THE VOCABULARY DEMEANING?

It is long past time for the informal expressions of prejudice and misunderstanding to be put to rest, in movies, in novels, in television programs, and, beyond popular culture, in schoolbooks. Naturally, when frontier characters of fiction or drama are speaking in the context of the past, they might be expected to use the terminology of their era. But pejoratives should not be thrown in carelessly. Whatever the medium, the writer should be aware of the influence exerted when a white character, major or minor, characterizes a body of people with terms like "hostiles" or "savages." And might it not be logical once in a while for some white character to say "man" instead of "buck" when talking about an Indian male? Or "woman" instead of "squaw" when mentioning a female? What an enormous advance it could represent in many quarters if a married Indian male could be considered, in dialogue and narration, a *husband* and his partner a *wife.* So simple a concept to convey, yet how rarely anyone tries.

[3]Robert Berkhover, Jr., *The White Man's Indian,* p. 71.

240

People who would never speak or write words like "darky" or "mulatto" or "mammy" or "pickaninny" take no notice at all of "redskin" or "half-breed" or "squaw" or "papoose." So pervasive has been the popular culture and history book misuse that millions of Americans would be stunned to discover that "squaw," for instance, is not a universal word in "Indian" for woman or wife but is instead (say most language experts) a corruption of a regionalism of the Algonquian tonque (dark-horse theory makes squaw a distortion of an Iroquois word denoting female sexual parts). Whatever its origin, the word has been almost universally a white convenience and is scarcely laudatory.[4]

One more thing about language: while derogations can sometimes be excused as appropriate to an individual character's dialogue, they are inexcusable in an author's expository or narrative passages. Do such libels and slanders still occur? Of course they do. But conscientious writers can learn to avoid them as perceptivity comes. For example, could the author of a nonfiction best-seller of 1970 sympathetic to the Indian have taken a somewhat different verbal stance in a frontier novel written earlier? Could Dee Brown, author of *Bury My Heart at Wounded Knee,* have written: "Five squaws were lined up in front of Westcott . . ." and "From out of the restless mass a papoose squawled"? Could his hero have ripped stolen dresses from five "squaws," leaving them naked to the waist? Could the author have put the word "squaw" into the mouth of a Plains Indian? Yes he could have—in *The Girl from Fort Wicked* (1964). And Brown, of course, is one of the friendly writers.

Anyone can make a mistake? Assuredly, the writer of this book included. And anyone can make improvements, as Dee Brown had done by the time of his *Action at Beecher Island* (1967), which contained conspicuously fewer language slights than his earlier novel, in both exposition and dialogue. Brown's act of awareness and rectification is to his credit and is an example that other writers could follow.

With both human error and the possibility of adjustment in mind, here is one short list of words and phrases that the world might stagger along without in narration, headlines, and ordinary conversation. Please feel free to add to it as similar phrases turn up:

[4]Verbal denigration can be carried even to the closing credits. The end titles of *Billy Two Hats* (theatrical release, 1974; television debut, 1978) contain this entry: "Squaw—Dawn Little Sky." *Bring Back Birdie* (a sequel to *Bye Bye Birdie*) reached Broadway in 1981 with "Indian Squaw" played by Janet Wong.

Another redskin bit the dust	Papoose
Buck	Scalper (relating to tickets)
Half-breed	Squaw
Heap big	Ugh!
Honest Injun	Warlike (describing specific Indian groups)
Indian giver	War paint
Lo, the poor Indian	War whoop
On the warpath	Wild Indian

An artificial or dated list? During the course of preparing this book, I encountered each of the words and phrases *in a contemporary work* at least once—and each time with a negative connotation. On *The Young Pioneers,* first shown on April 1, 1978, a pregnant Sioux, whose husband had been befriended by the gentle homesteader, was introduced by them to other whites as "Circling Hawk's woman." Ironically, the episode was obviously designed to be sympathetic to Indians. *The Brady Bunch* (a family comedy reaching new youngsters through reruns) has to be mentioned here for managing to get three of the loaded words into only twenty seconds of dialogue. Trying to snatch his play headdress from the head of his sister, a boy howls, "I'm gonna *scalp* her. . . . I'm the real Little Owl." Interceding, the housekeeper smilingly observes, "Oh, I think she makes a *heap* pretty *squaw.*" Children apparently will be developing images of the Indian from fleeting lines like those until image makers begin to recognize their real meaning. At present they spring forth unnoticed.

2. DO THE INDIANS TALK LIKE TONTO?

An entire chapter of this book has been devoted to the vagaries of supposed Indian talk. Let me merely remind the reader, then, that the practice of putting infantile mumblings into the mouths of real or imaginary Indian characters has not been abandoned. Moreover, it is not limited to Wild West stories or dramatizations. Advertisers are especially fond of the "ughs" and "me-gettums." A photograph of Jay Silverheels, the television protrayer of Tonto himself, turned up not too long ago in a newspaper promotion for a ski lodge with this printed message:

> TONTO SAY: "Okemo Mountain ski week plans save wampum 10 ways. Okemo want your tribe have much fun, not get scalped."

A broadcasting advertisement of 1980 began with a shouted, "Indians! Indians! Circle the Wagons!" Then a deep voice responded, "Relax, paleface. We want 'em dips and chips."

How much more discouraging, though, were the cartoon advertisements placed in newspapers and magazines by the Mobil Oil Corporation for a program appearing on public television. In one entry a foolishly grinning brave, holding a sports encyclopedia, tells a baseball expert, "Make-um move! Got-um answer in book!" In a later advertisement the half-naked fellow, prancing tomahawk in hand, yowls, "Make-um big rain dance, dope!"

A precursor of change in convention may have appeared during the television season of 1977–78, when, in an episode of *Little House on the Prairie*" an Indian spoke to the white characters in standard English—with no folderol about having been educated at Harvard. It was all done so naturally that the general audience probably did not notice that (as in the early days of American theater) the Indian was speaking in the same manner as the rest of the people in the drama. What if Tonto had been allowed to do the same thing all those years!

3. DO THE INDIANS BELONG TO THE FEATHER-BONNET TRIBE?

The mass media have long fostered the idea that Indians have one ethnic, national, and linguistic identity, that, aside, perhaps, from minor differences in dress or mode of transportation, all Indians look, think, and talk alike. For Hollywood the convenience was obvious from the beginning (just as it had been for the theater). If all Indians were alike, they could all dress and act alike. The Hurons of one picture could wear the same costume as the Seminoles of another. Better yet, they could all wear the costumes of the Plains Indians because those trailing feathered headdresses of the "braves" were so impressive and the princess outfits so cute. If minor distinctions were desired, the male extras could wear braids, scalp locks, or Prince Valiant wigs and headbands—just as long as the coiffures were readily available, easily put on, and resistant to disarray during rougher scenes.

With all Indians behaving identically, writers could draw upon, and repeatedly reuse, the great clichés: Indian warriors never fought

243

at night, howled constantly during attacks, tortured every prisoner, scalped all slain, worshiped a being called Manitou, longed for the Happy Hunting Ground, were expert outdoorsmen, did not practice farming, wandered like nomads, lusted after whiskey and white women, seemingly had no spouses of their own, floundered when attempting English, and spoke a common language called "Indian." When these behavior patterns were combined with the ubiquitous Indian clothes and wigs, audiences knew they were seeing Indians, whether they were being played by Joey Bishop, Victor Mature, or Boris Karloff. Nor should we forget what braids and buckskin dresses did (or did not do) to transform Donna Reed, Jean Peters, and Dame Judith Anderson.

If all the one-big-tribe foolishness had faded away as the mass media, and the United States, grew up, matters would be more encouraging. In fact, however, there are few, if any, discernible signs of enlightenment. The 1976 movie *Breakheart Pass* (televised nationally for the third time in 1981), undoubtedly broke all records for sustained howling by renegade Indians during an attack on a railroad train. One could almost visualize the sound man's tape loop marked "Indian War Whoops." On October 12, 1977, CBS presented a telefilm entitled *The Girl Called Hatter Fox.* It was based upon Marilyn Harris's novel (*Hatter Fox*), which described the rehabilitation of an unmanageable seventeen-year-old Indian girl. Possibly Hatter is Navajo—she is in the book, but the filmed version is vague about the whole thing. More than anything else, the Hatter of the television movie is Hollywood's omnipresent, nondenominational "Indian." The loose overall approach of the writers is reflected even in the dialogue of the central male figure, a softhearted young physician working for the government agency near Santa Fe. Out of Hatter's snarlings he identifies an expletive; it is one of the few "Indian" words he knows. No one speaks "Indian," of course, just as no one speaks "European." But many media writers have not learned that yet, dwelling as they do largely in Feather-Bonnet territory.

One special note here: Indians themselves sometimes encourage this misconception when they disregard their own heritage and dress up like Plains Indians to please the tourists. The large; colorful headdresses originally were marks of valor, worn by a relatively small percentage of western Indians who had earned them. Indians whose ancestors did not wear the familiar plains attire should think twice about disregarding traditional dress patterns and selling out to the Wild West crowd.

244

In *Run, Simon, Run,* a sometimes uneven television movie of 1970, the problem is examined dramatically through a sequence at a small local rodeo. To entertain the whites in attendance with a bit of "authentic culture," the girls of the Indian school perform a carefully rehearsed but Hollywood-influenced dance number. To Simon (Burt Reynolds), a well-liked Papago sitting in the Indian section of the grandstand, the contrived exhibition is an extreme embarrassment. He stands and hides his face. And soon his bleacher mates do likewise. In suddenly realized shame the young dancers break off the number and flee the arena. Their lesson might be studied elsewhere.

Show-business alterations can, at least, be distinguished from natural evolution, in which white culture has sometimes played a role. Perhaps that is why part-Indian author Leslie Marmon Silko in her novel *Ceremony* had wise old Betonie say about his rituals:

> "The people nowadays ... think the ceremonies must be performed exactly as they always have been done, maybe because one slip-up or mistake and the whole ceremony must be stopped and the sand painting destroyed. That much is true.... But long ago when people were given these ceremonies, the changing began, if only in the aging of the yellow gourd rattle or the shrinking of the skin around the eagle's claw, if only in the different voices from generation to generation, singing the chants. You see, in many ways, the ceremonies have always been changing."

4. ARE COMIC INTERLUDES BUILT UPON FIREWATER AND STUPIDITY?

Disheartened people, people with little to live for and not much hope, sometimes find solace in liquor. That is not funny. People who drink too much liquor, especially those not used to it, can behave foolishly. That should not be a source of long-term amusement to others. Within any family some individuals may drink excessively, and some may not drink at all. That should not be forgotten.

It is the special misfortune of the Indian that in comedy situations of fiction he is either the drunken fool or the sober dolt. The cavalcade of movie comedy (or comedy relief) stretching back to the early 1900s embodies instance after instance of Indians cavorting daffily after sipping the bottle and acting only slightly less inanely when not imbibing. Recall the countless sequences in which blanketed near-statues murmur "Ugh!" or burlesqued braves pursue a slapstick comic with raised tomahawks or fat "squaws" set their sights on whitemen, determinedly dog their trails, and sometimes catch them—though an Indian marriage ceremony can be quickly forgotten by the white groom.

Then notice how television has carried on the low-comedy tradition. Think, perhaps, of an "it-was-all-a-dream" plot of *Little House on the Prairie* (first shown for Halloween, 1979) in which white children pass themselves off as Indians to Indians by repeatedly saying, "Ugh!" The easily duped Indians are Chief Kilowatt and Sly Fox of the No Shoot tribe—"Kill many bluecoats." Supposedly in fun, almost every demeaning cliché is pulled out by the creators: scalps, screams, hodgepodge costumes, the torture stake, the uprising threat—even a giggling, fat little Indian girl, Little Pebble—"She looks like a whole quarry!"

Think, perhaps, of an earlier night when Carol Burnett paraded with guest star Steve Lawrence and other cast members in ludicrous misconstructions of Hopi ceremonial dress for a stomping rendition of "Singin' in the Rain." Think of the bizarre rock-and-roll dance number by a chorus of male "Indians" in a John Wayne-Glen Campbell special of 1979, the bouncing absurdity following Wayne's inspirational narration about Indians not owning the land any more than the sky or water (that convenient rationale for having relieved them of their property). Or think of the network variety show in which the stars joined a comic opera ensemble for a "witch doctor" routine set in Canada—the Indians, not surprisingly, louts and buffoons who speak Tontoese and noisily deride one of their number who uses elegant English.

No broadcaster would have dared present such nonsense in African costume and makeup, but apparently no one wondered whether Indians would mind ridicule of their customs and religion. Or is it that any stray protester could be brushed aside as easily as the giant Injun Joe in *Wagon Heels,* a much-televised Warner Brothers theatrical cartoon? Fierce as he is, Joe has an Achilles heel. Tickle him as you would a baby, and the mean-visaged colossus, who could use a tree trunk for a bow, spit back pioneers' bullets, and singlehandedly "massacre" Porky Pig's wagon train, will tumble off a cliff, pulling all of "Indian Territory" into the crater his body makes and leaving the broad land free for comic exploitation.

One public figure, at least, resisted such mindless humor in connection with, of all things, a National Myasthenia Gravis Foundation charity event at Madison Square Garden in 1980. Asked only whether he would mind being listed as a member of the honorary committee, Governor William J. Janklow of South Dakota noticed one item on the program: "An American Indian Firewater Pow Wow." "This is the twentieth century," fired back the governor, "Television, movies, and show-business personalities should stop promoting the stereotype of Indians being drunks."

The charity's national chairman, Tony Randall—who a few years earlier had grotesquely paraphrased the Gettysburg Address for a television special in which a burlesque Squanto and the "Thanksgiving Indians" had disported in Sioux costumes—blamed the errant title on publicists "with a flair for schmantzy words." What then, the doubtfully amended title, approved all around? "*Manhattan* Firewater Pow Wow" (italics supplied). Not even the *New York Times* (April 26, 1980) caught the compounded error (if error it was). Altering no "schmantzy" words, the publicists had grafted in the name of the tribe that had sold New York, and everyone was satisfied—except the last Manhattan, or anyone who found the "Firewater-Pow Wow" juxtaposition damaging enough in itself.

5. ARE THE INDIANS PORTRAYED AS AN EXTINCT SPECIES?

Do they seem to belong only in the pages of history or the dioramas of museums? Are they presented as creatures of the past who disappeared with the great buffalo herds? In popular fiction and drama the settings of Indian stories are almost always the past, a situation that can cause even adults to forget that more than 1.3 million Indians are living varied lives within the boundaries of the United States. Unfortunately literature and educational materials for children tend to encourage the focus on the past with hundreds of items telling what Indians *did* or *knew* or *were* like. Many of these materials handle the past intelligently but leave the Indian there. Others make a muddle of everything. A well-distributed book called *The Indians Knew,* by Tillie S. Pine, compares Indian technology of the past with white technology of the present. Not a single Indian enters the contemporary sections, in text or illustration. Worse yet, the illustrator, Ezra Jack Keats, jumbles the hairstyles, dwellings, and ceramics of the past-tense Indians.

Even an offbeat television comedy like *Soap,* for all its persiflage, can stumble into the past-tense blunder. When Jessica and Chester, two of the major characters, went to see a clergyman for marriage counseling in an episode of 1980, Jessica complained that Chester had been unfaithful at every possible occasion . . . before work, during work, after work, while she was in the delivery room, and so on. Why, she asked the pastor, was there so much infidelity in the contemporary world?

Clergyman: I think it's because there are no more Indians.

Jessica: (*Confused*) No more Indians? What do you mean?

Clergyman: I mean back then we spent too much time worrying about Indians to be fooling around. It was always: "Are the Indians burning our crops? Are the Indians stealing our horses?" The least fooling around went on in Apache country because they were the meanest Indians.

Jessica: Well, Your Reverence, how do you get rid of marriage problems?

Clergyman: *I* got a divorce! [*Audience laughter*] One day while I was out my wife called to get new carpet put in. When the guy got there, I think he was confused about what he had come to lay . . . so they left me with 30 yards of blue shag and . . . he must have been an Apache.[5]

Possibly related to the fossilized Indian is the alphabet Indian. An amazing number of picture books for young children put the Indians right in there with the apples, gnus, and xylophones that help the little ones remember their letters. Not only are specific human beings matched with inanimate objects and cuddly animals—as people of other groups rarely are—but the alphabet Indians rarely are drawn without their feather bonnets and weapons. In the picture book *Bear Party,* by William Pene Du Bois, there are pictures of little bruins in various costumes. The Spanish Bear has a guitar, the French Bear an accordion, the Chinese Bear a triangle. The Indian Bear turns up twice, once with a bow and arrow, the other time with raised hatchet.[6]

6. ARE THE INDIANS EITHER NOBLE OR SAVAGE?

The ancient dual view persists. Writers do not seem to know what to do with Indians if they do not fit into either the exalted or debased molds first cast in the age of discovery. Thus a television drama

---

[5] *Soap,* ABC Television, January 3, 1980, as transcribed by Eric Stedman.

[6] In reviewing *The Chisolms* for *TV Guide* (p. 48), Robert McKenzie fell into the established pattern of lumping Indians with natural disasters: "All they [the pioneers] had to worry about were things like, Indians, rattlesnakes, fires, bandits, storms, floods, and droughts." A few sentences later he made an invidious comparison: "An occasional Indian attack may be easier on the nerves, overall, than the steady rain of awful news that leaves us so depressed and uneasy these days."

presents a near-saint who discourses on the tragedy of cutting into mother earth while white characters look on admiringly—and one night later on the same channel screaming barbarians are attacking trembling women and children. Nowhere does there seem to be a place for individual Indians possessing both strengths and weaknesses in the manner of real people.

The dichotomy came strikingly to light during the *Bicentennial Minutes,* which CBS presented for two years leading to 1976. On July 11, 1974, George Kennedy told viewers that two hundred years ago that night an Indian massacre of the settlers of the Mohawk Valley was imminent. The next evening Glenn Ford gave credit to a Shawnee chief who defied his warriors by sparing the lives of some hostages. In prime time on other days Senator Walter D. Huddleston of Kentucky told everyone that two centuries earlier Daniel Boone, the greatest Indian fighter of his time, was getting ready to fight some more of them because Shawnees had tortured his son to death, while James Earl Jones pointed a finger at the Virginians who had raided and burned Shawnee villages.

An ironic juxtaposition of good and bad occurred on CBS Television on January 14, 1980. The *Lou Grant* program used a script obviously designed to generate understanding and sympathy for the Indian, albeit through too much exposition and too many orchestrated recitations of injustices mixed with another (effective) performance by the staple actor of such dramas, Ned Romero. And what was the network promotional announcement at the middle break? A frenzied plug for the "premiere" of *The Chisolms,* complete with customary menacing shots of Sioux. When *The Chisolms* itself appeared on January 19, 1980—"Siege"—it displayed so many of the traditional defamations and clichés that it surely undid any good offered by *Lou Grant,* and then some.

While Cooper divided his good and bad Indians according to stock (Algonquin and Iroquois), in most instances of fictional glorification or vilification the Indians are of the Feather-Bonnet tribe, or facsimile, a blurring of diversities being more convenient to surface treatment. Henry Wadsworth Longfellow set a profitable precedent in 1855 with *The Song of Hiawatha.* Picking up without recognition the errors in ethnologist Henry Schoolcraft's *Algic Researches* and omitting undignified or nonheroic trickster elements found in the folk character upon with he was basing his poetic saga, the rhyme maker gave a legendary Algonquin hero (Manabozho) the name of an actual Iroquois statesman. To tell the truth, he thought that they were the same person but liked the ring of Hiawatha and settled on that name. Many other ethnological errors followed that pattern in the poem, but Longfellow's noble Indian delighted a public that would have been uncomfortable with the impish and conniving aspects of the story deleted by the poet. In similar fashion other writers have eliminated charitable actions by Indians chosen from history to be villains.

An Indian too good to be true or too bad to be believed? Suspect shallow research and narrow viewpoint—especially if those feather bonnets are in view.

7. IS THE TONE PATRONIZING?

This kind of foolishness is sometimes readily recognized but at other times is deceptively backhanded (as in the business of Indians not "owning" land). Patronization is nothing new, of course. At its most transparent level it corresponds to the "good voice, natural rhythm" condescension toward blacks—though the opportunities for complimenting a seemingly perpetual fictional adversary may be minimal. Indians can, perhaps, be grateful that they have thus far avoided the "happy darky" stage of recognition.

Sometimes, however, so-called pals can be embarrassing when paying their respects. For instance, in a low-budget shoot-'em-up of the 1950s called *The Wild Dakotas* a young friend of the white hero is absolutely astounded to discover that an Arapaho can speak English. "All the chiefs can," reassures the hero. "They're wise men," he confides, "despite their red skins."

In almost the same vein, but two decades later, a television series, *The Waltons,* crowds bountiful laudatory exposition into a brief front-porch chat that includes an ancient Cherokee and his grandson. In a matter of seconds the folks of Walton's Mountain let drop the information that the Cherokees were the first Indians to have an alphabet, that the giant Sequoia trees were named for the inventor of that alphabet, and so on. The remainder of the television drama of 1977 concerns the old man's search for the graves of his ancestors—which turn up in convenient camera range right inside the Walton barn. As the complicated plot unravels, various Virginians gain all sorts of stunning insights into the plight of the Indians, and Jerado DeCordovier somehow manages to develop an appealing characterization of the 101-year-old Mr. Teskigi. But could it overcome the treacle?

Of late, patronization has had a way of turning into blundering attempts to show what good pals an Indian and a white can be. "See how we can tease each other locker-room style," the characters seem to be saying. In *The Outlaw Josie Wales* (1976), Chief Dan George, as sidekick to Clint Eastwood, issues a running line of self-deprecating humor on what an Indian is supposed to be able to do—like sneak up behind a white man or hear hoofbeats in the ground—but he also delights in climbing under the blanket of a young Navajo woman (who joins them on the trail) before his white companion can turn the trick. Cecil Colson (Sam Waterson), an oddball Indian of *Rancho Deluxe* (1975), offers his equally flaky white pal a lively idea for brightening a dull day: "Let's burn and pillage."

There are limits to being a jolly boy, however, and in *Relentless,* a CBS Television film broadcast on September 14, 1977, Will Sampson, the giant Indian of *One Flew Over the Cuckoo's Nest,* defined that limit for those who would notice. As an Indian lawman, Sampson seems unruffled by the continuing Lone Ranger-Tonto jests of his friendly deputy, Buck. Yet toward the end of the drama, when his aide asks, "You mean the man in the black mask, Kemo Sabe?" forbearance comes to an end.

"Hey . . . Buck," sighs Sampson. "That's enough. . . . No more."

Did tens of thousands of voices throughout the land echo that request for release from the good sports of the land?

8. IS INDIAN HUMANNESS RECOGNIZED?

Perhaps this is the only question that need be asked when looking at the Indian of popular culture, for when people are seen as people, conscious or unconscious slights tend to disappear. The anonymous "they" are far more vulnerable to suspicion or prejudicial treatment than are groups recognized as being composed of individuals—even if those individuals are characters of fiction.

In that light, do the Indians of a book or movie seem to belong to the human race? Do they have homes? Families? Emotions other than mindless fury? Anxieties not connected to warfare? Aside from the menacing chief or the lovely princess, do the Indian characters have personal names? Daily tasks? Amusements other than drinking or torturing? In sum, are they seen in something resembling full dimension? When they are not and incidental white characters are, the implication is obvious, the cliché imminent.

251

The humanness factor really goes back to the Golden Rule or ancient equivalent. Who should be disturbed by the sight or mention of "warlike Indians" or "savage redskins"? The same persons who would shudder at similar broadside references to people of other races or nations. Or the persons who would be uncomfortable as critics and audiences were during a revival in 1978 of the stage musical of 1928, *Whoopee.* As Richard Eder expressed it in the *New York Times* (July 21, 1978), the focal points of the second act are "caricature Indians, cigar store Indians and sentimental Indians all at once; and whatever cuteness they may have had . . . has thickened into pure embarrassment."

In another fifty years that embarrassment may be so widespread that a book like this one will be but a reminder of how things were. In the meantime, perhaps, the questions I have framed, after a long look at the Indian of popular culture, will be of some service. Just a few years before I began assembling materials for this book, Vine Deloria wrote: "The historical image of the Indians is pretty well set, we are the bad guys who burned the wagon trains and images are the white man's game."[7]

I like to believe that Vine Deloria would enjoy being proved wrong.

[7]Vine Deloria, *Custer Died for Your Sins,* p. 272.

Appendix
A Literary and Historical Chronology

THE information that follows is designed to aid the reader of this book but is in no way intended to be an inclusive profile of the Indian in history or popular culture. Although most of the plays and printed works contained in the chronology are examined in the main text, several representative titles are included simply as points of reference. The intent was to avoid repeated stops for historical or literary fill-in.

To conserve space, some titles are presented in their shorter form, while some proper names are abbreviated.

1493
The Tainos of the West Indies appear in a favorable, though childlike, light when Christopher Columbus writes of the people he calls "Los Indios." They are innocent, friendly, and naked.

1503
The letters of explorer Amerigo Vespucci reach printers and soon bring him fame throughout Europe. Later Vespucci letters, probably fraudulent, bring him criticism as a purloiner of Columbus's honors. In these letters the writer describes Indians who are ingenuous, friendly, and naked.

1507
The word "America" appears on a globe published by the scholars at Saint-Dié, France.

1511
Peter Martyr begins the Latin reports on the New World that will make him the Americas' first historian.

1520
Paracelsus theorizes on the separate genesis of Indians.

1524
Giovanni Verrazano, explorer of North America, describes extensively the physical appearance of the Indians he encounters, noting differences between groups. His is the first description of Indian life within what is now the United States.

1528–29
Performing Indians, assembled in Mexico by Hernán Cortés, entertain audi-

ences in eastern Europe. German artist Christoph Weiditz captures their exhibitions in cartoons, thus preserving images of the first touring Indian show.

1535

Partial Publication of Gonzalo de Oviedo's *Historia general y natural de las Indias,* which will include a detailed analysis of the southeast coast of the present United States and its peoples.

1537

In a papal bull Indians are declared to be "true men."

1560

South American Indians are a regular part of French ceremonials, having impressed audiences a decade earlier in an expositionlike re-creation of a Brazilian village staged at Rouen.

1580

In *Des Cannibales,* Michel de Montaigne portrays the Indians of "Brazil" as Noble Savages.

1582

Richard Hakluyt, British geographer and writer, begins a series of publications that bring together early accounts of exploration, including those of Hernando De Soto and Jacques Cartier.

1590

John White, artist and governor, on his return trip to Roanoke, discovers that the settlers have vanished and in his diary enters the first account of the "Lost Colony." "This," he writes, "could be no other but the deed of the savages our enemies."

1608

One year after the founding of Jamestown, John Smith is captured by Opechancanough ("Powhatan's" brother) and saved by Pocahontas, according to Smith's account.

John Smith's *A True Relation* is published, but contains no mention of the Pocahontas rescue. That comes in Smith's *General Historie* (1624).

1611

Using the accounts of actual shipwrecks, and the essays of Montaigne, Shakespeare creates a drama of life in a new world—*The Tempest.* A pivotal character is the sulking aboriginal servant, Caliban.

1616

Pocahontas—as Lady Rebecca—delights the English court.

1622

On March 22, Opechancanough directs a surprise attack on the settlers around Jamestown. This first major effort to eliminate the white colonist falls short of success only because Chanco, a Christian Indian, warns the English nearest the town. Warfare continues until 1638, then resumes in 1644, when the aged Opechancanough is killed and the Powhatan confederacy collapses.

1670

In *The Conquest of Granada,* John Dryden applies the term "Noble Savage" to early Europeans. It will soon be fitted to the American Indian.

1675

King Philip's War begins with an attack on the colonists at Swansea, on the Bristol peninsula of Rhode Island.

1677

William Hubbard's *Narrative of the Troubles with the Indians in New England* portrays them as "children of the devil" and the "dross of mankind."

1682

Publication of Mary Rowlandson's famous captivity narrative comes at the end of King Philip's War. At least thirty editions are issued.

1690

America's first newspaper, *Publick Occurrences,* is suppressed after one issue. Much of its news involves Indians, including some Christianized ones who had "newly appointed a day of Thanksgiving" for a "very Comfortable Harvest."

1699

Jonathan Dickinson's *Narrative of a Shipwreck in the Gulph of Florida* rivals Mary Rowlandson's captivity tale in quality and popularity.

Cotton Mather employs the captivity narrative as propaganda in *Decennium Luctuosum,* which presents the stories of Hannah Dustin (Dustan) and others. This work is later included in Mather's *Magnalia Christi Americana.*

1719

Daniel Defoe's *Robinson Crusoe* introduces the faithful Indian servant and companion, complete with garbled English.

1728

In his *History of the Dividing Line Run in the Year 1728,* Virginian William Byrd suggests that intermarriage will solve the Indian problem (the book is not published until 1841).

1744

The Massachusetts General Court declares a general bounty on Indian scalps: 250 pounds. In 1757 this already bounti-

ful reward is raised to 300—more than a year's pay for many educated colonists.

1752

Philip Freneau, the "father of American poetry," is born. His Indian poems include "The American Village," "The Indian Student," "The Dying Indian," and "The Prophecy of King Tammany."

1754

The French and Indian War, background for many frontier adventures, begins.

1762

Pontiac, an Ottawa, launches a three-year effort to expel the English through combined Indian action.

1763

Quaker John Woolman in his journal presents a human portrait of the Indians he meets on his journey to the Susquehanna River. First publication comes in 1774.

1766

Ponteach, Major Robert Rogers's pioneer play on an American subject, is written. Printed in England, and possibly never performed during the lifetime of the Rangers' commander, the drama has a noble Indian for its central character.

1777

Jane McCrea, daughter of a Presbyterian minister, is murdered and scalped—allegedly by the Indian allies of the British in New York. Her death figures in art and fiction, and the propaganda attached to the atrocity quickly attracts volunteers to the colonial side before the battle of Saratoga.

1779

Professor John Smith of Dartmouth brings an intelligent Indian character

255

into his *Dialogue Between an Englishman and an Indian,* presented at the college.

1791

"The Death Song of an Indian Chief" becomes America's first printed score when published in the March issue of the *Massachusetts Magazine.*

1793

In *The History of Maria Kittle,* Anna Eliza Bleeker uses an Indian as the central figure of a story patterned on the captivity tales.

1794

Anna Kemble Hatton's *Tammany,* sometimes called the first opera produced in the United States, has its bow. Only fragments of the work survive.

1799

Publication of Charles Brockden Brown's European-influenced *Edgar Huntly; or, Memoirs of a Sleepwalker,* marks the first significant use of American Indians in fiction. Careless latter-day claims of idealization notwithstanding, Brown's portrait of the Indians is unflattering.

1801

René de Chateaubriand's *Atala* begins the French romantic movment. Some of the Indian, or part-Indian, figures are idealized.

1808

James N. Barker's *The Indian Princess; or, La Belle Sauvage,* is staged in Philadelphia. This drama about Pocahontas is the first "Indian play" to reach the footlights.

1809

Washington Irving uses irony to reveal the shallowness of the European claims to Indian lands in *A History of New York.*

Later, in *The Sketch Book* (1819) and other writings, Irving contributes to the early nineteenth century idealization of the American Indian.

1811

Tecumseh's effort to confederate the Indian nations against the United States ends when his brother, Tenskwatawa ("the Prophet") is defeated by General William Henry Harrison at Tippecanoe. The Shawnee statesman becomes the subject of many pieces of fiction.

1817

The Seminole wars begin as settlers attack Indians in Florida and Seminoles retaliate. These bloody struggles, popular with screenplay writers, never come to an official end but subside following the government's campaign of attrition in 1841 and the removal of many Seminoles to the West.

1819

M. M. Noah's *She Would Be a Soldier* appears, a successful romantic-adventure drama containing a peace-treaty sequence full of irony and insight. The defeated chieftain is the most vivid character and bears no small resemblance to Tecumseh.

A several-year flurry of fiction and poetry built upon the romanticized Indian includes *Frontier Maid; or, the Fall of Wyoming* (1819); *Logan, an Indian Tale* (1821); *The Land of Powhatten* (1821); and *Ontwa, Son of the Forest* (1822). More enduring is *Yamoyden, a Tale of the Wars of King Philip* (1820), a six-canto tragic poem by James Eastburn and Robert Sands.

1823

James Fenimore Cooper introduces Natty Bumppo and Chingachgook (John

Mohegan) as elderly men in *The Pioneers,* the first of the Leatherstocking tales. Both men are uncomfortable in the Cooperstown of 1793, though Chingachgook (who dies in the novel) has learned passable English.

1826

The Leatherstocking tales gain their real impetus from *The Last of the Mohicans,* in which Natty Bumppo (Hawkeye), in his thirties, travels the forest trails with Chingachgook and his son, Uncas, during the French and Indian War. Magua is a memorable villain. With Pastor John Heckewelder's history as a guide, Cooper sees the Indians as "good" (Algonquin-Delaware) or "bad" (Iroquois-Huron).

1827

Cooper's *The Prairie* finds an octogenarian Natty Bumppo on the western frontier of 1804.

1829

Actor Edwin Forrest brings to life the stage's most noble, and popular, Indian chieftain in John Augustus Stone's *Metamora; or, the Last of the Wampanoags.* Forrest plays the role in virile fashion to the end of his career. In *The Wept of the Wish-ton-Wish* Cooper uses Metacomet/-Metamora/King Philip as an influential character in a tale of marriage between an Indian man and a white woman.

1830

Pocahontas; or, the Settlers of Virginia, by George Washington Custis, sets off the "Indian plays" that fill American theaters until the mid-1840s. The Noble Savage motif is dominant.

1832

The Black Hawk War breaks out in April after settlers ignore a truce flag. By August, Black Hawk's people are massacred, and the chief is a prisoner, paraded through streets like a circus animal.

1835

William Gilmore Simms's Indian romance, *The Yemassee,* is published. The first edition sells out in three days. Although Simms's work shows the influence of Cooper, his Indians are recognizable as ordinary mortals.

Washington Irving completes *A Tour of the Prairies,* the first of three works in which the Indian plays a major role (the others are *Astoria,* 1836, and *The Adventures of Captain Bonneville,* 1837.) Irving's approach is sympathetic, but he soon turns to European subjects and shows only passing interest in the Indian in later writings.

1837

First appearance of Robert Montgomery Bird's highly popular frontier novel, *Nick of the Woods.* Much in contrast to Cooper's ennobled Sagamores, the Indians of Bird's book are loathsome savages. Their image thereafter prevails in popular fiction, *Nick of the Woods* itself going through many editions.

Painter George Catlin opens his Indian gallery in New York City. Three years later his famous English exhibitions begin at Egyptian Hall in Piccadilly. Eventually they include performances by real Indians.

1838

Louisa H. Medina creates the most successful stage adaptation of *Nick of the Woods.*

Osceola, the great Seminole battle leader, dies after being captured under a flag of truce and imprisoned.

1841
Cooper's *The Deerslayer* portrays Natty Bumppo and Chingachgook as young men in the 1740s. *The Pathfinder* (set in 1759) has been published the year before.

1849
Francis Parkman, in *The Oregon Trail,* gives a firsthand account of prairie life, Indian and white

1853–54
The "Native American" or "Know Nothing" Party is openly established. Unconnected to Indians, it has been a secret society opposed to foreign-born and Roman Catholics.

1855
On November 10, Henry Wadsworth Longfellow's *The Song of Hiawatha* is published. It immediately becomes a literary sensation. Using the folklore researches of H. R. Schoolcraft and the meter and style of the Finnish epic *Kalevala,* the poet portrays a noble Indian amid a fair amount of muddled Indian legend.

John Brougham devastates the Indian play in general and the Pocahontas play in particular through his burlesque, *Po-Ca-Hon-Tas; or, The Gentle Savage.* The spoof (done in the pattern of his *Metamora; or, the Last of the Polywogs,* 1847) delights audiences year after year, undergoing occasional changes to reflect topical events. Among things parodied is *The Song of Hiawatha.*

1860
The first Pony Express ride begins in Saint Joseph, Missouri, on April 3.

The first Beadle dime novel is published: *Malaeska; the Indian Wife of the White Hunter* (a reprint). *Seth Jones; or, the Captives of the Frontier* appears shortly after with much success. Most of the Indians of the dime-novel genre are howling savages made for biting the dust, sometimes by the dozen. Authenticity is beyond consideration.

1864
Colonel J. M. Chivington and his ninety-day militia surprise and destroy a peaceful camp of Cheyennes and Arapahos at Sand Creek, Colorado.

1869
Buffalo Bill is introduced to the world of fiction in a dime novel by Ned Buntline (who writes only four of the hundreds of Buffalo Bill stories).

1872
After seeing himself impersonated by an actor in Ned Buntline's *Buffalo Bill: King of the Border Men,* W. F. Cody himself takes the stage in *The Scouts of the Prairie* (a melodrama hastily assembled by Buntline). The Buffalo Bill "Combinations," minus Buntline, amuse critics and delight audiences for a decade, gradually evolving into the outdoor Wild West shows. Indians in these fast and furious theatricals match the already well-established stereotypes, especially those of the mindless attacker and the pristine princess. Action is the dominant note, but Buffalo Bill "in person" is the magnet.

1876
"Custer's Last Stand." It serves as the basis or inspiration for innumerable books, plays, and films.

Cody's theatrical company tours with *The Red Right Hand; or, Buffalo Bill's First Scalp for Custer,* based on Cody's just-completed scouting duty that culminated in the slaying of Yellow Hand.

1877

Chief Joseph and the Nez Percé attempt the long march toward Canada, pursued by as many as three forces of military. About three hundred warriors stave off more than five thousand soldiers for two thousand miles, surrendering only thirty miles from freedom.

1882

The Buffalo Bill Combinations evolve into the outdoor Wild West shows. These spectacles (which continue through 1916) provide early moviemakers with impressive lessons in staging Indian raids on wagon trains and stagecoaches—and last-minute relief charges. The Plains Indians of the Wild West shows, Sioux especially, become the standard Indians of show business. Even the Apaches, principal exceptions to Feather Bonnet dominance, are turned into horseback Indians in popular media to match the exciting style of the Buffalo Bill warriors.

1884

Helen Hunt Jackson, whose *Century of Dishonor* had outlined (less than objectively) the wrongs inflicted on Indians by the government, gains much more attention with her historical romance *Ramona.* When the novel of old California at last fades from circulation, the love story of the Indians, Ramona and Allesandro, lives on through pageant and film.

1886

Geronimo surrenders to the soldiers of General Nelson Miles in Arizona. The Indian wars come to an end, though occasional skirmishes still occur.

1890

On the night of December 15, Sitting Bull is killed by Indian police attempting to arrest him at the Standing Rock Reservation. On December 29, the Seventh Cavalry carries out the massacre at Wounded Knee, about nine miles from the Pine Ridge Reservation. Brushes continue into early January, 1891, but the Sioux, realizing the delusion that was the ghost-dance phenomenon, give up the fight against the largest military force ever gathered to engage Indians.

1893

The Girl I Left Behind Me, a David Belasco–Franklin Fyles play built around a ghost-dance kind of uprising, bows in New York. The popular melodrama successfully combines most of the plot elements of cavalry movies yet to be.

1905

William C. De Mille, in his play *Strongheart,* portrays the problems of a college-educated Indian in love with a white woman.

E. M. Royle, in *The Squaw Man,* dramatizes the tragedy of an Indian woman married to but soon discarded by an English traveler in the West. Cecil B. De Mille uses E. M. Royle's play for his first motion picture—and films it twice thereafter.

1909

Geronimo dies—of pneumonia.

1911

Mary Austin's play *The Arrowmaker* depicts life in the Far West before the arrival of the white settlers.

1913

D. W. Griffith demonstrates his mastery of the Indian-attack genre with a two-reel film, *The Battle at Elderbush Gulch.* Its last-minute rescue sequence looks back to stage melodrama and forward to the epic Westerns, *Stagecoach* included.

1917

Buffalo Bill, the last major link to the actual cowboy-and-Indian era, dies at seventy. His Wild West tours ended in 1916.

1929

Laughing Boy, Oliver La Farge's novel of Navajo life, is published. It wins the Pulitzer Prize.

1933

Chingachgook is partly reanimated through the Lone Ranger's Tonto (radio 1933; novel, 1936; movies, 1938; television, 1948). Robinson Crusoe's Friday is a closer verbal cousin, however.

1939

The Indian returns to prominence in motion pictures through films like *Stagecoach* (John Ford), *Union Pacific* (Cecil B. De Mille), and *Drums Along the Mohawk* (Ford again). De Mille's *The Plainsman* (1937) had been a precursor of the howling-Indian revival. *Northwest Passage* and *Kit Carson* (both 1940) continue the slaughter, but World War II provides diversionary high-budget enemies after *They Died with Their Boots On* (1941).

1950

Broken Arrow signals a several-year trend toward noble Hollywood Indians—in films that never match the dramatic quality of the movie that makes the Apache chief Cochise a familiar figure and latter-day Metamora.

1969

An Indian author, N. Scott Momaday, wins the Pulitzer Prize for his novel *House Made of Dawn.*

Vine Deloria vividly presents an Indian point of view in a nonfiction book *Custer Died for Your Sins.*

Arthur Kopit's dramatically staged *Indians* brings theatergoers a harsh examination of the Buffalo Bill era, with comparisons to the Vietnam War thrown in.

1970

Moviemakers attempt, erratically, to reinterpret the wars of the West at the expense of the white man in *Soldier Blue* and *Little Big Man,* and concoct a pseudofactual mélange of anthropological blunders and white supremacy in *A Man Called Horse.* Inaccuracies and distortions abound, whatever Hollywood's message.

1972

Robert Redford annihilates Crows right and left to avenge the slaying of his Indian wife in the film *Jeremiah Johnson,* based upon the tales about a mountain man who ate his victims' livers.

1975

Television carries on the Noble Savage myth with *I Will Fight No More Forever,* which loosely depicts the long march of Chief Joseph and his Nez Percé.

1977

Leslie Marmon Silko, of both Indian and white heritage, produces an extraordinary novel about an Indian in transition, *Ceremony.*

1979

Ruth Beebe Hill's lengthy narrative, *Hanta Yo,* draws rapturous reviews from many critics (but not all) and skepticism from the Dakotas, whose concern about the novel's content increases sharply when it is announced as a forthcoming television epic in the *Roots* mold. One wry reviewer calls *Hanta Yo* a throwback to *Hiawatha.*

1981

National park ranger Bill Hay asks that Geronimo's body be moved from Fort Sill, Oklahoma, where he died still a prisoner, to the Arizona country that he loved.

BIBLIOGRAPHY

BOOKS

Adair, James. *History of the American Indians.* 1775. Reprint. Edited by Samuel Cole Williams. New York: Promontory Press, n.d.

Arnold, Elliott. *Blood Brother.* New York: Duell, Sloan, and Pearce, 1947.

———. *The Camp Grant Massacre.* New York: Simon & Schuster, 1976.

Bataille, Gretchen, and Charles Silet, editors. *The Pretend Indians: Images of Native Americans in the Movies.* Ames: Iowa State University Press, 1980.

Beal, Merrill D. *I Will Fight No More Forever.* Seattle: University of Washington Press, 1963.

Berkhofer, Robert F., Jr.. *The White Man's Indian.* New York: Alfred A. Knopf, 1978.

Bird, Robert Montgomery. *Nick of the Woods.* 1837. Reprint based on 1853 rev. ed. New Haven, Conn.: College & University Press, 1967.

Black, Nancy B., and Bette S. Weidman, editors. *White on Red: Images of the American Indian.* Port Washington, N.Y.: Kennikat Press, 1976.

Bode, Carl, Leon Howard, and Louis B. Wright. *American Literature: The 17th and 18th Centuries.* New York: Washington Square Press, 1966.

Bowman, John Clarke. *Powhatan's Daughter.* New York: Viking Press, 1973.

Brandon, William. *The American Heritage Book of Indians.* New York: American Heritage Publishing Co., 1961.

Brown, Dee. *Action at Beecher's Island.* Garden City, N.Y.: Doubleday & Co., 1967.

———. *The Girl from Fort Wicked.* Garden City, N.Y.: Doubleday & Co., 1964.

Brownlow, Kevin. *The War, the West, and the Wilderness.* New York: Alfred A. Knopf, 1979.

Busch, Niven. *Duel in the Sun.* New York: William Morrow & Co., 1944.

Capps, Benjamin. *The Indians.* New York: Time-Life Books, 1973.

Calder, Jenni. *There Must Be a Lone Ranger.* New York: Taplinger Publishing Co., 1974.

Cather, Willa. *Death Comes for the Archbishop.* Garden City, N.Y.: Alfred A. Knopf, 1927.

Chronicles of American Indian Protest. Compiled and edited by the Council on Interracial Books for Children. Greenwich, Conn.: Fawcett Publications, 1971.

Clark, Barrett H., ed. *America's Lost Plays.* Princeton, N.J.: Princeton University Press, 1940.

Cohen, J. M., ed. and trans. *The Four Voyages of Columbus.* Baltimore, Md.: Penguin Books, 1969.

Cook, Will. *Two Rode Together [Comanche Captives].* New York: Bantam Books, 1960.

Cooper, James Fenimore. *The Deerslayer.* 1841. Reprint. New York: Heritage Press, 1961.

———. *The Last of the Mohicans.* 1826.

Reprint. New York: Thomas Nelson & Sons, 1927.

———*The Wept of Wish-ton-Wish.* 1829. Reprint. Columbus, Ohio: Charles E. Merrill Publishing Co., 1970.

Darton, F. J. Harvey. *Children's Books in England: Five Centuries of Social Life.* Cambridge: At the University Press, 1932.

Debo, Angie. *A History of the Indians of the United States.* Norman: University of Oklahoma Press, 1970.

Defoe, Daniel. *Robinson Crusoe.* 1719. Reprint. New York: James Miller, 1863.

Deloria, Vine, Jr.. *Custer Died for Your Sins.* New York: Macmillan Co., 1969.

———. *We Talk, You Listen.* New York: Macmillan Co., 1970.

Downey, Fairfax. *Indian Wars of the U.S. Army (1776–1865).* Garden City, N. Y.: Doubleday & Co., 1963.

Edmonds, Walter D. *Drums Along the Mohawk.* Boston: Little, Brown, & Co., 1936.

Ellwood, Muriel. *Heritage of the River.* New York: Charles Scribner's Sons, 1945.

Fairman, Paula. *The Tender and the Savage.* Los Angeles: Pinnacle Books, 1980.

Fenin, George N., and William K. Everson. *The Western.* New York: Orion Press, 1962.

Fey, Harold E., and D'Arcy McNickle. *Indians and Other Americans.* Revised edition. New York: Harper & Brothers, 1959.

Fiedler, Leslie. *The Return of the Vanishing Native.* New York: Stein & Day, 1968.

Friar, Ralph and Natasha. *The Only Good Indian.* New York: Drama Book Specialists, 1972.

Garst, Shannon. *Custer, Fighter of the Plains.* New York: Julian Messner, 1944.

Giles, Janice Holt. *Hannah Fowler.* Boston: Houghton Mifflin Co., 1956.

Gluyas, Constance. *Rogue's Mistress.* New York: Signet Books, 1977.

———. *The Passionate Savage.* New York: Signet Books, 1980.

Grames, Selwyn Anne. *Royal Savage.* New York: Dell Publishing Co., 1980.

Grey, Zane. *The Vanishing American.* New York: Harper & Brothers, 1925.

Grice, Julia. *Emerald Fire.* New York: Avon Books, 1978.

Guerber, H. A. *The Story of the Thirteen Colonies.* New York: American Book Co., 1898.

Hall, James. *Tales of the Border.* 1835. Upper Saddle River, N.J.: Literature House, 1970.

Hallowell, A. Irving. *Culture and Experience.* New York: Schocken Books, 1967.

Harner, Michael, and Alfred Meyer. *Cannibal.* New York: William Morrow and Co., 1979.

Harris, Marilyn. *Hatter Fox.* New York: Random House, 1973.

Harris, Marvin, *Cannibals and Kings: The Origins of Cultures.* New York: Random House, 1977.

Haykluyt, Richard. *Virginia Richly Valued.* 1609. Ann Arbor, Mich.: University Microfilms, 1966.

Heckewelder, John. *History, Manners, and Customs of the Indian Nations.* 1818. Reprint. New York: Arno Press, 1971.

Henry, Will. *The Gates of the Mountains.* New York: Random House, 1963.

———. *No Survivors.* New York: Random House, 1950.

Hill, Ruth Beebe. *Hanta Yo.* Garden City, N.Y.: Doubleday & Co., 1979.

Honour, Hugh. *The New Golden Land.* New York: Pantheon Books, 1975.

Hunter, John Dunn. *Memoirs of a Captivity Among the Indians of North America.* Edited by Richard Drinnon. New York: Schocken Books, 1973.

Hurlimann, Bettina. *Three Centuries of Children's Books in Europe.* Cleveland: World Publishing Co., 1968.

Ives, John. *Fear in a Handful of Dust.* New York: E. P. Dutton, 1979.

Jackson, Helen Hunt. *Ramona.* 1884. Reprint. Boston: Little, Brown & Co., 1921.

Josephy, Alvin M. *The Indian Heritage of America.* New York: Alfred A. Knopf, 1968.

Keiser, Albert. *The Indian in American Literature.* New York: Oxford University Press, 1933.

Krapp, George Philip. *The English Language in America.* New York: Frederick Ungar Publishing Co., 1960.

La Farge, Oliver. *Laughing Boy.* Boston: Houghton Mifflin Co., 1929.

L'Amour, Louis. *Hondo.* New York: Fawcett Publications, 1953.

———. *War Party.* New York: Bantam Books, 1975.

Lankford, John, ed. *Captain John Smith's America: Selections from His Writings.* New York: Harper & Row, 1967.

LeMay, Alan. *The Searchers.* New York: Harper & Row, 1954.

———. *The Unforgiven.* New York: Harper & Brothers, 1957.

Longfellow, Henry Wadsworth. *The Song of Hiawatha.* 1855. Reprint. Garden City, N.Y.: Doubleday & Co., 1947.

McBride, Joseph, and Michael Wilmington. *John Ford.* New York: DaCapo Press, 1975.

Manfred, Frederick. *Scarlet Plume.* New York: Trident Press, 1964.

Marshall, S. L. A. *Crimsoned Prairie.* New York: Charles Scribner's Sons, 1972.

Mason, F. Van Wyck. *Wild Drums Beat.* New York: Pocket Books, 1954.

Mencken, H. L. *The American Language.* New York: Alfred A. Knopf, 1937.

Miller, Randall M., editor. *The Kaleidoscopic Lens: How Hollywood Views the Ethnic Groups.* (n.p.): Jerome S. Ozer, Publisher, 1980.

Momaday, N. Scott. *House Made of Dawn.* New York: Harper & Row, 1968.

Moody, Richard, ed. *Dramas from the American Theatre, 1762–1909.* Cleveland: World Publishing Co., 1966.

Morison, Samuel Eliot. *Admiral of the Ocean Sea.* Boston: Little, Brown & Co., 1942.

Moses, Montrose J., ed. *Representative Plays by American Dramatists.* 3 vols. New York: E. P. Dutton & Co., 1918.

Muir, Percy. *English Children's Books.* New York: Frederick A. Praeger, 1954.

Myers, Albert Cook, ed. *William Penn's Own Account of the Lenni Lenape or Delaware Indians.* Somerset, N.J.: Middle Atlantic Press, 1970.

Nachbar, Jack, editor. *Focus on the Western.* Englewood Cliffs, N.J.: Prentice-Hall, 1974.

Noel, Mary. *Villains Galore.* New York: Macmillan Co., 1954.

Norman, Charles. *Discoverers of America.* New York: Thomas Y. Crowell, 1968.

O'Connor, John E.. *The Hollywood Indian: Stereotypes of Native Americans in Films.* Trenton: New Jersey State Museum, 1980.

Olsen, Theodore V. *Soldier Blue (Arrow in the Sun).* Garden City, N.Y.: Doubleday & Co., 1969.

———. *The Stalking Moon.* Garden City, N.Y.: Doubleday & Co., 1965.

———. *Summer of the Drums.* Garden City, N.Y.: Doubleday & Co., 1972.

Parkman, Francis. *The Oregon Trail.*

1847. Reprint. New York: Lancer Books, 1968.

Pearce, Roy Harvey. *Savagism and Civilization: A Study of the Indian and the American Mind.* Revised edition. Baltimore: Johns Hopkins Press, 1965.

Place, J. A. *The Western Films of John Ford.* Secaucus, N.J.: Citadel Press, 1974.

Prager, Arthur. *Rascals at Large.* Garden City, N.Y.: Doubleday & Co. 1971.

Quinn, Arthur Hobson. *A History of the American Drama (from the Beginning to the Civil War).* 2d ed. New York: Appleton-Century-Crofts, 1943.

————. *Representative American Plays from 1767 to the Present Day.* 7th ed. New York: Appleton-Century-Crofts, 1953.

Quinn, David Beers. *England and the Discovery of America, 1481–1620.* New York: Alfred A. Knopf, 1974.

Rennert, Jack. *100 Posters of Buffalo Bill's Wild West.* New York: Darien House, 1976.

Reynolds, Quentin. *The Fiction Factory.* New York: Random House, 1955.

Ringe, Donald A. *James Fenimore Cooper.* New York: Twayne Publishers, 1962.

Rockwood, Roy [Edward Stratemeyer]. *Bomba, the Jungle Boy.* New York: Cupples & Leon Co., 1926.

Rogers, Gayle. *Nakoa's Woman (The Second Kiss).* New York: David McKay Co., 1972.

Rogers, John (Chief Snow Cloud). *Red World and White: Memories of a Chippewa Boyhood.* Norman: University of Oklahoma Press, 1973.

Ryan, Tom. *The Savage.* New York: Signet Books, 1979.

Sadker, Myra Pollack, and David Miller Sadker. *Now upon a Time.* New York: Harper & Row, 1977.

Sale, Richard. *The White Buffalo.* New York: Simon & Schuster, 1975.

Sanders, Thomas E., and Walter W.

Peek. *Literature of the American Indian.* Beverly Hills, Calif.: Glencoe Press, 1973.

Sauer, Carl Ortwin. *Sixteenth-Century North America: The Land and the People as Seen by the Europeans.* Berkeley: University of California Press, 1971.

Savage, Christina. *Love's Wildest Fires.* New York: Dell Publishing Co., 1977.

Sell, Henry Blackman, and Victor Weybright. *Buffalo Bill and the Wild West.* New York: Oxford University Press, 1955.

Seton, Ernest Thompson. *Rolf in the Woods.* Garden City, N.Y.: Doubleday-Doran & Co., 1911.

Silko, Leslie Marmon. *Ceremony.* New York: Viking Press, 1977.

Slaughter, Frank G. *Fort Everglades.* Garden City, N.Y.: Doubleday & Co., 1951.

Slotkin, Richard. *Regeneration Through Violence: The Mythology of the American Frontier.* Middletown, Conn.: Wesleyan University Press, 1973.

Smith, Henry Nash. *Virgin Land: The American West as Symbol and Myth.* Twentieth Anniversary Printing: Cambridge, Mass.: Harvard University Press, 1970.

Solomon, Stanley J.. *Beyond Formulas: American Film Genres.* New York: Harcourt Brace Jovanovich, 1976.

Spears, Jack. *Hollywood: The Golden Era.* New York: A. S. Barnes & Co., 1971.

Stensland, Anna Lee. *Literature by and about the American Indian.* Urbana, Ill.: National Council of Teachers of English, 1979.

Stone, Grace Zaring. *The Cold Journey.* New York: William Morrow & Co., 1934.

Stonequist, Everett V.. *The Marginal Man: A Study in Personality and Cultural Conflict.* New York: Russell and Russell, 1961.

266

Sutherland, James, ed. *Robinson Crusoe and Other Writings.* Boston: Houghton Mifflin Co., 1968.

Swann, Lois. *The Mists of Manittoo.* New York: Charles Scribner's Sons, 1976.

Swanson, Neil H. *Unconquered.* Garden City, N.Y.: Doubleday & Co., 1947.

Terrell, John Upton. *Apache Chronicle.* New York: Thomas Y. Crowell Co., 1972.

Textbooks and the American Indian. San Francisco: American Indian Historical Society, 1970.

Thompson, Howard, ed. *The New York Times Guide to Movies on TV.* Chicago: Quadrangle Books, 1970.

Tournier, Michel. *Friday.* Translated by Norman Denny. Garden City, N.Y.: Doubleday & Co., 1969.

Tuska, Jon. *The Filming of the West.* Garden City, N.Y.: Doubleday & Co., 1976.

Utley, Robert M.. *Frontier Regulars: The United States Army and the Indian, 1866–1890.* New York: Macmillan Co., 1973.

Vega, Garcilaso de la. *The Florida of the Inca.* 1605. Translated by John Grier Varner and Jeanette Johnson Varner. Austin: University of Texas Press, 1962.

Wagenknecht, Edward. *The Movies in the Age of Innocence.* Norman: University of Oklahoma Press, 1962.

Walker, Warren S. *Leatherstocking and the Critics.* Chicago: Scott, Foresman & Co., 1965.

Welch, James. *Winter in the Blood.* New York: Harper & Row, 1974.

West, Jessamyn. *The Massacre at Fall Creek.* New York: Harcourt Brace Jovanovich, 1975.

Widdemer, Margaret. *The Golden Wildcat.* Garden City, N.Y.: Doubleday & Co., 1954.

Winter, William. *The Life of David Belasco.* 2 vols. 1918. Reprint. Freeport, N.Y.: Books for Libraries Press, 1970.

Wright, Will. *Sixguns and Society: A Structural Study of the Western.* Berkeley: University of California Press, 1975.

PERIODICALS

Allen, Jerry. "Tom Sawyer's Town." *National Geographic,* July, 1956, pp. 120–140.

Axtell, James. "Who Invented Scalping?" *American Heritage,* April, 1977, pp. 96–99.

Battle, Don. "The Man Who Killed Alessandro." *Westways,* February, 1962, pp. 14–15.

Billington, Ray A.. "The Wild West Through European Eyes." *American History Illustrated,* August, 1979, pp. 16–23.

Case, Dale E. "Theodore Roberts." *Films in Review,* April, 1972, pp. 213–30.

Davidson, Bill. "Fact or Fiction?" *TV Guide,* May 20, 1976, pp. 4–8.

Dinan, John A. "Dime Novels Live Again." *Antiques Journal,* July, 1975, pp. 22–25, 56.

Ehly, Jean. "Horrifying Story of an Indian Captive." *Western Frontier Annual,* no. 1 (1975), pp. 26–27, 53–55.

Folsom, James K. "The Only Good Indian." [book review]. *American West,* March, 1974. p. 52.

"Gunsmoke." [program review]. *Variety,* September 19, 1973.

Heinrich, June Sark. "Native Americans: What Not to Teach." *Interracial Books for Children* 8 (1977):26–27.

Heuman, Bill. "The Word Merchants." *Writer's Digest,* March, 1964. pp. 32–38.

"Hollywood's Revenge." *Time,* April 9, 1973, p. 54.

"I Will Fight No More Forever." [program review]. *Variety,* April 23, 1975.

"Legend Maker of the West—Erastus Beadle." *Real West Annual,* 1970, pp. 43–45, 56ff.

McKenzie, Robert. "The Chisolms." *TV Guide,* March 29, 1980, p. 48.

Melton, Horace A. "King of the Dime Novels." *Western Frontier Annual,* no. 1 (1975), pp. 22–25, 65–66.

Metcalf, P. Richard. "Who Should Rule at Home? Native American Politics and Indian-White Relations." *The Journal of American History,* vol. 61, (December, 1974): 651–65.

Millichap, Joseph R. "George Catlin." *American History Illustrated,* August, 1977, pp. 4–9, 43–48.

Nolan, Paul T. " 'Truth' and a Buffalo Bill Play." *Real West Annual,* 1970, pp. 37–39.

Reeder, Kik. "The Real Robinson Crusoe: A Classic Revisited." *Interracial Books for Children* 5 (1974): 1–3.

Robinson, Hubbell. "The 45th Academy Awards." *Films in Review,* May, 1973, pp. 257–62.

"Tragic Mystery of Lizzie Fletcher." *West,* May, 1973, pp. 28–31, 66.

Wagenknecht, Edward. "Griffith's Biographs." *Films in Review,* October, 1975, pp. 449–67.

"War Party." *Akwesasne Notes,* May, 1971, p. 28.

Wechsberg, Joseph. "Winnetou of der Wild West." *Saturday Review,* October 20, 1962, pp. 52ff.

NEWSPAPERS

Birney, Hoffman. "Blood Brother" [book review]. *New York Times,* March 2, 1947.

Burgess, Anthony. "Said Mr. Cooper to His Wife: 'You Know, I Could Write Something Better than That.' " *New York Times Magazine,* May 7, 1972.

Canby, Vincent. " 'Horse' Sequel Retreads Mystic Rite." *New York Times,* July 29, 1976.

Dunham, Barbara Tumarkin. "Kiowa Indians Stay Loyal to Their Heritage." *Philadelphia Inquirer.* September 6, 1976.

Eder, Richard. "Connecticut 'Whoopee.' " *New York Times,* July 21, 1978.

————. "Love-Death Western." *New York Times,* April 24, 1976.

Flaste, Richard. "American Indians: Still a Stereotype to Many Children." *New York Times,* September 27, 1974.

Garnett, David. "John's Royal Wife." *New York Times Magazine,* April 5, 1964.

"The Girl I Left Behind Me," *New York Times.* January 26, 1893.

Hayes, Diane. "They Lived to Tell." *Western Advertiser,* May 26, 1977.

Kleiman, Dena. "How Pioneer Women Lived." *New York Times,* October 17, 1975.

"Navajo War Code Was Unbroken." *New York Times,* January 7, 1979.

New York Times, drama notes, January 23, 1893.

O'Connor, John J. "Historical Dramas—Fact or Fancy?" *New York Times,* May 25, 1975.

Schickel, Richard. "Why Indians Can't Be Villains Any More." *New York Times,* February 9, 1975.

Stabiner, Karen. "Experts for Hire: Authenticity Hollywood Style." *New York Times,* December 31, 1978.

Turner, Frederick. " 'Tribe' Is a White Man's Concept." *New York Times,* January 8, 1978.

Van Horne, Harriet. "Brando's Oscar: Grandstanding but Effective." *Philadelphia Inquirer,* April 3, 1973.

Walker, Stanley. "Let the Indian Be the Hero." *New York Times Magazine,* April 24, 1960.

Wilson, Earl. "No Reservations." *Bucks County* (Pa.) *Courier Times,* December 2, 1974.

Wilson, Jane Adeline. "Captive Among the Comanches." *New York Tribune,* February 2, 1854.

CREDITS AND PERMISSIONS

Except where otherwise indicated, illustration credits from left to right are separated by semicolons and from top to bottom by dashes.

p. 11: George Catlin sketch of himself, New York Historical Society.

p. 12: Sections of illustrations for Vespucci letter, 1509 (above left), *Dati's Lettera,* 1493 (below left), cannibal scene after Hans Staden, 1557 (center), ship woodcuts for *Mundus Novus,* 1505, and illustrations for Columbus's letter, 1493 (middle left), British Library; sections of Grynaeus map, 1555 (above right), Royal Geographic Library, London; sections of *The People of the Islands Recently Discovered . . . ,* ca. 1505 (below right) Bayerisches Staatsbibliothek, Munich.

p. 13: Bibliothèque Nationale, Paris—Germanisches Nationalmuseum, Nuremberg.

p. 14: Geronimo photograph, 1905, Western History Collections, University of Oklahoma, Norman—George Catlin gallery at the Louvre, Howard McCracken Collection.

p. 15: Sitting Bull, Bureau of American Ethnology, Smithsonian Institution.

p. 32: British Museum.

p. 33: Stefano della Bella illustration, Metropolitan Museum of Art, New York—America with spear by Philippe Galle, Bibliothèque Nationale, Paris; America by Marten de Vos.

p. 34: Frederick A. Stokes Company, 1916—Bureau of American Ethnology, Smithsonian Institution.

p. 35: Pocahontas as Lady Rebecca, National Portrait Gallery, Smithsonian Institution—Abby Aldrich Rockefeller Collection, Colonial Williamsburg.

p. 36: Copyright © 1967 by John Alcorn. Reprinted by permission of DELACORTE PRESS/SEYMOUR LAWRENCE.

p. 37: Old drawing by W. L. Sheppard—Brougham scene, New York Public Library.

p. 38: Alfred Jacob Miller, *The Trapper's Bride,* Walters Art Gallery, Baltimore.

p. 39: *Cortez and Marina,* Popular Library, 1963.

p. 52: Dayley illustration for early edition.

p. 53: J. D. Watson illustration, George Routledge and Sons; Thwaites illustration, James Miller.

p. 54: *The Lone Ranger* comic, King Features, 1947.

271

p. 56: Forrest portrait by Frederick S. Agate, Smithsonian Institution.

p. 57: *Red Ryder* panels by Fred Harman, McNaught Syndicate, 1953.

p. 93: Alfred Jacob Miller, *Indian Girls Swinging,* Walters Art Gallery, Baltimore.

p. 94: D. Appleton and Co.—C. C. Nahl painting, Denver Public Library.

p. 97: *The Last of the Mohicans,* Marvel Comics, 1976—Curtis Publishing.

p. 100: Engraving after Bernard Picart, 1723, Library of Congress.

p. 101: *Royal Savage,* Dell; *The Tender and the Savage,* Pinnacle—*The Savage* and *The Passionate Savage,* Signet.

p. 102: Woodcut, Edward E. Ayer Collection, Newberry Library, Chicago; Dick Calkins, *Skyroads,* ca. 1929—Tony Johannot illustration for *The Last of the Mohicans,* 1827, Bibliothèque Nationale, Paris; *Fort Everglades,* Perma Books.

p. 103: Dell; Avon; Pocket Books—Popular Library *(Roanoke Warrior);* Lion.

p. 104: *The Golden Wildcat,* Popular Library; others, Bantam.

p. 133: *Chato* porcelain, CYBIS, 1974.

p. 147: Illustration for John Williams, *The Redeemed Captive Returning to Zion,* first printed in 1706.

p. 148: *Current Events,* Xerox Corp.—*Osceola, Seminole Leader,* illustrated by Ben F. Stahl, Morrow, 1976; painting of Jane McCrea by John Vanderlyn, Wadsworth Atheneum, Hartford.

p. 149: *Geronimo,* Paramount, 1939.

p. 150: Bibliothèque Nationale, Paris; *Guerrier Iroquois* by Grasset de St. Sauveur, Library of Congress—William L. Clemens Library, University of Michigan.

p. 152: Jesuit martyr by Dahlstrom for *Stories of Niagara Falls,* Stewart, 1971.

p. 153: LePage Du Pratz, ca. 1758, Bureau of American Ethnology, Smithsonian Institution.

p. 168: Old print in *Harper's Encyclopedia of United States History . . . ,* 1915.

p. 187: E. B. Swisher, Philadelphia.

p. 190: *Buffalo Bill,* 1944—*Windwalker,* 1981.

p. 191: Ace, 1963; Pocket Books, 1971—Pocket Books, 1972.

p. 192: Ace, 1960—Western History Collections, University of Oklahoma, Norman.

p. 202: *Our Native Land,* D. Appleton and Co.

p. 204: American Museum of Natural History—William Harmsen Collection, Denver.

p. 205: Bantam, 1976; Bantam, 1979; Fawcett, 1966.

p. 228: Don Brautigan cover, *National Lampoon,* June, 1978.

p. 232: Montage includes sections of Frank O'Neal, *Short Ribs,* NEA, Inc., 1975; *The Last of the Mohicans,* Marvel Comics, 1976; Allen Saunders and Elmer Woggan, *Big Chief Wahoo,* Field Newspaper Syndicate—Cleveland Indians logo (center); T. K. Ryan, *Tumbleweeds,* King Features, 1975—Rik Bollen, *Catfish,* New York News, 1974—Al Capp, *Lil Abner* (below right).

GENERAL INDEX

TITLE INDEX

Shadows of the Indian,

designed by Edward Shaw and Terry Bernardy, with illustration layout by the author, was set in 12-point Baskerville by Datagraphics and printed offset on 60-lb. Bookmark by McNaughton & Gunn with binding by Becktold Company.